The Longman Companion to

Britain in the Era of the Two World Wars,
1914 – 45

Longman Companions to History

General Editors: Chris Cook and John Stevenson

Now available

The Longman Companion to

Britain in the Era of the Two World Wars, 1914 – 45

Andrew Thorpe

Longman
London and New York

Longman Group UK Limited,
Longman House, Burnt Mill,
Harlow, Essex CM20 2JE, England
and Associated Companies throughout the world

Published in the United States of America
by Longman Publishing, New York

© Longman Group UK Limited 1994

First published 1994

ISBN 0–582 07771–0 CSD
ISBN 0–582 07772–9 PPR

British Library Cataloguing-in-Publication Data

A catalogue record for this book is
available from the British Library

Library of Congress Cataloging-in-Publication Data

Thorpe, Andrew.
The Longman companion to Britain in the era of the two world wars,
    1914–45 / Andrew Thorpe.
        p. cm. — (Longman companions to history)
    Includes bibliographical references and index.
    ISBN 0–582–07771–0 (CSD). — ISBN 0–582–07772–9 (PPR)
    1. Great Britain—History—20th century.—2 World War, 1914–1918—.
Great Britain. 3. World War, 1939–1945—Great Britain.   I. Title II. Title:
Britain in the era of the two world wars, 1914–45.
III. Series.
DA566.T54 1993
941.083—dc20   92-43347
                                                                                    CIP

Set by 5 in 9½/11 Baskerville
Transferred to digital print on demand 2001
Printed and bound in Great Britain by Antony Rowe Ltd, Eastbourne

Contents

Acknowledgements

The publishers would like to thank the following for permission to reproduce copyright material: E P Craig for extracts from tables in F W S Craig, *British Electoral Facts 1832–1980* (1981); Batsford for extracts from a table in J E Cronin, *Labour and Society in Britain 1918–79* (1983); Oxford University Press for extracts from tables in R Currie, A Gilbert and L Horsley, *Churches and Churchgoers: patterns of church growth in the British Isles since 1700* (1977) and from F V Meyer, *Britain's Colonies in World Trade* (1948); The Royal Statistical Society for a table from H E Browning and A A Sorrell, 'Cinemas and cinema-going in Great Britain', *Journal of the Royal Statistical Society* 117 (1954); Croom Helm for extracts from tables in M Pegg, *Broadcasting and Society 1918–1939* (1983); Routledge & Kegan Paul for extracts from tables in G D G Cole, *A History of the Labour Party from 1914* (1948); Longman UK Ltd for extracts from tables in G C Allen, *British Industries and their Organization* (5th edn, 1970); HMSO for material from Department of Employment and Productivity, *British Labour Statistics: Historical Abstract 1886–1968* (1971); the Central Statistical Office for material from: the *Annual Abstract of Statistics* no 84 (1947), *Statistical Digest of the War* (1951), the Ministry of Agriculture, Fisheries and Food, *A Century of Agricultural Statistics: Great Britain 1866–1966* (1968); Cambridge University Press for extracts from tables in the following: B R Mitchell, *British Historical Statistics* (1988), B R Mitchell and P Deane, *Abstract of British Historical Statistics* (1962); Macmillan Ltd for extracts from tables from the following: D E Butler and G Butler, *British Political Facts* (5th edn, 1985), C Cook and J Ramsden (eds), *By-Elections in British Politics* (1973), A H Halsey (ed), *British Social Trends since 1900* (2nd edn, 1988) and G Routh, *Occupation and Pay in Great Britain 1906–79* (1980).

Preface

This handbook tries to provide a useful and accessible companion for teachers and students of British history in the period between the outbreak of the First World War in 1914 and the end of the Second World War in 1945. By its very nature and scale it cannot hope to be comprehensive, and those carrying out advanced research will doubtless find it of very limited value. But it is not really intended for them, and there are other volumes to which they can turn. On the other hand, those works are not often easy to use, or even to get hold of, for the average student or teacher; and it is to fill that gap that this volume has been produced. The necessity of staying within the strict confines of space imposed by the need to produce a work of manageable length has obviously necessitated ruthless selection of material, and no claim is made that the volume is comprehensive. If its existence saves others a fraction of the time and trouble it has taken the author to put together, then it will have served its purpose.

I would like to thank Dr John Stevenson, for first suggesting that I write this volume, and the staff of Longman Higher Education for all their assistance and cooperation. The book is dedicated to Arthur Barratt and Mary Barratt, and to the late Margaret Barratt, Joseph Thorpe and Kathleen Thorpe, my grandparents, all of whom lived right through this period and who, between them, experienced most of its fluctuations, joys and heartaches.

Andrew Thorpe
August 1992

Political history

1. Political chronology

1914
Aug.   Britain declares war on Germany and Austria-Hungary. Two cabinet ministers resign in protest. MacDonald resigns as chairman of the Labour Members of Parliament (MPs); succeeded by Henderson.
Nov.   First battle of Ypres. Britain declares war on Turkey.

1915
Apr.   Allied landings at Gallipoli.
May   Formation of Asquith Coalition, with Conservatives under Bonar Law (Colonial Secretary) and Labour under Henderson (President of the Board of Education) joining the government.
Dec.   Robertson appointed Chief of Imperial General Staff; Haig succeeds French as British commander in chief on Western Front.

1916
Jan.   Allied evacuation of Gallipoli. Conscription introduced.
Apr.   Easter Rising in Dublin: quickly suppressed.
Jun.   Battle of Jutland confirms British naval superiority.
Jul.   Battle of the Somme opens. Lloyd George appointed War Secretary.
Dec.   Asquith resigns, and goes into opposition to new Lloyd George Coalition government. Lloyd George, supported by about one-third of Liberal MPs plus Conservatives and Labour, appoints five-man war cabinet including Law as Chancellor of the Exchequer plus Curzon, Henderson and Milner with no formal departmental duties.

1917
Mar.   Revolution in Russia overthrows Tsar; broad-based Provisional government formed under Prince Lvov.
Apr.   USA declares war on Germany.
Jul.   Start of third battle of Ypres (Passchendaele).
Aug.   Henderson forced to resign from war cabinet; replaced by George Barnes.
Nov.   Bolshevik revolution in Russia. End of third battle of Ypres with no substantial territorial gains.
Dec.   Allies take Jerusalem.

1918
Jan.   Lloyd George makes declaration of British war aims. President

Wilson of USA announces 'Fourteen Points' for basis of a peace settlement.

Feb. Representation of the People Act gives vote to all men over 21 and some women over 30.

Mar. Treaty of Brest-Litovsk ends war between Germany and Russia. German offensive on Western Front breaks 40 miles through the British lines.

Jun. Labour party adopts new constitution with socialist commitment.

Jul. Final German offensives.

Aug. Start of Allied offensives on Western Front.

Nov. Austria-Hungary and then Germany surrender. Labour withdraws from Coalition government.

Dec. General election gives overwhelming victory to Lloyd George Coalition, most of its MPs being Conservatives. Labour emerges as largest opposition party since the Sinn Fein MPs refuse to take their seats.

1919

Jan. Paris peace conference opens. First Dáil Eireann elected, and Irish Republic proclaimed.

Jan–Feb. Engineers' strike at Belfast and on Clyde.

Feb. Establishment of National Industrial Conference. Appointment of Coal Commission under Justice Sankey averts a mining strike.

Apr. De Valera elected president of Sinn Fein. Amritsar Massacre in India.

Aug. Sinn Fein declared illegal.

Sept. Railway strike. Dáil Eireann banned, and republican violence increases.

Oct. Railway strike ends on terms broadly favourable to the railway workers. War cabinet replaced by full cabinet, with Curzon succeeding Balfour as Foreign Secretary.

Dec. Lady Astor (Conservative) becomes first woman MP to take her seat.

1920

Jan. Treaty of Versailles comes into force.

Apr. Abolition of conscription.

Jun. Start of recruiting for 'Black and Tans' by government to counter the Irish Republican Army (IRA).

Aug. Formation of Communist party of Great Britain (CPGB). Economy moves into severe recession.

Oct. 'Datum line strike' in mining industry.

Nov. Mining strike ends in stalemate.

Dec. Government of Ireland Act passed, partitioning the six Ulster counties from the rest, and giving a separate parliament to North and South.

1921
Mar. Anglo-Soviet trade agreement signed. Legislation passed to return coal mines to private ownership.
Apr. Start of mining lockout, but miners not supported by their allies in the Triple Industrial Alliance.
May Sinn Fein win majority of seats in Southern Irish parliament, but refuse to take them or recognize the assembly.
Jul. Miners return to work on employers' terms. Resignation of Addison from cabinet in protest at abandonment of radical social reform.
Oct. Irish treaty talks in London.
Dec. Irish treaty agreed, setting up an Irish Free State (excluding the six counties of the north) with Dominion status.

1922
Feb. Geddes Report recommends big cuts in public expenditure.
Mar.–Jun. National engineering lockout; ends in defeat for unions.
Sept. Chanak crisis.
Oct. Carlton Club meeting of Conservative MPs votes to fight next election independently of Lloyd George. Lloyd George resigns and is succeeded as Prime Minister by Law, who succeeds Austen Chamberlain as party leader.
Nov. General election produces Conservative majority of 73. MacDonald replaces Clynes as leader of the Labour party.
Dec. Irish Free State comes into existence.

1923
Jan. Agreement reached on repayment of war debt to USA.
May Law resigns as Prime Minister due to ill-health, and is succeeded by Baldwin.
Oct. Baldwin declares the need for protective tariffs.
Dec. General election. No party emerges with a majority, but Conservatives have most seats so Baldwin remains Prime Minister.

1924
Jan. Conservative government defeated in parliament. MacDonald forms first Labour government, dependent on Liberal support.
Feb. Britain recognizes the Soviet Union.
Aug. London conference on reparations accepts the Dawes Plan.
Sept. Prosecution of Communist J R Campbell withdrawn by the Attorney-General.
Oct. Government defeated on a censure motion over the Campbell Case. Government resigns; Conservatives win election (majority, 209).
Nov. Baldwin forms Conservative government, which includes for-

mer Coalitionists like Austen Chamberlain (Foreign Secretary), Churchill (Chancellor of the Exchequer) and Birkenhead (India Secretary).

1925

Apr. Britain returns to the gold standard.

Jul. 'Red Friday': government, under threat of a Trades Union Congress (TUC) embargo on coal transportation, gives a nine-month subsidy to maintain miners' wage levels pending the report of a Royal Commission under Samuel.

Dec. Contributory pensions introduced; minimum age for pensions reduced from 70 to 65. Signature of Locarno treaty. Borders of Northern Ireland and Irish Free State emerge unchanged from work of boundary commission.

1926

Mar. Samuel report suggests measures for reform of coal industry but accepts that wages will have to be cut in the short term.

May Miners are locked out for refusing to accept pay cuts; General Strike follows, but TUC surrenders after nine days.

Oct. Lloyd George replaces Asquith as Liberal leader.

Nov. Imperial conference in London recognizes equal status of Dominions with Britain.

Dec. Miners return to work on employers' terms.

1927

May Trade Disputes and Trade Unions Act attacks unions, replaces 'contracting out' of the political levy with 'contracting in', and declares the General Strike illegal.

Aug. Unemployment Insurance Act reforms system and reduces benefits.

1928

Apr. Women between 21 and 30 given the vote for parliamentary elections.

May Parliament rejects Revised Prayer Book.

1929

Mar. Local Government Act abolishes Poor Law guardians and reforms local authority responsibilities and finance.

May General election produces no overall majority but Labour is the largest party; MacDonald forms the second Labour government.

Aug. Young Plan further reduces German reparations payments.

Oct. Wall Street 'Crash' in New York. Diplomatic relations with Soviet Union restored. 'Irwin Declaration' promises eventual Dominion status for India.

1930

Apr. London Naval Treaty signed.

May Resignation of Mosley from government over its failure to accept his policy for tackling rising unemployment.
Nov. Round Table Conference on India.

1931
Feb. Committee on National Expenditure set up under Sir George May to suggest ways of cutting public spending.
Mar. Formation of Mosley's New party.
Jul. European financial crisis. May Report predicts large budget deficit and recommends massive cuts in expenditure. Increasing pressure on sterling as a result.
Aug. Collapse of Labour government following its failure to agree on cuts in unemployment benefits. MacDonald forms a National government with the support of the Conservatives, Liberals and a few Labourites. Henderson elected leader of Labour party.
Sept. National government reduces public expenditure and increases taxes. Britain forced off the gold standard following renewed pressure on sterling. Second Indian Round Table Conference opens in London.
Oct. Liberal party splits into Liberal Nationals ('Simonites') and official Liberals ('Samuelites'). General election sees National government win an overall majority of 493; Labour reduced to 46.
Nov. Formation of second National government by MacDonald. Emergency tariffs imposed pending introduction of permanent import duties. Samuel replaces Lloyd George as Liberal leader.

1932
Feb. World disarmament conference opens at Geneva.
Mar. Tariff of 10 per cent imposed on most imports.
Apr. Tariffs on manufactures increased to 20 per cent or more.
Jul. Start of trade war with Ireland (until 1938).
Aug. Imperial conference in Ottawa agrees on measures of imperial preference.
Sept. Resignation of Snowden and free trade ('Samuelite') Liberals from government in protest at the Ottawa agreements.
Oct. Foundation of the British Union of Fascists. Lansbury succeeds Henderson as Labour leader.
Nov. Opening of third Indian Round Table Conference in London.

1933
Jan. Hitler becomes German Chancellor.
Apr. Anglo-German trade agreement.
Apr.–July Government imposes embargo on Soviet exports as a result of the trial of British engineers working in the USSR.
Jun. World economic conference meets in London.
Nov. Samuelite Liberals go into opposition.

1934

Feb. Anglo-Soviet trade agreement.

Oct. London naval conference fails to reach agreement on disarmament.

1935

Jan–Feb. Unemployment Assistance Board crisis, ending in a government retreat on the issue of new benefit scales.

Apr. Formation of 'Stresa Front' between Britain, France and Italy.

May Celebration of King George V's Silver Jubilee.

Jun. MacDonald resigns as Prime Minister, and is succeeded by Baldwin. Anglo-German naval agreement signed.

Aug. Government of India Act passed.

Sept. Foreign Secretary Hoare declares support for collective security through the League of Nations.

Oct. Italy attacks Abyssinia; League of Nations imposes sanctions on Italy. Lansbury resigns as Labour leader; succeeded by Attlee pending the general election.

Nov. General election produces overall majority of 243 for National government.

Dec. Hoare–Laval Pact; Hoare forced to resign as Foreign Secretary, and is succeeded by Eden. Attlee re-elected Labour leader.

1936

Jan. George V dies and is succeeded by Edward VIII.

Mar. London Naval Convention between Britain, USA and France.

Jul. Outbreak of Spanish Civil War.

Aug. End of British military occupation of Egypt.

Sept. Major powers meet in London to discuss non-intervention in Spanish Civil War.

Oct. 'Battle of Cable Street' in east London as British Union of Fascists (BUF) marchers and anti-Fascist protestors clash.

Dec. Abdication of Edward VIII; succeeded by George VI. Public Order Act bans the wearing of political uniforms.

1937

Apr. Indian constitution comes into force.

May Coronation of George VI. Baldwin resigns as Prime Minister; succeeded by Neville Chamberlain.

Jul. New Irish constitution changes name of Irish Free State to Eire and claims greater independence from Britain.

1938

Feb. Eden resigns as Foreign Secretary; succeeded by Halifax.

Mar. Austria annexed by Germany.

May Anglo-Irish agreement reached regarding treaty ports; trade war ends.

Sept. Following three meetings with Hitler, the last at the Munich

Conference, Chamberlain accepts the German annexation of the Sudetenland, the German-speaking part of Czechoslovakia.

Oct. Resignation of Duff Cooper as First Lord of the Admiralty in protest at the Munich agreement.

1939

Mar. German invasion of Bohemia and Moravia (Czechoslovakia). British guarantee to Poland.

Apr. Hitler denounces the Anglo-German naval agreement. Conscription introduced. British guarantees to Greece and Romania.

Apr.–Aug. Inconclusive negotiations between Britain, France and the Soviet Union for an anti-German alliance.

Jul. Ministry of Supply set up.

Aug. German–Soviet Pact of non-aggression, with secret protocols for the partition of Poland and the Baltic states.

Sept. German invasion of Poland is followed by Anglo-French declaration of war on Germany. Period of 'Phoney War' follows.

1940

Apr. German invasion of Denmark and Norway.

May British troops evacuate Norway. Chamberlain resigns after government majority sharply reduced in a vote of confidence. Germany invades Low Countries and France. Churchill becomes Prime Minister of a Coalition government including Labour: war cabinet includes Chamberlain and Halifax (Conservative) plus Attlee and Greenwood (Labour). British Union of Fascists banned and its leaders interned.

Jun. British troops evacuate France. Italy declares war on Britain.

Jul. Germans occupy Channel Islands.

Jul.–Sept. Battle of Britain.

Sept. Start of London Blitz.

Nov. German air raids on Coventry.

1941

Mar. Lend-Lease introduced.

May HMS *Hood* and German battleship *Bismarck* sunk.

Jun. Germany invades the Soviet Union.

Jul. Anglo-Soviet alliance formed.

Aug. Atlantic Charter issued.

Dec. Japanese attack on US naval base at Pearl Harbor (Hawaii); Germany and Italy declare war on United States.

1942

Mar. Japanese take Singapore.

May Twenty-year treaty between Britain and Soviet Union agreed.

Jun. Fall of Tobruk (Libya) to Axis forces leads to a sharp decline in morale and increased criticism of Churchill's government.

9

Oct.–Nov. Battle of El Alamein, ending in British victory.
Dec. Publication of Beveridge Report.

1943
Jan. Casablanca conference between Churchill and Roosevelt: Allies state that they will be satisfied only by unconditional surrender of their enemies.
Feb. Surrender of German forces at Stalingrad.
Jul. Allied invasion of Sicily; Mussolini forced to resign by his cabinet.
Sept. Allies invade Italian mainland.
Oct. Britain, USA and Soviet Union agree to set up United Nations.
Nov. Tehran conference between Churchill, Roosevelt and Stalin.

1944
Jun. Allies enter Rome. Allied invasion of Normandy on D-Day (6 June).
Aug. Education Act passed.
Oct. Churchill and Stalin meet at Moscow conference.

1945
Feb. Yalta conference between Churchill, Roosevelt and Stalin.
Apr. Mussolini killed by Italian partisans. Suicide of Hitler.
May Surrender of Germany. Labour party leaves Coalition. Churchill remains as Prime Minister of a 'Caretaker' government pending a general election.
Jul. General election produces an overall Labour majority of 146. Attlee forms first majority Labour government.
Jul.–Aug. Potsdam conference.
Sept. Surrender of Japan.

2. The monarchy

Monarchs

1910–36	George V
1936	Edward VIII
1936–52	George VI

Civil List

1901	£470 000
1931	£420 000
1938	£410 000
1952	£475 000

Source: D Butler and G Butler, *British Political Facts 1900–85* (6th edn, 1986), p 419

Genealogical chart

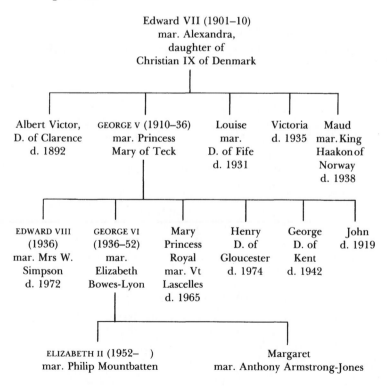

Edward VII (1901–10) mar. Alexandra, daughter of Christian IX of Denmark

Albert Victor, D. of Clarence d. 1892

GEORGE V (1910–36) mar. Princess Mary of Teck

Louise mar. D. of Fife d. 1931

Victoria d. 1935

Maud mar. King Haakon of Norway d. 1938

EDWARD VIII (1936) mar. Mrs W. Simpson d. 1972

GEORGE VI (1936–52) mar. Elizabeth Bowes-Lyon

Mary Princess Royal mar. Vt Lascelles d. 1965

Henry D. of Gloucester d. 1974

George D. of Kent d. 1942

John d. 1919

ELIZABETH II (1952–   ) mar. Philip Mountbatten

Margaret mar. Anthony Armstrong-Jones

11

3. Ministers

Prime Ministers

1908	7 Apr.	Herbert Henry Asquith (Earl of Oxford and Asquith)
1916	7 Dec.	David Lloyd George (Earl Lloyd-George of Dwyfor)
1922	23 Oct.	Andrew Bonar Law
1923	22 May	Stanley Baldwin (Earl Baldwin of Bewdley)
1924	22 Jan.	(James) Ramsay MacDonald
1924	4 Nov.	Stanley Baldwin (Earl Baldwin of Bewdley)
1929	5 Jun.	(James) Ramsay MacDonald
1935	7 Jun.	Stanley Baldwin (Earl Baldwin of Bewdley)
1937	28 May	(Arthur) Neville Chamberlain
1940	10 May	Winston Leonard Spencer Churchill (Sir)
1945	26 Jul.	Clement Richard Attlee (Earl Attlee)

Chancellors of the Exchequer

1908	16 Apr.	David Lloyd George (Earl Lloyd-George of Dwyfor)
1915	27 May	Reginald McKenna
1916	11 Dec.	Andrew Bonar Law
1919	14 Jan.	(Joseph) Austen Chamberlain (Sir)
1921	5 Apr.	Sir Robert Stevenson Horne (Viscount Horne)
1922	25 Oct.	Stanley Baldwin (Earl Baldwin of Bewdley)
1923	27 Aug.	(Arthur) Neville Chamberlain
1924	23 Jan.	Philip Snowden (Viscount Snowden)
1924	7 Nov.	Winston Leonard Spencer Churchill (Sir)
1929	8 Jun.	Philip Snowden (Viscount Snowden)
1931	9 Nov.	(Arthur) Neville Chamberlain
1937	28 May	Sir John Allsebrook Simon (Viscount Simon)
1940	13 May	Sir (Howard) Kingsley Wood
1943	28 Sep.	Sir John Anderson (Viscount Waverley)
1945	28 Jul.	(Edward) Hugh John Neale Dalton (Baron Dalton)

Secretaries of State for Foreign Affairs

1905	11 Dec.	Sir Edward Grey (Viscount Grey of Falloden)
1916	11 Dec.	Arthur James Balfour (Earl of Balfour)
1919	24 Oct.	Earl Curzon (Marquess Curzon)
1924	23 Jan.	(James) Ramsay MacDonald

1924	7 Nov.	(Joseph) Austen Chamberlain (Sir)
1929	8 Jun.	Arthur Henderson
1931	26 Aug.	Marquess of Reading
1931	9 Nov.	Sir John Allsebrook Simon (Viscount Simon)
1935	7 Jun.	Sir Samuel John Gurney Hoare (Viscount Temple-wood)
1935	22 Dec.	(Robert) Anthony Eden (Sir) (Earl of Avon)
1938	1 Mar.	Viscount Halifax
1940	22 Dec.	(Robert) Anthony Eden (Sir) (Earl of Avon)
1945	27 Jul.	Ernest Bevin

Major ministerial resignations and dismissals

1914   2 Aug.   Viscount Morley (Lord President of the Council) and John Burns (President of the Local Government Board) resigned over decision to enter war.

1915   31 Dec.   Sir John Simon (Home Secretary) resigned in protest against introduction of conscription.

1916   3 May   Augustine Birrell (Chief Secretary for Ireland) resigned following the Easter Rising in Dublin.

1917   12 Aug.   Arthur Henderson (Member of the War Cabinet) was forced to resign for supporting Labour's attendance at proposed Stockholm conference of socialist parties to discuss peace plans.

1921   14 Jul.   Christopher Addison (Minister without Portfolio) resigned over government's abandonment of social reform.

1922   9 Mar.   Edward Montagu (India Secretary) resigned in protest against government's pro-Greek, anti-Turkish policy.

1927   28 Aug.   Viscount Cecil (Chancellor of the Duchy of Lancaster) resigned over government's failure to pursue disarmament.

1930   19 May   Sir Oswald Mosley (Chancellor of the Duchy of Lancaster, outside the Cabinet) resigned over government's failure to implement radical proposals for dealing with unemployment.

1931   2 Mar.   Sir Charles Trevelyan (President of the Board of Education) resigned after the failure of his Education Bill.

1932   28 Sep.   Sir Herbert Samuel (Home Secretary), Sir Archibald Sinclair (Scottish Secretary) and Viscount Snowden (Lord Privy Seal), plus the Liberal junior ministers, resigned following Ottawa agreements on protection and imperial preference.

1935	18 Dec.	Sir Samuel Hoare (Foreign Secretary) was forced to resign following the revelation of the Hoare–Laval Pact.
1936	22 May	J H Thomas (Colonial Secretary) was forced to resign after leaking budget secrets.
1938	20 Feb.	Anthony Eden (Foreign Secretary) resigned in protest at Chamberlain's policy towards Italy.
1938	16 May	Viscount Swinton (Air Secretary) resigned after Commons criticism of 'slow' pace of strengthening the Royal Air Force.
1938	1 Oct.	Alfred Duff Cooper (First Lord of the Admiralty) resigned over Munich Agreement.
1940	5 Jan.	Leslie Hore–Belisha (War Secretary) was dismissed after clashing with Army over military preparedness.

4. Elections

Chronology of legislation

1915–18 Newly-appointed ministers temporarily relieved of having to fight a by-election.

1915 Local elections and preparation of electoral registers abandoned, and life of present parliament, due to expire at end of 1915, extended.

1918 Representation of the People Act: (a) universal suffrage granted to men aged 21 and over in parliamentary elections; (b) women over 30 given the parliamentary vote if they or their husbands are local government electors; (c) local government franchise was given to all householders; (d) ex-servicemen can vote at 19, while conscientious objectors are disenfranchised for five years; (e) people in receipt of poor relief are no longer disenfranchised; (f) except for the City of London and the twelve university constituencies, seats redistributed on the principle of constituencies of equal population; (g) registration of voters greatly simplified.

1919 Newly-appointed ministers relieved of the obligation to fight a by-election if appointed within nine months of contesting an election.

1926 Abolition of requirement that ministers resign and fight by-elections on appointment.

1928 Representation of the People (Equal Franchise) Act gives the vote to all women at the age of 21.

1939 Electoral truce agreed between three main parties on outbreak of war. Local Elections and Register of Electors (Temporary Provisions) Act, renewed annually until 1944, suspends local elections for duration of war.

1940 Life of parliament extended for duration of war.

1944 Permanent Boundary Commission set up to review constituencies every three to seven years; existing constituencies with more than 100,000 electors to be divided immediately.

1945 Local government vote given to all adults.

General elections, 1910–45

	Seats	Total votes	% share of vote
3–19 December 1910 (Turnout 81.6%)			
Conservatives	237 ⎫		
		2 420 566	46.3
Liberal Unionists	35 ⎭		
Liberals	272	2 295 888	43.9
Irish Nationalists	84	131 375	2.5
Labour	42	371 772	7.1
Others	0	8 768	0.2
14 December 1918 (Turnout 57.2%)			
Coalition Unionist	332	3 472 738	32.5
Coalition Liberal	127	1 396 590	12.6
Coalition Labour	4	53 962	0.4
Coalition Independent	1	9 274	0.1
Coalition Nat. Dem.	9	156 834	1.5
(Coalition)	(473)	(5 089 398)	(47.1)
Conservatives	50	671 454	6.1
Liberals	36	1 388 784	13.0
Labour	57	2 245 777	20.8
Irish Nationalists	7	238 197	2.2
Sinn Fein	73	497 107	4.6
Others	11	656 101	6.2
15 November 1922 (Turnout 73.0%)			
Conservatives	344	5 502 298	38.5
National Liberals	53	1 471 317	9.9
Liberals	62	2 668 143	18.9
Labour	142	4 237 349	29.7
Others	14	513 223	3.0
6 December 1923 (Turnout 71.1%)			
Conservatives	258	5 514 541	38.0
Liberals	158	4 301 481	29.7
Labour	191	4 439 780	30.7
Others	8	291 893	1.6
29 October 1924 (Turnout 77.7%)			
Conservatives	412	7 854 523	46.8
Liberals	40	2 928 737	17.8
Labour	151	5 489 087	33.3
Others	12	367 932	2.1

General elections, 1910–45 (cont.)

	Seats	Total votes	% share of vote
30 May 1929 (Turnout 76.3%)			
Conservatives	260	8 656 225	38.1
Liberals	59	5 308 738	23.6
Labour	287	8 370 417	37.1
Others	9	312 995	1.2
27 October 1931 (Turnout 76.4%)			
Conservatives	470	11 905 925	55.0
National Labour	13	341 370	1.5
Liberal Nationals	35	809 302	3.7
Liberals	33	1 372 595	6.5
National	3	100 193	0.5
(National Government)	(554)	(14 529 385)	(67.2)
Independent Liberal	4	103 528	1.2
Labour	46	6 324 737	29.3
Independent Labour	3	260 344	1.2
Unendorsed Labour	3	64 549	0.3
Others	5	373 830	1.5
14 November 1935 (Turnout 71.1%)			
Conservatives	387	10 496 300	47.8
National Labour	8	339 811	1.5
Liberal Nationals	33	866 354	3.7
National	1	53 189	0.3
(National Government)	(429)	(11 755 654)	(53.3)
Liberals	21	1 443 093	6.7
Labour	154	8 325 491	38.0
Independent Labour	4	139 577	0.6
Others	7	333 239	1.4
5 July 1945 (Turnout 72.8%)			
Conservatives	197	9 101 099	36.2
Liberal Nationals	11	737 732	2.9
National	2	133 179	0.5
(Cons. and allies)	(209)	(9 972 010)	(39.6)
Liberals	12	2 252 430	9.0
Labour	393	11 967 746	48.0
Others	25	903 009	3.4

Source: F W S Craig, *British Electoral Facts 1832–1980* (Chichester, Parliamentary Research Services, 1981), pp 20–35

By-election swing by parliament

Parliament	Government	Contests	Mean swing to Conservative
1918–22	Coal.	55	−11.4
1922–3	Con	16	−3.0
1923–4	Lab	7	−0.2
1924–9	Con	52	−7.7
1929–31	Lab	30	+6.7
1931–5	Nat	45	−15.8
1935–Sept. 39	Nat	64	−3.9
Sept. 1939–45	Coal.	64	+12.8

Source: C Cook and J Ramsden, *By-Elections in British Politics* (1973),
Appendix B, p 389

5. Party politics

Conservative party

1910
Party loses two general elections, with 273 seats in January and 272 in December.

1911
Jun.   Sir Arthur Steel-Maitland becomes party chairman and sets about the reorganization of the party.
Nov.   A J Balfour succeeded as leader by Andrew Bonar Law.

1914
Aug.   Party supports British entry into war.

1915
May   Conservatives enter Asquith's Coalition government, with eight (mostly minor) posts; Law becomes Colonial Secretary.

1916
Dec.   Party withdraws support from Asquith. Law advises King to appoint Lloyd George as Prime Minister and Conservatives support his Coalition government. Law (Chancellor of the Exchequer), Curzon and Milner become members of the five-man war cabinet. Sir George Younger becomes party chairman.

1918
Dec.   Party fights general election in alliance with Lloyd George Liberals, with approved candidates of both parties receiving the 'coupon' from Law and Lloyd George. 'Couponed' Conservatives win 332 seats; a further 50 Conservatives also elected.

1921
Mar.   Law retires because of illness. Succeeded as leader by Austen Chamberlain.

1922
Oct.   Party meeting at the Carlton Club rejects advice of its leaders and votes to fight forthcoming general election independently of the Coalition. Law and Stanley Baldwin the major speakers in favour of this move. Chamberlain resigns party leadership; Law replaces him and forms a government excluding most of the Coalitionists, and

pledges that there will be no attempt to introduce tariffs before a further election.

Nov. General election: Conservatives win 344 seats and comfortable majority.

1923

Mar. Sir Stanley Jackson becomes party chairman, succeeding Viscount Younger who becomes treasurer and between then and 1929 overhauls the party's finances.

May Law retires through ill-health and dies soon afterwards. Succeeded by Baldwin.

Oct. Baldwin calls for tariffs, and in deference to Law's pledge dissolves parliament.

Dec. General election: Conservatives win only 258 seats and fall well short of a majority.

1924

Jan. Baldwin is defeated by Labour and Liberal votes in parliament, and resigns the premiership.

Oct. Conservatives win sweeping victory at general election, with 412 seats, with Baldwin having revived Law's pledge. Baldwin forms his second government, which includes most of the former Coalitionists: Churchill (Chancellor of the Exchequer), Austen Chamberlain (Foreign Secretary) and Lord Birkenhead (India Secretary); only Balfour and Horne remain outside.

1925

Apr. Balfour enters cabinet.

1926

Nov. J C C Davidson becomes party chairman and sets about an extensive reorganization and modernization of the party.

1928

Feb. Robert Topping becomes principal agent.

1929

May Baldwin, rejecting alternative strategies, appeals to the country on the slogan 'Safety First'. Although gaining slightly more votes than Labour, the party wins fewer seats (260). Baldwin resigns immediately, rather than negotiate with Lloyd George for Liberal support.

Nov. Conservative Research Department (CRD) set up by Davidson to work on policy proposals.

1930

Mar. Neville Chamberlain becomes chairman of Conservative Research Department; Joseph Ball, formerly of MI5, its director. Period of virtual civil war in the party as Lords Beaverbrook and Rothermere exploit Conservative discontent with Baldwin and his failure to come out for protectionism.

May One of the results of this is Davidson's resignation; he is succeeded by Neville Chamberlain.

Oct. Party policy moves to overt protectionism.

1931

Jan. Churchill resigns from shadow cabinet over protectionism and India.

Feb. Topping becomes the party's first general director (until September 1945).

Mar. Leadership crisis; Chamberlain resigns party chairmanship (succeeded by Lord Stonehaven), possibly to free himself to take over the leadership, but Baldwin finally defeats his critics and is confirmed as leader.

Aug. Conservatives enter National government under Ramsay Mac-Donald, with four ministers in a ten-strong cabinet.

Oct. General election, fought under the auspices of the National government, in which Conservatives win 470 seats. Baldwin remains Lord President and, in effect, deputy Prime Minister. Conservatives have eleven ministers in a twenty-strong cabinet.

1931–5

Series of revolts by Conservative back-benchers, including Churchill, against the government's liberal policy on India. Conservatives gradually increase representation in cabinet.

1935

June Baldwin succeeds MacDonald as Prime Minister.

Nov. National government wins general election; Conservatives have 387 of its 429 seats, and 15 out of 22 cabinet posts.

1936

Mar. Douglas Hacking becomes party chairman.

1937

May Baldwin retires; succeeded by Neville Chamberlain.

1938

Feb. Anthony Eden, Foreign Secretary, resigns in protest against the government's foreign policy.

Oct. Bulk of party supports Chamberlain's settlement of the Czecho-slovakian crisis at Munich conference, though Duff Cooper resigns as First Lord of the Admiralty and some Conservative MPs, most notably Churchill, express bitter opposition.

1939

Sep. On outbreak of war Chamberlain offers Labour a place in a Coalition government, but is rebuffed. Churchill enters cabinet as First Lord of the Admiralty.

1940

May Chamberlain resigns as Prime Minister after expressions of back-bench discontent with conduct of war. Lord Halifax (Foreign Secretary) stands aside to allow Churchill to become premier. Conservatives have three members (one of them Chamberlain) in Churchill's five-man war cabinet.

Oct. Chamberlain resigns through ill-health; Churchill becomes party leader.

1942

Mar. Thomas Dugdale becomes party chairman.

1944

Oct. Ralph Assheton becomes party chairman.

1945

May Following victory in Europe, Labour withdraws from the Coalition. Churchill forms a Caretaker government pending a general election.

July General election sees heavy defeat for the Conservatives, who with their allies can win only 209 seats. Churchill remains party leader until 1955.

Labour party

1914

Aug. MacDonald resigns as chairman of Labour MPs when parliamentary party supports entry into the war; succeeded by Henderson (who is also party general secretary).

1915

May Labour supports new Asquith Coalition: Henderson enters cabinet as President of the Board of Education, to advise the government on labour matters.

1916

Dec. Henderson enters Lloyd George's five-man war cabinet as a Minister without Portfolio.

1917

Aug. Henderson forced to resign from cabinet over Stockholm conference; Labour remains in the government, with George Barnes taking Henderson's place. William Adamson becomes chairman of parliamentary party.

1918

Jan.–Jun. Party conferences accept the new party constitution drawn up by Henderson and Sidney Webb. It allows for individual membership of the party, while Clause Four commits the party to 'socialist' aims. The party's policies are set out more fully in the programme *Labour and the New Social Order*.

Dec. Labour wins 57 seats at the general election and is largest opposition party, but most of its leading figures, including Mac-Donald and Henderson, are defeated.

1921
Feb. Clynes replaces Adamson as parliamentary chairman.

June Rejection of Communist party's application for affiliation.

1922
Oct. Rejection of renewed Communist party application for affiliation.

Nov. Labour wins 142 seats at the general election. MacDonald challenges and defeats Clynes by 61 votes to 56, and becomes first person to be styled 'leader' of Labour party.

1923
Dec. Labour wins 191 seats at general election.

1924
Jan. Baldwin is defeated in parliament. King asks MacDonald to form first Labour government, which survives with Liberal support.

Sep. Government defeated on a motion to set up an investigation of its handling of Campbell Case. MacDonald calls a general election.

Oct. Party conference rejects Communist affiliation, and declares that Communists may not be endorsed as Labour candidates nor accepted as individual members. Labour loses election, winning only 151 seats.

1926
May General Strike.

Nov. Sheffield becomes first major city to come under Labour municipal control.

1927
Apr. Trade Disputes Act replaces 'contracting out' of the political levy with 'contracting in', a severe blow to party finances.

1928
Oct. Adoption of new programme, *Labour and the Nation*, more moderate and vague than *Labour and the New Social Order*. Communists barred as trade union delegates to the party conference.

1929
May General election sees Labour gain 287 seats. MacDonald forms second minority Labour government, dependent on Liberal support.

1930
May Sir Oswald Mosley resigns as Chancellor of the Duchy of

Lancaster over the failure of the government to adopt the radical 'solution' to unemployment proposed in his 'memorandum'.

1931

Aug. Cabinet splits over demand to cut unemployment benefits. MacDonald stays on as head of National government, with a few Labour supporters. Labour goes into opposition; Henderson elected party leader.

Oct. General election results in a heavy defeat for Labour, which wins only 46 seats. Henderson loses his seat, but remains party leader while George Lansbury leads the parliamentary Labour party (PLP).

Nov. Reconstitution of National Joint Council (National Council of Labour from 1934) with representatives of national executive committee and PLP but dominated by TUC general council.

1932

Aug. Independent Labour party (ILP) disaffiliates from the Labour party. Socialist League formed as a group of 'loyal grousers' aiming to radicalize the party.

Oct. Henderson, still outside parliament, resigns the party leadership; succeeded by Lansbury.

1934

Mar. Labour wins control of London County Council for first time.

Oct. New party programme, *For Socialism and Peace*, adopted. James Middleton succeeds Henderson as general secretary.

1935

Oct. Lansbury resigns in protest against its support for economic sanctions against Italy over its invasion of Abyssinia. Attlee elected leader pending the general election.

Nov. General election gives Labour 154 seats. Attlee confirmed as leader (with 58 votes on first ballot and 88 on second) despite challenges from Morrison (44, 48) and Arthur Greenwood (33, eliminated).

1936

Jan. Rejection of appeal for Communist affiliation.

1937

May Following party leadership's hostility towards its 'Unity Campaign' the Socialist League is forced to dissolve itself.

Oct. Party conference changes method of election for the party's national executive committee, giving more power to local parties. *Labour's Immediate Programme* outlines the measures that a majority Labour government would implement in a five-year term of office.

1939

Jan. Sir Stafford Cripps, Aneurin Bevan and others expelled for their support of a popular front.

Sept. Party agrees to wartime electoral truce but refuses to join Chamberlain's government.

1940

May Labour refuses Chamberlain's offer of coalition, but agrees to serve under Churchill. Attlee and Greenwood enter the five-man war cabinet. Bevin and Morrison join later.

1942

Feb. Policy statement *The Old World and the New Society* calls for retention of controls, planning and public ownership.

1944

Mar. Morgan Phillips becomes general secretary.

1945

May Labour withdraws from Coalition.

July General election gives Labour a massive victory; with 393 seats. Attlee forms the first majority Labour government.

Liberal party

1914

Aug. Liberal government under Asquith takes Britain into First World War. John Morley, John Burns and junior minister C P Trevelyan resign in protest.

1915

May Formation of Asquith Coalition with Liberals retaining the more important posts. Lloyd George becomes Minister of Munitions.

1916

Jan. Sir John Simon resigns from cabinet over conscription.

July Lloyd George becomes War Secretary.

Dec. Asquith loses support of Conservatives and resigns as Prime Minister; replaced by Lloyd George. The party splits as Asquith takes about two-thirds of Liberal MPs into opposition.

1918

Dec. Lloyd George and the Coalition Liberals fight 'coupon' election in alliance with the Conservatives. Lloyd George remains Prime Minister, although there are far fewer Coalition Liberals (127) than Conservatives. Asquith loses his seat and his followers are reduced to 36, led by Sir Donald Maclean.

1920

Feb. Asquith wins Paisley by-election.

Mar.   Coalition Liberal MPs reject Lloyd George's idea of 'fusion' with the Conservatives, and instead form their own constituency parties.

1922
Oct.   Lloyd George resigns premiership after Carlton Club meeting of Conservatives votes to abandon Coalition.
Nov.   The two Liberal groups fight general election separately: Lloyd George (National) Liberals win 53 seats to Asquithians' 62.

1923
Dec.   The two factions reunite to face Baldwin's attack on free trade. Asquith and Lloyd George issue a joint manifesto and the organizations are merged, but Lloyd George retains control over his headquarters and political fund. Liberals win 158 seats.

1924
Jan.   Liberals help Labour to oust Baldwin's government and give general support to the minority Labour government.
Sep.   Labour government falls on a Liberal motion regarding its handling of the Campbell Case.
Oct.   Lloyd George refuses to turn over his political fund for party use: only 339 Liberal candidates can be run, winning only 40 seats. Asquith is among those defeated.

1925
Feb.   Asquith goes to House of Lords. Lloyd George is elected chairman of parliamentary party; seven MPs who oppose him, led by Walter Runciman, form the Radical Group. The Liberal 'Million Fund' is launched to raise £1 million and so free the party from financial reliance on Lloyd George, but fails to make an impact. The Liberal Land Committee publishes the 'Green Book', *The Land and the Nation*, and Lloyd George forms the Land and Nation League.

1926
May   Asquith attacks Lloyd George for not supporting the government more strongly in the General Strike.
Oct.   Asquith resigns party leadership; succeeded by Lloyd George.

1927
Jan.–Feb.   Lloyd George purges party organization of Asquithians, who form the Liberal Council to work against him. Sir Robert Hutchison becomes chief whip and Sir Herbert Samuel is appointed chairman of the organization committee.

1928
Feb.   Publication of the report of the Liberal Industrial Inquiry, *Britain's Industrial Future* (the 'Yellow Book') advocating loan-financed public works to solve the nation's industrial ills. It forms the basis of the 1929 manifesto.

1929

May Liberals gain over 5 million votes but only 59 seats in the general election. Lloyd George, hoping to bargain between the two major parties, is forced into general support of a minority Labour government by Baldwin's decision to resign immediately.

Dec. The party splits over the government's Coal Bill.

1930

Nov. Hutchison resigns as chief whip in protest at continuing support for the government; succeeded by Sir Archibald Sinclair. Simon starts talks with the Conservatives about a possible defection of right-wing Liberals.

1931

Jun. Simon, Hutchison and Ernest Brown resign the Liberal whip.

Jul. Lloyd George falls seriously ill.

Aug. Liberals support the newly formed National government. Samuel (acting leader) and Lord Reading enter the ten-man cabinet.

Sep. A group of twenty-one MPs led by Simon declare their independent support of the National government.

Oct. Simon forms Liberal National group. At general election, seats won by thirty-five Liberal Nationals ('Simonites'), thirty-three Liberals ('Samuelites') and four anti-government Liberals (Lloyd George and his family).

Nov. The Liberals gain three places, and the Liberal Nationals two, in the new twenty-strong cabinet. Lloyd George resigns party leadership; succeeded by Samuel.

1932

Feb. Import Duties Bill introduced: Samuelite free traders are allowed to oppose this while remaining in the government by the 'agreement to differ'.

Jun. Maclean (deceased) is replaced in the cabinet by a Conservative.

Sep. Following the Ottawa agreements on imperial preference, the Samuelite ministers resign, but the Liberal Nationals stay in the government. However, the Liberals continue to give general parliamentary support to the government.

1933

Nov. Samuelites move into opposition.

1935

Nov. At the general election the Liberals are reduced to twenty-one. Samuel loses his seat; succeeded as leader by Sinclair.

1939

Sept. Liberals refuse to join Chamberlain's government but accept electoral truce.

1940

May Liberals join the Churchill Coalition, but gain no seats in war cabinet; Sinclair becomes Air Secretary.

1945

July Liberals win twelve seats at the general election. Sinclair loses his seat and is succeeded as leader by Clement Davies.

6. Other parties

British Fascisti/Fascists

Formed in 1923 by assorted members of middle-class pressure groups plus some young 'toughs', and inspired by Mussolini's Italy, with which it maintained some links. But most of its policies were little more than extreme anti-socialism, plus increasing anti-Semitism in the 1930s. In 1926 its offer of help to the government during the General Strike was rejected. In 1927 it adopted the blue shirt as a uniform. It was never more than a few hundred strong. Most of its abler members left to join the British Union of Fascists (BUF) in 1932, and it finally collapsed in 1934. It never fought a parliamentary election, and its main significance was in training some of the people who eventually became the leading administrators of the BUF.

British Socialist party (BSP)

Marxist party formed in 1911–12 from an amalgamation of left-wing groupings, especially the Social Democratic party (formerly Federation), but also left-wing members of the Independent Labour party. The party claimed to be committed to revolutionary socialism, but its remoteness from working-class struggles meant that it lost out to the more radical syndicalist movements of the time, and by 1914 its membership had halved to around 20 000. It was heavily defeated in the three pre-war by-elections that it fought. The war added to its difficulties, with its leading figure, H M Hyndman, taking a strongly pro-war, anti-German stance at odds with the feelings of the majority. After the Easter 1916 conference the Hyndmanites left to form the National Socialist party (Social Democratic Federation from 1920, when it affiliated to the Labour party; dissolved October 1939). The BSP now took an anti-war stance based on pacifism rather than the revolutionary defeatism of Lenin and the Russian Bolsheviks. From January 1916 the BSP was affiliated to the Labour party, and at the 1918 election twelve of its sixteen candidates secured Labour endorsement, but none was elected, although a Coalition Liberal MP, C Malone, did join the party in June 1920. In the following month the BSP became the largest part of the newly formed Communist party of Great Britain.

British Union of Fascists (BUF)

Organization formed in October 1932 by Sir Oswald Mosley. In part it evolved from the New party, although it also included fascists from other organizations. The party's original programme favoured a corporate state, full employment and high wages via autarky and public works, intense anti-socialism, fervent patriotism, and a dictatorship. At first support rose steadily, and then spectacularly in the first half of 1934 as Lord Rothermere lent the support of his newspapers to the new movement. However, the Fascists' brutal treatment of hecklers at the Olympia rally (7 June 1934) plus Hitler's suppression of his Nazi opponents in the Night of the Long Knives (30 June) helped Rothermere decide to withdraw his support; and this, along with the continuing revival of the economy and the BUF's increasing anti-Semitism, meant that membership fell from 50 000 to around 5 000 by the end of the year. The movement was soon in severe difficulties and at the 1935 election put up no candidates, adopting the slogan 'Fascism next time'. In 1936 it became the British Union of Fascists and National Socialists, reflecting the increasing influence of Nazi Germany. By now it was concentrating especially on local campaigns, and it returned to prominence in 1936 when one of these – the anti-Semitic campaign in the East End of London – threatened to get out of hand. In October 1936 Fascists were prevented by thousands of protestors from marching through the area in the 'Battle of Cable Street'. The Public Order Act, which followed, outlawed political uniforms, so that the black shirt could no longer be worn. Financial difficulties in 1937 led to severe cut-backs and the secession of some leading figures into the National Socialist League. Membership rose again to around 22 500 in 1938–9 because of Mosley's opposition to war with Germany; but after the outbreak of war BUF candidates were annihilated at by-elections. In May 1940 Mosley and 747 other Fascists were imprisoned under Defence Regulations. That July, the BUF's activities were suspended. It had never won a parliamentary seat.

Common Wealth (CW)

Left-wing body formed in 1942. It based its appeal on Christian morality, and its policy was one of extreme socialization, although it eschewed the term 'socialism' in favour of 'Common Ownership'. Its main appeal was to the middle classes. The major figure was the former Liberal MP Sir Richard Acland. CW stood in by-elections where Conservative candidates were not being opposed by Labour owing to the electoral truce, and won startling victories at Eddisbury in 1943, Skipton in 1944 and Chelmsford in 1945. But at the 1945 election only one CW candidate (unopposed by Labour) won. He, like Acland, soon joined the Labour party.

Communist party of Great Britain (CPGB)

Formed in August 1920 from an amalgamation of left-wing groups (the British Socialist party, the Communist Unity Group of the Socialist Labour party, the Communist party (British section of the Third International) and parts of the shop stewards' movement). Most of its members came from the BSP. The party declared its adherence to the Third (Communist) International in Moscow and its commitment to the dictatorship of the proletariat, and applied for affiliation to the Labour party. The last was rejected repeatedly in the early 1920s by Labour, as were further applications in 1936 and 1943. In the early years, repeated attempts were made to work through the Labour party, but the rejection of affiliation plus Labour's refusal to accept Communists as party members or candidates (1924) or trade union delegates to party conference (1927) made this more difficult to sustain, as did low membership throughout the 1920s (never over 11 000). The only Communist MPs were Malone (1920–2), J T Walton Newbold (Motherwell, 1922–3), and Shapurji Saklatvala (North Battersea, 1922–3, 1924–9). By 1928 a substantial section favoured a new line, and the Communist International also wanted a change, so a new leadership of younger men – Harry Pollitt, Rajani Palme Dutt and William Rust – emerged to take the party into extreme sectarianism in the 'class against class' period, when all other parties were condemned as fascist. But this failed. All the party's candidates at the 1929 and 1931 elections were defeated (most very heavily) and from 1933 onwards, after the rise of Hitler in Germany, the CPGB once again began to call for united action with Labour and the ILP. With the continuing march of fascism abroad and the USSR's desire for a diplomatic *rapprochement* with the western powers, the party was forced to adopt the 'popular front' in 1935–6, aiming to unite all opponents of fascism and the National government. However, this also failed, although there was an increase in membership and the election of a single MP, William Gallacher at West Fife, in 1935. At the outbreak of war the USSR was neutral and so the CPGB returned to sectarianism, attacking the war and Labour's support for it. But the German attack on the Soviet Union in June 1941 meant that it switched to wholehearted support for the war effort, and this line, plus British admiration of Soviet resistance, helped to increase party membership to record levels – 60 000 in 1943 – and to elect two MPs, Gallacher and Phil Piratin at Mile End (London) in 1945. But nineteen other candidates were defeated, most heavily. During the interwar period the CPGB did play an important role in some areas, such as the organization of the unemployed, rank-and-file movements in the trade unions, and tenants' struggles. But its influence was generally greater the less it stressed its Communism.

31

Imperial Fascist League (IFL)

Formed in November 1928 along patriotic anti-socialist lines, the
IFL moved towards ferocious anti-Semitism in 1930 when Arnold
Leese emerged as its leading figure. IFL members wore uniforms and
attacked Jews verbally and physically. The IFL never had more than a
hundred active members, and never fought parliamentary elections.
It refused to collaborate with the British Union of Fascists, which
Leese saw as a Jewish plot to take the teeth out of British fascism.
With Leese's imprisonment in 1937 the League collapsed. It was to
Leese, rather than Mosley, that some of the founders of the National
Front were to look for inspiration in the 1950s and 1960s.

Independent Labour party (ILP)

Formed in 1893, the ILP played a leading role in the formation
of the Labour Representation Committee (Labour party) in 1900.
It campaigned for Labour to adopt socialism and provided a way
for individuals who were not members of trade unions to join
the Labour party. The ILP also provided some of Labour's best-
known leaders. The ILP was more critical than Labour of the First
World War, arousing considerable right-wing and some Labour
hostility. However, their line appealed to many radical Liberals,
like Sir Charles Trevelyan, who worked with ILPers in the Union
of Democratic Control and joined the ILP during or after the
war. The Labour party's 1918 constitution, however, allowed for
individual membership and declared a commitment to socialism. In
search of a new role, the ILP moved leftwards, helped in 1922 by
an influx of left-wing MPs from Clydeside under the leadership of
John Wheatley. In 1925 it adopted 'Socialism in our Time', a radical
programme in sharp contrast to Labour's increasing moderation. By
the late 1920s some members were looking to abandon the Labour
party, and this view was strengthened by the performance of the
second Labour government (1929–31), during the life of which some
ILP MPs acted as a separate group. At the 1931 election nineteen
ILP candidates were not endorsed by the Labour party; five
were elected. In August 1932 the party voted to disaffiliate from the
Labour party, but a substantial minority abandoned the ILP instead.
Cooperation with the Communists in 1933–4 had further adverse
results, with members either defecting to that party or returning to
Labour in disgust. By the end of 1934 the ILP was in collapse: in
1935 it could hold only four seats in its Clydeside heartland. The
party opposed the Second World War, but made little impact in
by-elections. At the 1945 election it retained three seats, but after
the death of its leader, Maxton, in 1946 the remaining MPs returned
to Labour.

Irish Nationalist party

Group founded in 1873 as the Home Rule League, which aimed to gain self-government for Ireland. By 1900 it had recovered from the trauma of the Parnell divorce case, and at each election between then and 1910 it won most of the seats in Ireland, with 84 in December 1910. This meant it held the balance of power in parliament, and so was able to force Asquith's Liberal government to pass home rule legislation, but at the outbreak of war in 1914 this was suspended for the duration of the conflict. Divisions over the war, and the Easter Rising in Dublin in 1916, discredited the party and at the 1918 election it could win only 7 seats, with the more extreme Sinn Fein winning 73.

Liberal National party ('Simonites')

Group formed shortly before the 1931 election under the former Liberal cabinet minister Sir John Simon. Simon, discontented with the leadership of Lloyd George and Samuel and their support of the Labour government, had been negotiating with the Conservatives from November 1930 onwards, and in June 1931 he and two others resigned the Liberal whip. With the formation of the National government, 23 Liberal MPs declared that their first allegiance was to MacDonald, and they formed a separate group in time to fight 41 seats at the 1931 election, winning 35. Simon (Foreign Secretary) and Runciman (President of the Board of Trade) entered the cabinet after the election, and this representation was increased to three in 1932 and four in 1935. Despite Samuelite approaches they remained committed to the National government, being prepared to accept protection, and did not resign with the Samuelites in 1932. In 1935 they won 33 seats, and remained in the government until the fall of Chamberlain in May 1940. However, they were unrepresented in Churchill's war cabinet and in 1945 won only eleven seats. The Woolton–Teviot Agreement of 1947 drew them still closer to the Conservatives, and the party ceased to exist as a separate group in 1966.

National Democratic party (NDP)

Formed as the Socialist National Defence Committee in May 1915 to represent 'patriotic labour', it was renamed the British Workers' National League in March 1916, British Workers' League (BWL) in March 1917, and National Democratic and Labour party in May 1918. Its leading figure was Victor Fisher. By February 1917, when an electoral pact was agreed with the Conservatives, it had 81 branches; within a year this had grown to 221. At the 1918 election the NDP ran 26 candidates, and 10 were elected, its most spectacular successes being the defeat of Labour's most prominent leaders, MacDonald and Henderson. The party never made much impact in parliament, and in December 1921 it reverted to its former name, the BWL. At the 1922 election its nine MPs ran as National (Lloyd George) Liberals; all were defeated. In 1925 it changed its name to the Empire Citizen's League, which was dissolved around 1927.

National Labour party

Group formed prior to the 1931 election as a vehicle for MacDonald and his fellow Labour supporters of the National government, who had been expelled from the Labour party. At the election they won thirteen seats, and four ministers remained in the post-election cabinet – MacDonald himself, J H Thomas (Dominions Secretary), Lord Snowden (Lord Privy Seal) and Lord Sankey (Lord Chancellor). However, the movement was never strong and had little real organization outside Westminster. In 1932 Snowden resigned from the government and was replaced by a Conservative; in 1935 MacDonald was replaced as Prime Minister by Baldwin, and Sankey was dropped from the cabinet. Although MacDonald's son, Malcolm, joined the cabinet as Colonial Secretary in June 1935, both he and his father lost their seats at that year's general election, which saw the party reduced to eight MPs elected on Conservative sufferance. The MacDonalds soon returned at by-elections, but with the resignation of Thomas over the budget leak scandal in May 1936, and Ramsay MacDonald's retirement the following year, National Labour ceased to have any meaning. When Malcolm MacDonald was made High Commissioner in Canada in 1941, the remaining MPs agreed not to elect a replacement leader, and the organization wound itself up shortly before the 1945 election.

National party

Body of eight Conservative MPs opposed to the Lloyd George Coalition, formed in August 1917 by Henry Page Croft and Sir Richard Cooper. It combined a radical anti-German line with protectionism and the extension of conscription to Ireland. Although it gained the support of the right-wing *Morning Post*, it was largely ignored elsewhere; the Conservative leader, Law, dismissed it as irrelevant. At the 1918 election only Croft and Cooper among its 26 candidates were successful. In April 1921 the party was wound up and its two MPs rejoined the Conservative party.

New party

Party formed by Sir Oswald Mosley in February 1931 to support his proposals for a radical policy of streamlined government, public works and imperial economic self-sufficiency. It was backed by three other Labour MPs – Lady Cynthia Mosley, John Strachey and Robert Forgan. They were expelled from the Labour party for 'gross disloyalty'. The Ulster Unionist MP W E D Allen also joined; in October a Liberal MP, C R Dudgeon, followed suit. At the Ashton-under-Lyne by-election in April 1931, Allan Young won 16 per cent of the votes and helped to ensure that Labour lost the seat. However, Mosley was increasingly tempted by fascism, and this resulted in the resignation of Young and Strachey in July 1931. At that October's general election, all the party's candidates were defeated, most very heavily. In December 1931 the party's newspaper was closed down, and Mosley concentrated on the organization of a group of young 'toughs' in what was increasingly referred to as 'Nupa'. These fascist leanings were confirmed by his enthusiastic response to Mussolini's Italy, which he visited in early 1932. The remains of the New party were merged into the British Union of Fascists later in the year.

Plaid Cymru (PC)

Welsh nationalist party formed in 1925 as a reaction against continuing anglicization and the failure of Lloyd George's government to help Wales. Initially concerned solely with the preservation of Welsh language and culture, by the 1930s it had evolved more detailed proposals for dominion status for Wales within the British Empire. The leading figure was the writer Saunders Lewis, who became its president in 1926. The party ran four parliamentary candidates between 1929 and 1935, but all were defeated. In September 1936 Lewis and two others set fire to an RAF bombing school in north Wales. They gave themselves up immediately and were imprisoned. PC presented the men as martyrs and support increased. However, by the outbreak of war PC was still very much a minority, intellectual-dominated sect, with little appeal even in the Welsh-speaking north, a fact shown by its modest, though improved, performances in the two wartime by-elections it fought. It did not win a parliamentary seat until 1966.

Scottish National party (SNP)

Formed in April 1928 as the National party of Scotland to campaign for greater self-government. Initially it was led by left-wingers like R B Cunninghame Graham and R E Muirhead, but its radicalism put off other nationalists, who formed the Scottish party (SP) in

October 1932. The two groups came together again in April 1934 as the SNP, and after this the left was increasingly marginalized. The party fared better in elections than its Welsh counterpart: up to the merger in 1934, seven of fifteen SNP candidates, and the single SP candidate, saved their deposits. From then until and including the 1945 general election, there were twenty-three SNP candidates, of whom ten saved their deposits and one who was elected MP for Motherwell at a by-election in April 1945, although he lost the seat in the 1945 general election. The party did not win another seat until 1967.

Sinn Fein

Group (meaning 'Ourselves Alone') formed in 1905–8. Its pre-war impact was limited, but Sinn Feiners took a leading part – not least as martyrs – in the Easter Rising of 1916, and as the idea of Home Rule became discredited, it came to prominence, winning 73 seats at the 1918 election and pushing the Nationalists into near-oblivion. The Sinn Feiners refused to take their seats at Westminster and formed a Dáil in Dublin. During the struggle against the British that followed, Sinn Fein took the leading role, but the movement split in 1921–2 over the Anglo-Irish treaty. The Irish civil war which followed saw 'free staters' like Michael Collins, who were prepared to accept partition and Dominion status under the Crown, opposed by 'republicans' who wanted an Irish republic and nothing less, under the leadership of Eamon de Valera. Eventually the free staters won, and in 1926 de Valera, having modified his stance, formed a new party, Fianna Fáil. The rump of Sinn Fein remained behind the activities of the Irish Republican Army (IRA), which continued spasmodic violence during the interwar period. Its most spectacular terrorist outrages came in January–August 1939, when it launched a series of explosions and fires in London, Liverpool, Coventry, Birmingham and other cities, which resulted in at least seven deaths and dozens of injuries, as well as considerable damage to property. Fianna Fáil dominated Irish politics from 1932 onwards.

7. Pressure groups

Co-operative Women's Guild   formed in 1883, which at first largely confined itself to issues of consumerism and Co-operative politics, but which by the interwar period was taking a much broader view of its role, for example in the areas of housing, health, divorce law reform, and encouraging female unionization.

Council of Action   formed at a joint conference of the TUC, NEC of the Labour party and parliamentary Labour party in August 1920 to attempt to prevent British arming of Poland in its war against Soviet Russia. The council could claim success, in so far as the British government ceased overt arms shipments. However, Lloyd George had been planning to end shipments anyway, and the response to the council's call was due more to war-weariness than to any great sympathy with the Bolsheviks. Local councils were set up and their increasing radicalism and calls for 'direct action' against the government led to the council being wound up early in 1921.

Economic League   formed 1919 to counter socialism and advertise the merits of private enterprise. It co-ordinated anti-union activities and acted against what it saw as 'subversion'.

Empire Crusade (EC)   launched in December 1929 by Lord Beaverbrook, proprietor of newspapers including the *Daily Express*, to campaign for Empire Free Trade, which aimed to make the Empire into a unitary trading block with high tariffs against the products of non-Empire countries. The Crusade prospered among protectionist Conservatives in some parts of Britain in 1930, to the extent that some party members, encouraged by Beaverbrook, sent their subscriptions to the EC instead. EC candidates ran against Conservatives at some by-elections, and one was elected in 1930. However, the Conservative party's move towards protectionism cut the ground from under Beaverbrook, and after March 1931 the EC made little impact.

Empire Industries Association (EIA)   formed 1924 to campaign for protection and imperial preference; its main support came from Conservative business people, many of them MPs.

Federation of British Industries (FBI)   formed 1916 to embrace trade associations and employers' organizations, and represent them in all matters except industrial relations. In this period it was not insignificant, but it had less impact on government than in the period after 1945.

India Defence League   formed 1933 to oppose the National government's liberal Government of India Bill. Supported mainly by right-wing Conservatives, including Churchill. Although it failed to prevent the legislation, it made its passage more difficult, and showed how much diehard imperialist sentiment remained in the Conservative party.

Left Book Club   formed by the left-wing publisher Victor Gollancz in May 1936. It offered each month a book selected by Gollancz, John Strachey and Harold Laski for its members to buy at a special cheap rate. The selections covered diverse topics but there were many about the Soviet Union and foreign affairs, and before the war they generally favoured the Communist party's 'popular front' line. The Nazi–Soviet Pact of August 1939 damaged its image, and its membership fell from its peak figure of 60 000. The club remained in existence until 1948.

National Confederation of Employers' Organizations (NCEO) formed 1919 as a complement to the Federation of British Industries, to represent employers on industrial relations issues.

National Federation of Women's Institutes   formed 1917 to propagate the virtues of motherhood and housewifery in rural areas. Starting with 137 branches and originally financed by the Board of Agriculture, it had 1 405 branches by the time the board pulled out in 1919. By 1937 it had over 300 000 members.

National Minority Movement   formed in 1924 out of the British Bureau of the (Moscow-based) Red International of Labour Unions ('Profintern'). A Communist front organization aiming to increase the power of the left in established unions and to work for a united front, it made some progress in the mid-1920s. But its activities were increasingly circumscribed by the unions after the General Strike, and the move to 'class against class' in 1928–9, which favoured the organization of new Communist unions, weakened it further, although it continued to exist until 1935.

National Unemployed Workers' Movement   organization formed under Communist guidance in 1921 with the aim of acting as a trade union for unemployed people, to increase benefits, defend claimants and publicize the plight of unemployed people. Its leading figure, Wal Hannington, was a Communist, and it was generally under firm Communist control. It had a large, though shifting, membership, and organized hunger marches and represented claimants at benefit tribunals, but its successes were mundane and the Communists' hope that it would help recruit members to the party and destabilize capitalism came to very little. Its activities virtually ended in 1939 although it was not formally dissolved until 1945.

National Union of Townswomen's Guilds formed 1929 from earlier women's groups, with the aim of organizing women in places with a population exceeding 4 000 (the upper limit for Women's Institutes). By 1939 it had 54 000 members.

Trades Union Congress (TUC) formed 1868 to coordinate action between the unions affiliated to it. At its apex was a parliamentary committee which aimed to press for favourable legislation. The TUC played a major part in the formation of the Labour party in 1900. In 1921 the parliamentary committee was replaced by a larger and more powerful general council. The TUC coordinated the General Strike, 1926, but thereafter it moved, under its general secretary, Walter Citrine, towards a more accommodating stance with state and employers. The TUC played a major role in reorienting the Labour party after the débâcle of 1931.

Union of Democratic Control (UDC) formed shortly after the outbreak of war in 1914 to campaign for the democratic control of foreign and defence policy and an end to the 'secret diplomacy' which had supposedly led to the war. Many radical Liberals and socialists joined; their experience of working together, and radicals' disillusionment with the Liberal party, led many, like E D Morel, and C P Trevelyan, subsequently to join the Labour party.

War Emergency Workers' National Committee (WEWNC) formed 5 August 1914 as a collective voice for the constituent parts of the Labour movement, which, given the resignation of MacDonald as chairman of the PLP and the differing opinions held by various sections of the movement, might otherwise have fragmented. The WEWNC became the main forum of Labour during the war, concerned with industrial, social and economic as well as political issues. It was vital in keeping MacDonald in touch with the movement, and in promoting the cooperation which was to lead to the new Labour programme and constitution in 1918.

8. Machinery of government

Chronology of legislation and principal events

1915 Ministry of Munitions set up for duration of war plus a maximum of one year, to coordinate and maximize production of weapons and ammunition.

1916 Creation of five new ministries: two, Pensions and Labour, were to be permanent; the other three, Food, Shipping, and the Air Board, were intended as temporary only.

1917 Ministry of National Service set up under a director-general responsible for improving allocation of human resources; however, he had no powers of compulsion (the first director-general, Neville Chamberlain, soon resigned). Ministry of Reconstruction set up to plan post-war Britain.

1919 Ministry of Health set up as new department with comprehensive powers over health, housing and local government, replacing old Local Government Board and taking over certain functions of Board of Education. Ministry of Transport set up, with powers over all forms of domestic land and water transportation. Ministry of Agriculture and Fisheries set up to replace (and with wider powers than) the old Board of Agriculture.

1920 Ministry of Food's abolition postponed until 1922. Mines Department set up (under Board of Trade) to oversee coal industry.

1921 Ministries of Munitions and Shipping abolished.

1925 Honours (Prevention of Abuses) Act made the trade in honours illegal.

1926 Post of Secretary for Scotland upgraded to a Secretaryship of State.

1936 Sir Thomas Inskip appointed to a new office, Minister for Co-ordination of Defence.

1937 Ministers of the Crown Act revised and in many cases raised ministerial salaries; gave a pension of £2 000 a year to former Prime Ministers; and granted a salary (£2 000) to the Leader of the Opposition for the first time.

1939 Ministry of Supply set up with wide-ranging powers over materials, in readiness for the coming war.

1942 Ministry of Works and Planning replaced the Commissioners of Works; it had greater powers, especially over planning.

1943 Ministry of Town and Country Planning set up to take over Ministry of Works' functions in coordination of planning.

1944 Education Act replaced the old Board of Education with a more powerful Ministry. Ministry of National Insurance set up, taking over responsibilities of Home Office regarding workmen's compensation; of Home Office and Ministry of Health regarding national health insurance and pensions; and of Ministry of Labour regarding unemployment insurance and assistance.

1945 Ministry of Fuel and Power created to coordinate effective development of fuel resources, to oversee mining and quarrying, and generally to promote efficient use of fuel and power. Ministry of Civil Aviation formed to organize and encourage development of civil aviation.

Number of civil servants (000)

	Non-industrial	Industrial	Post Office
1910	55	—	155
1914	70	—	209
1918	221	—	197
1919	194	—	201
1923	124	—	181
1928	106	—	192
1933	118	—	195
1938	152	184	224
1944	505	658	258
1946	452	366	294

Source: Department of Employment and Productivity,
British Labour Statistics: Historical Abstract 1886–1968
(1971), p 299

9. Local government

Chronology of legislation and principal events

1914–18 Local elections suspended during wartime.

1919 Big Labour gains in London elections; heavy Liberal losses. Ministry of Health replaces old, less powerful, Local Government Board. Public Libraries Act puts county and county borough councils in sole charge of public libraries for their area, and repeals restrictions on how much can be spent on the library service. Massive Labour gains in local elections; Liberals heavily defeated and, as a result, form municipal anti-socialist pacts with the Conservatives in places like Bristol, Derby and Sheffield.

1922 Councils permitted by law to set up pension funds for their employees. After three years of gains, Labour loses heavily in the municipal elections.

1925 Rating and Valuation Act greatly simplifies the collection of rates, replacing separate payments to different councils and the Poor Law authorities by a single payment which is then divided.

1926 Boards of Guardians (Default) Act allows the Minister of Health to appoint a new board of guardians in place of an elected board which is not carrying out its functions properly. Sheffield becomes the first major city to come under Labour control.

1928 Ministry of Labour starts industrial transference scheme, to help able-bodied unemployed people to move from depressed to more prosperous areas.

1929 Neville Chamberlain's Local Government Act, a massive reform. (a) Functions: (i) as from 30 April 1929 separate Poor Law authorities are abolished, and their functions transferred to county and county borough councils, the directly elected boards of guardians being replaced by public assistance committees set up as subcommittees of the councils concerned; (ii) county councils take over responsibility for roads; (iii) county councils are given additional town planning powers. (b) Finance: (i) agricultural land and buildings are totally exempted from rates; (ii) industrial and transport undertakings are relieved of 75 per cent of their rates burden; (iii) a number of old Exchequer grants to local authorities are abolished; (iv) to compensate, a system of block grants from central to local government is set up; (v) limits on the borrowing powers of local government are abolished. Separate legislation reforms Scottish local administration on similar principles.

1930 Labour makes a net loss in council seats at the local elections for the first time since 1922.

1931 Heavy Labour losses in the local elections.

1932 Labour makes a few gains in the local elections but loses control of Sheffield (regained 1933).

1934 Labour wins control of London County Council for the first time, while the remaining Liberal councillors are all defeated. Special Areas (Development and Improvement) Act follows increasing concern at the plight of the distressed areas, and appoints two unpaid commissioners, one for the 'Special Areas' of England and Wales (south Wales, Tyneside, and west Cumberland), and one for central Scotland, each with an annual budget of £1 million, but with strict limits on how it can be spent. This marks the first major excursion into regional policy for British government.

1936 Sir Malcolm Stewart, Special Areas commissioner for England and Wales, resigns, urging stronger powers be given to his successor. First Labour net losses at local elections since 1931, and last until 1947.

1937 Special Areas (Amendment) Act offers rates and tax subsidies for up to five years to firms setting up works in these areas, and leads to the establishment of a number of trading estates, with premises ready-made for firms to set up in business.

1939–44 Local elections suspended for duration of war.

1940 Barlow Report on the Distribution of the Industrial Population published, recommending that government should plan the use of land throughout the whole country, and that factory development in the south-east should be restricted, and new industry directed to areas threatened by heavy unemployment.

1945 Local Authorities Loans Act restricts the borrowing powers of local authorities, subjecting all applications to Treasury scrutiny. Local Government Boundary Commission set up to review, and where necessary alter, the boundaries of local authorities. Massive Labour gains in the local elections: Liberals largest party in only one town (Huddersfield) and second in only three others.

Local councils under Labour control

	London County	London boroughs	Provincial England and Wales		Scotland burghs
			counties	boroughs	
1913	—	—	—	—	—
1919	—	12	3	n/a*	n/a
1922	—	4	1	n/a	n/a
1925	—	8	2	n/a	n/a
1928	—	8	—	21	n/a
1931	—	3	—	16	n/a
1934	1	15	3	39	11
1937	1	17	3	42	15
1945	1	23	10	120	37

Notes

There were no elections 1914–18 or 1939–44 inclusive

*Here, and elsewhere, n/a means that figures are not available

Source: G D H Cole, *A History of the Labour Party from 1914* (1948), pp 458–9

Social history

1. Population and migration

Chronology of legislation and principal events

1914–18 Issue of condoms to troops to prevent spread of venereal disease introduces many to barrier methods of contraception for first time. (Previously, contraception had been through abstinence, the 'withdrawal method', and illegal abortions.)

1914 Aliens Restriction Act, passed on outbreak of war, imposes strict restrictions on movement and actions of foreign nationals in Britain: they can now be prevented from entering or leaving the country, deported, and told where they may or may not travel and reside within the UK. British Nationality and Status of Aliens Act defines British nationality more closely than before, setting stringent conditions for naturalization, and limiting the types of property that aliens can own.

1915 National Registration Act sets up a register of all men and women between the ages of 15 and 65.

1918 Publication of Dr Marie Stopes's books, *Married Love* and *Wise Parenthood*, stressing the need for a full sex life for men and women, and emphasizing the merits of family planning.

1919 Aliens Restriction (Amendment) Act further redefines the position of foreign nationals in Britain: (a) aliens causing disaffection in armed forces or industry are to be imprisoned; (b) former enemy aliens are barred from working in the Merchant Navy, and strict restrictions are placed on other aliens working as merchant seamen; (c) aliens are barred from Civil Service; (d) all aliens, subject to appeal, are to re-adopt names they had in 1914; (e) former enemy aliens are to be deported immediately, unless they obtain a licence from a new advisory committee; (f) visits to Britain by former enemy aliens are severely restricted; (g) aliens' property rights are severely circumscribed.

1921 First birth control clinics established.

1925 Lifting of some of the restrictions imposed on former enemy aliens in accordance with an international agreement.

1939 National Registration Act sets up national register of entire population, and provides for issue of identity cards to all.

1940–1 Detention of foreign nationals seen as a threat to national security, many of them being imprisoned on the Isle of Man.

United Kingdom population figures (000)

	Men	Women	Total
1914	22 358	23 690	46 048
1919	20 385	24 214	44 599a
1924	21 500	23 386	44 866b
1929	21 887	23 798	45 685
1934	22 409	24 271	46 680
1939	22 962	24 800	47 762
1944	23 604	25 339	48 943c
1945	23 654	25 454	49 108c

Notes
a   Refers to civilian population only except in
    Scotland and Ireland
b   Figures after 1921 exclude Irish Free State
c   Includes members of HM Forces overseas,
    but excludes members of Armed Forces of
    other countries in UK

Sources: *Statistical Abstract* 70 (1927), pp 4–5; 80
(1937), pp 4–5; 84 (1947), p 7

Birth and death rates (per 000 population)

	Births	Deaths
1914	23.9	14.4
1919	19.1	14.8
1924	19.3a	12.6a
1929	16.7	13.6
1934	15.3	12.0
1939	15.3	12.2
1944	17.9	11.5
1945	16.2	11.4

Note
a   Figures after 1921 exclude Irish Free State

Sources: *Statistical Abstract* 70 (1927), p 7; 76
(1933), pp 6–7; 84 (1947), pp 17, 23

Selected urban populations (000)

	1911	1921	1931	1951
Greater London	7 256	7 488	8 216	8 348
Belfast	387	415[a]	438[b]	444
Birmingham	526	919	1 003	1 113
Bristol	357	377	397	443
Cardiff	182	200	224	244
Coventry	106	128	167	258
Edinburgh	401	420	439	467
Glasgow	784	1 034	1 088	1 090
Leeds	446	458	483	505
Liverpool	746	803	856	789
Luton	50	57	69	110
Manchester	714	730	766	703
Newcastle upon Tyne	267	275	283	292
Norwich	121	121	126	121
Sheffield	455	491	512	513

Notes
a   refers to 1926
b   refers to 1937

Sources: Censuses

Immigration and emigration: net migration balance, 1911–51

	Balance
1911–21	–919 000
1921–31	–672 000
1931–51	+465 000

Source: A H Halsey (ed)
British Social Trends since 1900 (2nd edn, 1988),
p 562

War casualties: civilian

First World War

In air raids by Zeppelins and aeroplanes, the casualty figures were 1 414 killed and 3 416 wounded.

Source: J B S Haldane, *APR* (1938), p 41

Second World War

	Number
1940	22 215
1941	19 543
1942	3 791
1943	3 002
1944	9 329
1945	2 404
Total	60 284

Source: *Statistical Abstract*,
84 (1947), p 33

War casualties: service personnel

First World War

	Total	Killed	Missing	Wounded	Prisoners of war
Army	2 471 152	673 375	n/a	1 643 469	154 308
Navy	74 289	43 244	n/a	25 323	5 722
Air Force	16 623	6 166	n/a	7 245	3 212
Total	2 562 064	722 785	n/a	1 676 037	163 242

Source: J M Winter, *The Great War and the British People* (1986), p 73

Second World War

	Total	Killed	Missing	Wounded	Prisoners of war
Army	569 501	144 079	33 771	239 575	152 076
Navy	73 642	50 758	820	14 663	7 410
Air Forces	112 296	69 606	6 736	22 839	13 115
Total	755 439	264 443	41 327	277 077	172 592
Women's Auxiliary Services	1 486	624	98	744	20
Merchant Navy	45 329	30 248	4 654	4 707	5 270

Source: Central Statistical Office, *Statistical Digest of the War* (1951), p 13

2. Education

Chronology of legislation and principal events

1918 Education ('Fisher') Act raises school-leaving age from 12 to 14; states that all young people between 14 and 16 in work will attend compulsory part-time instruction ('continuation schools'); states that provision of nursery schools will be greatly expanded; and central government guarantees to pay 50 per cent of local authority expenditure on education. Education (Scotland) Act reforms the separate Scottish system, raising the school-leaving age, abolishing secondary school fees, setting up continuation classes, and promising larger central government subsidies, as well as replacing the old school boards with new, large education authorities. A national non-contributory pension scheme for teachers is set up.

1919 University Grants Committee set up to administer state funding for universities. Compulsory Greek abolished at Cambridge University. Oxford University admits women to degrees for the first time.

1920 Compulsory Greek abolished at Oxford University. University College, Swansea, opens.

1922 Geddes Report recommends cuts of £18 million in education expenditure, with the raising of the school starting age from 5 to 6 and a cut in teachers' salaries; ultimately the government accepts neither proposal, and cuts of only £6.5 million are made. The teachers' superannuation scheme becomes contributory.

1925 Publication of Hadow Report, *The Education of the Adolescent*, calling for a break at 11 between 'primary' and 'secondary' education, with the latter being provided by a binary system of 'grammar' schools for more academic students and 'modern' schools for the rest between 11 and a new leaving age of 15.

1926 University of Reading established.

1929 Local Government (Scotland) Act transfers responsibility from the new authorities set up in 1918 to the four large cities and the county councils.

1931 Trevelyan's Education Bill, proposing the raising of the school-leaving age to 15 with maintenance grants in case of need, is heavily amended by Catholic Labour MPs and then defeated in House of Lords. Teachers' pay cut by 10 per cent in National government's 'economy' package.

1932 Ray Report proposes large economies by such means as replacing student grants with loans, raising staff-pupil ratios, closing smaller schools, etc, but is largely ignored by government.

1933 Government Circular 1421 comes into effect, stating that fees must be charged in all maintained secondary schools, thus eliminating the 'free secondary schools' which had grown up in many parts of the country. Fees charged would be dependent on the parents' income.

1936 Education Act and Education (Scotland) Act raises school-leaving age from 14 to 15, with effect from 1 September 1939, but if they had a job children could still leave at 14.

1938 Spens Report supports the introduction of universal free secondary education from age 11, based on intelligence testing, and a tripartite system of secondary education, with grammar, technical and secondary modern schools, between which there would be 'parity of esteem'.

1939 Raising of school-leaving age suspended on outbreak of war.

1943 Norwood Report on the secondary curriculum reports in favour of traditional subjects and no great innovations.

1944 Education ('Butler') Act, the major reform of the period, replaces the old Board of Education with a new ministry; abolishes 'elementary' education; states that in future all children will receive free primary and secondary education, divided at age 11; requires local authorities to submit plans for implementing this (in practice most were to opt for the tripartite Spens system, though few technical schools were ever developed); declares that the school-leaving age will be raised to 15 immediately (done 1947) and to 16 as soon as possible (done 1973); makes religious education and morning assemblies compulsory (nothing else is said about the curriculum); tells local authorities to expand the provision of nursery schools for the under-5s and special schools for disabled children and those with special needs; and makes independent schools subject to the education inspectorate for the first time (they are otherwise unaffected). London County Council adopts a system of comprehensive secondary schools.

1945 Education (Scotland) Act reforms Scottish education on lines similar to the Butler Act, but no religious instruction is prescribed. Cambridge University creates its first Chair of Electrical Engineering.

Expenditure (£ million)

	Central government	Local government
1914	19.5	31.8
1919	25.6	42.6
1924	47.7	72.3
1929	49.5	81.1[a]
1934	51.1	83.4
1939	61.6	100.4
1944	79.5	120.5
1945	85.3	128.1

Notes
a   There was a minor change in the method
    of accounting in 1929

Sources: *Statistical Abstract* 70 (1927),
pp 110–11, 164–5; 80 (1937), pp 158–9,
218–19; 84 (1947), p 215

University education

	Total no. taking courses	% of full-time students taking					Teaching staff
		Arts	Science	Medicine	Technology	Agriculture	
1922/3	58 952	40.9	17.4	26.6	12.5	2.7	n/a
1927/8	57 755	53.3	16.7	19.0	9.1	1.9	3 169
1932/3	64 115	50.2	16.7	22.4	9.0	1.6	3 629
1937/8	62 270	45.4	15.8	27.1	9.7	2.0	3 907
1942/3	48 029	33.9	16.5	33.5	13.7	2.4	n/a
1947/8	96 504	44.9	18.5	20.3	12.9	3.4	6 536

Source: Calculated from figures given in B R Mitchell, *British Historical Statistics* (1988), p 811

3. Health, social welfare and poverty

Chronology of legislation and principal events

1914 Local authorities obliged to provide meals for children, even in the school holidays. Pensions and allowances granted to civilians injured while on war work.

1915 Local authorities obliged to set up depots for the sale of milk for infants at cost price.

1916 Midwives (Scotland) Act makes their training more rigorous.

1917 Venereal Disease Act bans the treatment of such diseases except by qualified medical practitioners, and controls the supply and bans the advertisement of remedies.

1918 Workmen's Compensation (Silicosis) Act allows for the creation of special compensation schemes for workers exposed to silica dust. Maternity and Child Welfare Act allows local authorities to establish grant-aided antenatal and child welfare clinics. Midwives Act makes their training more rigorous.

1919 Ministry of Health and Scottish Board of Health set up. Scope of national health insurance scheme extended to those earning between £160 and £250 per annum. Nurses Registration Act and Nurses Registration (Scotland) Act obliges nurses to be registered, and imposes penalties for unregistered persons acting as nurses.

1920 National Health Insurance contributions, benefits and doctors' fees increased. Old age pensions granted to blind people at the age of 50.

1921 Public Health (Tuberculosis) Act increases the obligation of local authorities to treat and prevent tuberculosis. Obligatory registration for dentists introduced. All dismissals of local Medical Officers of Health are made subject to approval by the Minister of Health.

1923 Entitlement to workmen's compensation liberalized.

1924 Old Age Pensions Act gives the full pension of 10s (50p) to all persons over 70 earning less than 15s (75p) per week, and at reduced rates to those earning up to 34s (£1.70).

1925 Widows', Orphans' and Old Age Contributory Pensions Act permits people covered by national health insurance to pay extra contributions which, after two years, will entitle them to a pension of 10s (50p) per week between the ages of 65 and 70, or if widowed; and 5s (25p) per week for their orphans until they reach age 14.

1926 Adoption of Children Act (extended to Scotland, 1930) allows couples to adopt children legally, subject to court approval. Legitimacy Act eases the legitimization of children born to unmarried parents. Midwives and Maternity Homes Act (and Midwives and Maternity Homes (Scotland) Act 1927) tighten the regulations against unqualified midwives, and require nursing homes to be registered. Public Health (Smoke Abatement) Act lays down more stringent regulations against smoke pollution.

1927 Registration and inspection of nursing homes made compulsory (extended to Scotland 1938).

1929 Poor Law guardians abolished, and their functions transferred to local authorities, which also take over Poor Law hospitals. Infant Life (Preservation) Act states that abortion after the twenty-eighth week of pregnancy is infanticide, with the perpetrators liable to life imprisonment, except where the life of the mother is in danger.

1930 National Health Insurance (Prolongation of Insurance) Act extends the entitlement of unemployed workers whose entitlement to benefits has run out for another year; repeated 1931.

1931 Many benefits are reduced by 10 per cent as a result of the National government's economy package.

1932 Children and Young Persons Act states that juvenile courts should be different in personnel from ordinary courts, instead of just being the same courts sitting in special session, as hitherto; raises the maximum age for referral to a juvenile court from 16 to 17; abolishes corporal punishment for offenders under 14, and severely curtails it for those up to 17; empowers the courts to take children into local authority care; and strictly regulates juveniles' hours of work. National Health Insurance and Contributory Pensions Act reduces benefits under these schemes.

1933 Pharmacists obliged to be registered with the appropriate professional society.

1934 Poor Law Act and Poor Law (Scotland) Act allow certain types of income to be disregarded when assessing entitlement to public assistance.

1936 Voluntary Hospitals (Paying Patients) Act allows voluntary hospitals to treat paying patients. Midwives Act creates a full-time salaried midwifery service and bars unqualified midwives from attending births.

1937 Coal Mines (Employment of Boys) Act makes it illegal to employ boys under 16 on the night shift in coal mines. Scope of widows', orphans' and old age contributory pensions extended. Physical Training and Recreation Act encourages the development of recreational and social facilities by local authorities. National Health Insurance scheme extended to workers aged 14 and 15, at lower rates of contribution and benefit than adults.

1938 Age for entitlement to old age pensions for blind people reduced from 50 to 40; duties of local authorities to make general provision for blind people increased. Young Persons (Employment) Act sets maximum working weeks of 44 hours for 14 to 16 year olds and 48 hours for 16 to 18 year olds.

1939 Cancer Act aims to treat cancer earlier and more effectively by increasing provision for treatment, allowing for state loans to the National Radium Trust, and regulating the advertisements of treatments and 'cures'. Adoption of Children (Regulation) Act gives welfare authorities more power to supervise adoption, restricts the activities of adoption agencies, and bans payment of money in respect of adoption. Personal Injuries (Emergency Provisions) Act, passed on the outbreak of war, provides pensions and allowances to persons injured on war service.

1940 Old Age and Widows' Pensions Act reduces the pensionable age of women to 60 and gives a supplementary pension of 5s (25p) to pensioners in need on the basis of a household means test; contributions are increased to cover the cost.

1941 Determination of Needs Act abolishes the household means test for unemployment assistance and supplementary pensions: entitlement to be decided instead by a needs test which only takes into account the needs of the applicant. The unemployment assistance fund and board are abolished; in future, all payments will be made directly by the Exchequer. National Health Insurance, Contributory Pensions and Workmen's Compensation Act increases rates of contribution and benefit, and extends the scope of the schemes to cover those earning between £250 and £420 a year, so bringing in many non-manual workers for the first time. Advertisement of abortion and certain 'patent cures' banned.

1942 Beveridge Report on *Social Insurance and Allied Services* published.

1943 Nurses Act and Nurses (Scotland) Act provide for the enrolment of assistant nurses and regulate the activities of nurse-supplying agencies. Pensions and Determination of Needs Act replaces the household means test for public assistance with a test of personal need. Pensions appeal tribunals set up.

1944 Disabled Persons (Employment) Act aims to improve the employment prospects of disabled people by setting up training courses and a register of disabled persons, and obliging large employers to employ a quota of disabled people. Ministry of National Insurance set up to take over the powers of the Home Office regarding workmen's compensation, the powers of the Home Office and the Ministry of Health regarding national health insurance and pensions, and the powers of the Ministry of Labour regarding unemployment insurance and assistance.

1945 Introduction of family allowances, payable to the mother, of 5s (25p) per week for the second and each subsequent child.

Infant mortality

	Deaths of infants per 1 000 live births	
	England and Wales	Scotland
1913	108	110
1918	97	100
1923	69	79
1928	65	86
1933	64	81
1938	53	70
1943	49	65
1946	43	54

Sources: *Statistical Abstract* 70 (1927), p 34; 80 (1937), p 44; 84 (1947), p 28

Number and causes of deaths

	Number of deaths	% caused by					
		Influenza	Tuberculosis	Cancer	Heart disease	Bronchitis	Pneumonia
1913	578 044	1.2	7.1	7.6	10.3	7.6	4.0
1918	690 233	16.5	7.3	6.8	8.5	6.8	6.3
1923	526 858	1.8	7.1	10.7	12.6	7.1	7.5
1928	543 664	1.7	6.3	11.9	16.2	5.2	7.0
1933	579 467	4.4	5.5	12.2	21.0	4.4	6.2
1938	559 598	0.9	4.4	13.6	24.0	5.2	5.8
1943	574 125	2.4	4.3	14.3	24.3	6.0	5.0
1945	559 233	0.5	4.2	15.1	26.5	5.8	4.1

Note
Figures relate to Great Britain until 1921, United Kingdom from 1922; deaths outside the country (eg on active service abroad) not included

Source: Calculated from figures in *Statistical Abstract* 70 (1927), pp 32–3; 80 (1937), pp 42–3; 84 (1947), p 32

Health services (per 1 000 of population)

	Hospital beds	Nurses	Medical practitioners
1901	n/a	2.13	0.64
1911	5.48	n/a	0.62
1921	6.03	3.24	0.59
1931	n/a	3.85	0.66
1938	6.41	n/a	n/a
1941	n/a	n/a	0.75
1949	6.32	n/a	n/a
1951	n/a	4.75	0.89

Source: A H Halsey (ed) *British Social Trends since 1900* (2nd edn, 1988), pp 442, 452

4. Housing

Chronology of legislation and principal events

1914–18 Virtual cessation of house-building due to wartime demands on human and material resources.

1915 Rent rises lead to a rent strike in Glasgow. Increase of Rent and Mortgage Interest Act 'controls' rents of all houses under a certain rateable value at pre-war levels. Mortgages are not to be foreclosed, and interest payments are not to be increased. The Act is to remain in force until six months after the end of the war.

1918 Tudor Walters Report sets down relatively high standards for public housing, later followed by the Addison Act.

1919 Increase of Rent and Mortgage Interest (Restrictions) Act continues controls, which would otherwise have expired. The rateable value of 'controlled' properties is increased, and increases in rent are restricted to a maximum of 10 per cent, and mortgage interest increases to a maximum of 0.5 per cent, so long as the rate charged does not exceed 5 per cent altogether. Housing, Town Planning, &c. ('Addison') Act and Housing, Town Planning, &c. (Scotland) Act oblige local authorities to conduct a speedy survey of housing needs and report their proposals for satisfying them to the Health Ministry, and promise a state subsidy for all the costs of council-house building that cannot be met by a 1d ($\frac{1}{2}$p) in the £ increase in the rates. The Acts also introduce the principle of town planning in relation to undeveloped land. Housing (Additional Powers) Act offers government subsidies for houses built by private enterprise.

1920 Increase of Rent and Mortgage Interest (Restrictions) Act maintains controls until 1923, increasing the rateable value of properties to which they apply and restricting increases in rent to 40 per cent over the 1914 level, and in mortgage interest rates to 1 per cent, subject to a maximum of 6.5 per cent.

1920 Foundation of Welwyn Garden City.

1921 End of the Addison scheme marked by the withdrawal of all subsidies except those for houses currently being built.

1923 Increase of Rent and Mortgage Interest Restrictions (Continuance) Act continues the operation of the 1920 Act until 1925, but adding the proviso that a property would be 'decontrolled' once the current tenancy ended. This meant a gradual decline in the number of controlled rents (but controls renewed in 1925, 1927, 1929 and 1931). Housing ('Chamberlain') Act provides central government subsidies to private house-builders (or local authorities, if they could do the work more efficiently) to build moderately priced houses for sale.

1924 Prevention of Eviction Act passed by the first Labour government to protect tenants from 'unreasonable' eviction, its aim being to prevent landlords evicting tenants just so that they could then raise the rents on what would become, under the 1923 Act, 'decontrolled' properties. Housing (Financial Provisions) ('Wheatley') Act inaugurates a fifteen-year scheme of central government subsidies for the construction, by local authorities, of houses to let.

1926 Housing (Rural Workers) Act offers a twenty-year subsidy to local authorities in rural areas to assist private enterprise in building new housing at affordable rents for agricultural workers; the houses are not to be let to anyone who could afford to pay a higher rent (Act extended in 1931, 1938 and 1942).

1927 Greater London Regional Planning Committee set up.

1930 Housing ('Greenwood') Act and Housing (Scotland) Act give local authorities power to designate and take over 'clearance areas' of slum property, with the people affected having to be rehoused in new housing (for which central government subsidies are made available) before slum clearance can start. Work starts on the Wythenshawe estate, south of Manchester, which is intended ultimately to house 100 000 people.

1932 Town and Country Planning Act and Town and Country Planning (Scotland) Act extend local authorities' planning powers to cover built-up areas for the first time, giving them scope to envisage major urban reconstruction.

1933 Subsidies under the Housing Act 1924 abolished earlier than originally envisaged. Rent controls lifted from the housing of the middle and upper-working classes, leaving only poorer 'Class C' housing under control.

1935 Work starts on the massive Quarry Hill flats development in Leeds, to replace slum housing (all 938 flats were completed by 1941). Housing Act and Housing (Scotland) Act oblige local authorities to survey overcrowding in their area and to define the worst-affected areas as 'development areas'; central government grants are made available for the construction of new housing to relieve overcrowding. Councils are also given greater freedom to set and vary rent levels in the properties they own. Restriction of Ribbon Development Act aims to control the spread of new housing, usually built by speculative private builders for sale, along major roads leading out of urban areas.

1938 Housing (Financial Provisions) Act and Housing (Financial Provisions) (Scotland) Act introduce a standard scale of subsidy for all new public housing schemes.

1939 Housing (Emergency Powers) Act allows local authorities to repair and use any property they deem suitable for use as housing.

1939–45 Massive air-raid damage to housing, plus the virtual cessation of new construction and the limitation of repairs to emergencies due to wartime demands on human and material resources, lead to severe overcrowding and a massive housing shortage.

1943 Ministry of Town and Country Planning set up to coordinate planning, and many local authorities begin to produce detailed plans for the post-war rebuilding of their cities and towns, eg *Oxford Replanned, Sheffield Replanned, Exeter Phoenix.*

1944 Town and Country Planning Act gives local authorities greater powers to acquire land needed for planning purposes, with compensation payable on the basis of pre-war land values. The government announces plans to supply prefabricated temporary bungalows for erection by local authorities to ease the chronic housing shortage.

Annual average number of houses built (000s)

	1913–7	1918–22	1923–7	1928–32	1933–7	1938–9	1940–5
Annual average	30.1	38.1	169.7	200.9	339.7	307.4	27.1

Source: Calculated from figures in B R Mitchell, *British Historical Statistics* (1988), pp 390, 394

Types of tenure

(%)	1914	1938	1951
Owner-occupied	10	32	31
Rented from local authority	—	10	17
Rented from private landlord	90	58	52

Source: A H Halsey (ed) *British Social Trends since 1900* (2nd edn, 1988), p 377

5. Gender and sexuality

Chronology of legislation and principal events

1914–18 Women enter industry in unprecedented numbers, replacing men who have gone to fight in the war, by the process of 'dilution'. Many men use condoms for first time when they are issued to troops to control spread of venereal disease.

1916 National Society for Combating Venereal Disease founded.

1918 Women over 30 who are themselves, or who are the wives of, local government electors, are given the vote in parliamentary elections, and are allowed to sit as MPs. At the 1918 general election, Countess Markiewicz becomes the first woman elected to parliament, but as a Sinn Feiner she does not take her seat. Publication of Dr Marie Stopes's books *Married Love* and *Wise Parenthood*, stressing virtues of a full sex life for both partners and of family planning. Affiliation Orders Act increases maximum payment due a week from the father of an illegitimate child for his or her upkeep from 5s (25p) to 10s (50p).

1919–22 Women are combed out of most of the new areas of employment they entered during the First World War.

1919 Sex Disqualification (Removal) Act lifts legal restrictions on women entering the professions. Lady Astor (Conservative) wins a by-election and becomes the first woman to take her seat in parliament. Oxford University admits women to degrees for the first time.

1920 Legislation prevents women from working in lead manufacture and at night, and limits their ability to do shift work of any kind. Married Women (Maintenance) Act extends Affiliation Orders Act to the children of a failed marriage who are in the custody of the mother.

1921 Law changed to allow a man to marry his brother's widow. First birth control clinics established.

1922 Age of consent raised from 13 to 16.

1923 Divorce laws liberalized and equalized by allowing a woman to obtain a divorce on the grounds of her husband's adultery alone.

1925 Guardianship of Infants Act establishes legal equality between parents in event of marital breakdown: in determining custody, courts are to give the child's welfare paramount consideration.

1927 Board of Education recommends sex education in schools.

1928 Banning and prosecution of Radclyffe Hall's novel about lesbianism, *The Well of Loneliness.*

1929–31 Margaret Bondfield, Minister of Labour, becomes the first woman cabinet minister.

1929 First latex condoms appear in Britain.

1930 Church of England liberalizes its attitude towards barrier methods of contraception.

1931 Senior Liberal peer, Lord Beauchamp, is forced to flee Britain when it seems likely his homosexuality is about to be exposed.

1932 London Rubber Company starts to manufacture latex condoms, producing around 2 million a year for the rest of the 1930s, with further supplies being imported from Germany. The (Christian) White Cross League published *Threshold of Marriage*, with instructions on how to achieve simultaneous orgasm.

1936 Employment of Women and Young Persons Act relaxes restrictions on some shift working, while continuing to prohibit night work.

1937 Matrimonial Causes ('Herbert') Act (and Divorce (Scotland) Act 1938) make divorce easier to obtain: after a three-year 'cooling-off' period, either party can obtain a divorce on the grounds of adultery, desertion for three years, cruelty, insanity, rape, sodomy or bestiality. In addition, marriages can be nullified for wilful non-consummation, or if, at the time of marriage, one of the parties had been insane, infected with venereal disease, or pregnant with another man's child.

1939–45 Millions of women enter industry to replace men on war service.

1944 Suspension of the three-year waiting period to allow quick divorces for people who had married since the outbreak of war. Education Act prohibits local education authorities from operating a marriage bar, but does not grant equal pay to women teachers.

Female participation in labour force

	Single	Married	(% of women in paid work) Widowed/divorced	All
1911	69.3	9.6	29.4	35.3
1921	68.1	8.7	25.6	33.7
1931	71.6	10.0	21.2	34.2
1951	73.1	21.7	21.0	34.7

Source: A H Halsey (ed) *British Social Trends since 1900* (2nd edn, 1988), p 172

Women in selected fields of employment (000s)

	Domestic servants	Textile workers	Clerical workers	Dressmakers, etc
1911	1 663	604	183	469
1931	1 600	374	1 358	311
1951	797	413	1 409	474

Sources: F. Roberts, *Women's Work 1840–1940* (1988), pp 34–40; Census 1951

Women: union membership

	Number	% of working women
1913	433 000	8.0
1918	1 209 000	21.7
1923	822 000	14.9
1928	795 000	13.7
1933	731 000	12.0
1938	926 000	14.7
1943	1 916 000	29.5
1946	1 618 000	24.5

Source: A H Halsey (ed) *British Social Trends since 1900* (2nd edn, 1988), pp 186–7

6. Crime and police

Chronology of legislation and major disturbances

1914 A series of attacks on Germans follows outbreak of war.

1918

Aug. Police strike in London, organized by National Union of Police and Prison Officers (NUPPO): Lloyd George increases their pay and seems to suggest that NUPPO will be recognized after the war.

1919 Sporadic outbursts of violence against Irish in many cities.
Jan. Race riot in Glasgow; mutinies in Kent among soldiers being sent back to France.
Feb. Arab seamen attacked on Tyneside.
Mar. Rioting among Canadian soldiers in north Wales leads to five deaths.
May–Jun. Series of racial attacks in London, Liverpool, Newport and Cardiff.
Jul. Riots break out among recently demobilized soldiers, resulting in the burning down of Luton town hall. NUPPO calls a further police strike; while there is some response in London and Birmingham, it is greatest on Merseyside, where the strike leads to looting and rioting; troops shoot one rioter dead. The Riot Act is read for the last time in British history. All the strikers are dismissed and never reinstated, and lose their pension rights. Police Act prohibits police officers from striking or inciting strike action, bars them from trade union membership, and sets up a hierarchically-organized Police Federation which cannot affiliate to outside bodies like the TUC, to represent officers.

1920 Emergency Powers Act allows the government to declare a state of emergency and, in effect, rule by decree in the event of actions (particularly strikes) likely to affect essential supplies. It gives the government power to maintain supplies by any means short of military or industrial conscription.

1923 Special constables are made a permanent feature.

1926 Some violent clashes during the General Strike.

1930 Legislation for free legal aid to poor people being tried for an offence.

1931   The Communist-led National Unemployed Workers' Movement (NUWM) organizes a march of unemployed people from south Wales to the Trades Union Congress at Bristol to demand stronger action against the newly formed National government; there are violent clashes in Bristol, and the rest of the autumn sees a series of sporadic outbreaks in Dundee, Glasgow, London and Manchester.

1932
Sep.   Riots break out in Liverpool and Birkenhead against the means test and low rates of public assistance, lasting for about a week, with police baton charges, attacks on property and looting. Similar disturbances take place on a lesser scale in West Ham, Croydon and South Shields. A NUWM-organized Hunger March leads to violent clashes with police in Hyde Park.
Nov.   Discontent among Belfast unemployed people leads to riots and two deaths.

1933–4   A series of rural disturbances take place, associated with the campaign against tithes; particularly affected are Suffolk and Cornwall.

1935
Jan.–Feb.   Unemployment Assistance Board crisis sees considerable unrest in major cities and south Wales.

1936   A year of increasing attacks on Jews in the East End of London leads to
Oct.   'Battle of Cable Street', when 1 900 uniformed Fascists attempting to march through the Jewish East End of London are confronted by over 100 000 demonstrators, and Mosley is forced by police to reroute his march away from Cable Street. A revenge 'pogrom' follows a week later, with much damage to Jewish property and many assaults on Jews.
Dec.   Public Order Act bans the wearing of political uniforms, outlaws the use of inflammatory and insulting language, and gives power to the police to ban or change the route of any march they consider likely to cause a breach of the peace, or to ban all political marches in an area for a three-month period.

1939
Jan.   Start of an IRA bombing campaign on the British mainland, which continues until mid-1940. A series of bombings and arson attacks follow: in the worst incident, five people were killed and many more injured by a bomb blast in Coventry; there are also attacks in London, Liverpool and Birmingham.
Jul.   Prevention of Violence (Temporary Provisions) Act is passed to counter the campaign, imposing strict immigration controls, allowing

the deportation or detention of suspects, and providing for the compilation of a register of all Irish people living in Britain.

1945 Inspectors of Constabulary given greater powers by Police Act.

Police: numbers

	England & Wales	Scotland	Ireland[a]
1913	54 552	5 859	11 844
1918	55 860	5 593	10 818
1923	56 845	6 523	n/a
1928	57 436	6 607	2 884
1933	58 418	6 526	2 787
1938	60 028	6 799	2 820
1943	43 644	5 373	2 897
1946	51 779	6 488	2 871

Note
a   Northern Ireland only after 1918

Sources: *Statistical Abstract* 70 (1927), p 69; 80 (1937), 105; 84 (1947), p 46

Crimes known to the police

	England & Wales	Scotland
1910	103 000	38 000
1915	78 000	34 000
1920	101 000	39 000
1925	114 000	33 000
1930	147 000	37 000
1935	234 000	60 000
1940	305 000	62 000
1945	478 000	86 000

Source: C Cook and J Stevenson, *The Longman Handbook of Modern British History 1714–1987* (2nd edn, 1988), p 140

Daily average prison population

	Male	Female	Total
1910	19 333	2 685	22 018
1914	15 752	2 484	18 236
1916	9 244	2 067	16 311
1919	7 595	1 604	9 199
1920	8 279	1 404	9 683
1930	10 561	785	11 346
1938	10 388	698	11 086
1940	8 443	934	9 377
1943	11 430	1 360	12 790
1946	14 556	1 233	15 789

Source: A H Halsey (ed) *British Social Trends since 1900* (2nd edn, 1988), p 627

7. The news media

Chronology of principal events

1896 Foundation of *Daily Mail* by Alfred Harmsworth (later Lord Northcliffe) as first mass-readership popular daily. Followed by *Daily Express* (**1900**) and *Daily Mirror* (**1903**).

1908 Northcliffe takes over *The Times*.

1912 Foundation of *Daily Herald*, a Labour paper.

1916 Sir Max Aitken (later Lord Beaverbrook) takes full control of *Daily Express; Daily Chronicle* becomes first national paper to offer its 'registered readers' free insurance (against air raids).

1918 Lloyd George takes over *Daily Chronicle*. Wickham Steed replaces Geoffrey Dawson as editor of *The Times*.

1920 Launch of *Sunday Express*.

1921 London evening paper, *Globe*, closes; *Westminster Gazette* switches from evening to morning publication.

1922 Death of Lord Northcliffe: *The Times* sold to J J Astor, and Dawson returns as editor; Northcliffe's brother, Lord Rothermere, takes over *Daily Mail*. Formation of British Broadcasting Company, a private monopoly, under John Reith as director-general.

1923 London evening paper, *Pall Mall Gazette*, absorbed by Beaverbrook's *Evening Standard*.

1924 Formation of Kemsley Newspapers, which later buys up numerous provincial titles during interwar period. At 1924 general election, party leaders' speeches are broadcast for first time.

1925 Sunday *People* bought by the Odhams Press.

1926 *Daily Graphic* closes. British Broadcasting Company becomes state-owned British Broadcasting Corporation (BBC), but with considerable autonomy in day-to-day matters. During General Strike, printers are called out on strike: main newspapers available are government's *British Gazette* and TUC's *British Worker*; the BBC accordingly rises to greater prominence. While essentially backing the government, it tries to maintain a fairly neutral line.

1928 *Westminster Gazette* absorbed by *Daily News*. Rothermere launches a drive to buy up provincial newspapers. A legal decision outlaws many newspaper competitions as lotteries, and in the developing circulation war papers turn instead to offering free gifts to people who 'register' as readers.

1929 First British sound newsreels produced.

1930 Pro-Liberal papers, *Daily News* and *Daily Chronicle*, combine to form *News Chronicle*. *Daily Worker* launched as official Communist party paper. Odhams Press takes over half the shares in the *Daily Herald* and it is relaunched as a popular daily, but with TUC retaining editorial control. Beaverbrook and Rothermere launch their Empire Crusade movement.

1931 Amalgamation of the weeklies, *New Statesman* and *Nation*. Rothermere floats his shares in *Daily Mirror*.

1932 George V is the first monarch to make a Christmas broadcast.

1933 *Daily Express* becomes largest-selling daily, overtaking *Daily Mail* which had held the position since before 1914.

1934 Rothermere press backs Mosley's British Union of Fascists between January and June.

1935 *Daily Mirror* begins to move leftwards politically.

1936 Ullswater Report on Broadcasting supports BBC's monopoly and rejects introduction of advertising. First BBC TV broadcasts to a tiny number of households. Launch of Penguin Specials by Allen Lane and Left Book Club by Victor Gollancz make books on current affairs available to thousands of readers at special low prices. Press maintains a discreet stance during the Abdication Crisis.

1937 *Morning Post* absorbed by *Daily Telegraph*. Resignation of Reith as director-general of the BBC.

1938 Launch of *Picture Post*.

1939 Television closes down for duration of war.

1940 Introduction of newsprint rationing means newspapers shrink to one-third of their pre-war size. Defence Regulation 2D gives the Home Secretary power to ban any publication seen as fomenting opposition to successful prosecution of the war effort.

1941 *Daily Worker* closed down under Defence Regulation 2D.

1942 Churchill demands the closure of *Daily Mirror* under Defence Regulation 2D, but it escapes with a strong warning as to its future conduct. Ban on *Daily Worker* lifted later in year.

1944 Dawson retires as editor of *The Times*.

National morning press: circulation (000s)

	1910	1930	1937	1947
Daily Chronicle	400a	—	—	—
Daily News	320a	—	—	—
News Chronicle	—	1 451	1 324	1 623
Daily Express	425	1 693	2 204	3 856
Daily Sketch	50	926b	683	772
Daily Mail	900	1 845	1 580	2 077
Daily Mirror	630	1 072	1 328	3 072
Daily Telegraph	230	175	559	1 016
Morning Post	60	120c	—	—
Morning Leader	250d	—	—	—
Standard	80e	—	—	—
The Times	45	186	191	268
Daily Herald	—	1 119	2 033	2 135
Total	3 390	8 568	9 093	15 449

Notes
a   Combined as *News Chronicle*, 1928
b   Absorbed *Daily Graphic*, 1926
c   Absorbed by *Daily Telegraph*, 1937
d   Absorbed by *Daily News*, 1912
e   Ceased publication 1917

Sources: N Blewett, *The Peers, the Parties and the People:
The General Elections of 1910* (London, 1972), p 301;
Report of the Royal Commission on the Press, 1947–1949
(Cmd 7700; London, 1949), p 190

Number of newspapers

	1921	1930	1939	1945
National and London morning	14	11	9	9
London evening	4	3	3	3
Provincial morning	41	31	25	25
Provincial evening	89	82	77	75
National Sunday	14	11	10	10
Provincial Sunday	7	7	6	6
Weekly	1 485	1 423	1 303	1 162

Source: *Report of the Royal Commission on the Press, 1947–1949* (Cmd 7700;
London, 1949), pp 188–9

Cinema attendances

1934	903 million
1938	987 million
1942	1 494 million
1946	1 635 million

Source: H E Browning
and A A Sorrell,
'Cinemas and cinema-
going in Great Britain',
*Journal of the Royal
Statistical Society* 117
(1954), p 134

Radio audience

Year	Licences issued	Estimated % of population able to listen
1922	36 000	0.3
1927	2 395 000	21.1
1932	5 263 000	42.8
1937	8 480 000	68.5
1942	9 019 000	n/a
1946	10 770 000	n/a

Sources: M Pegg, *Broadcasting and Society
1918–1939* (1983), p 7; A Briggs, *History of
Broadcasting in the United Kingdom, vol. III: The
War of Words* (1970), p 736

8. Religion

Chronology of legislation and principal events

1907   Union of Bible Christians, Methodist New Connexion and United Methodist Free Churches to form United Methodist Church.

1914   Welsh Church Act disestablishes Anglican Church in Wales but with effect from the end of the war; it finally takes place in 1920.

1916   Roman Catholic archdiocese of Cardiff set up.

1917   Roman Catholic episcopal see of Brentwood set up; Church of England opposes any significant relaxation of divorce laws.

1919   Church of England Assembly (Powers) Act or 'Enabling' Act creates a Church Assembly (later General Synod) which increases Church's autonomy from parliament. Formation of Church of England's Industrial Christian Fellowship to spread Bible's 'social message'.

1920   Britain normalizes diplomatic relations with Vatican. Church of England's Lambeth Conference opposes artificial contraception, urges 'fellowship' rather than conflict in industry, and calls for Church to become 'a reservoir of social service'.

1921   Church of Scotland Act confirms Church's independence in all spiritual matters. R H Tawney, *The Acquisitive Society*, calls for Church to play a leading role in creating a socialist society.

1924   Roman Catholic episcopal see of Lancaster set up. Interdenominational Conference on Christian Politics, Economics and Citizenship (Copec) meets, with William Temple emerging as the leading figure in the social teaching of the Church of England. Bishop Henson of Durham, speaking for many conservative churchmen, condemns Copec.

1926   General Strike and coal dispute: Catholic Cardinal Bourne condemns the strike; Archbishop of Canterbury condemns it but tries to mediate between the two sides. Industrial Christian Fellowship attempts to mediate during the coal lockout.

1928   Rejection of Revised Prayer Book by parliament suggests that the Church of England is less autonomous than it wishes to be.

1929 Reunion of most Scottish Presbyterians, as majority of United Free Church of Scotland amalgamates with Church of Scotland. Copec dissolved.

1930 Lambeth Conference eases Church of England's prohibition of artificial methods of birth control, and condemns racialist doctrines. Hairdressers' shops forced by law to close on Sundays.

1931 Catholics oppose Trevelyan's abortive Education Bill due to its perceived hostility towards Catholic schools.

1932 Union of Wesleyan Methodists, Primitive Methodists and United Methodists to form Methodist Church. Sunday Entertainments Act allows opening of cinemas and musical entertainments on Sundays at discretion of local authorities.

1933 Bishop Headlam of Chichester writes to *The Times* criticizing public hostility towards Nazi Germany, a position he maintains until 1939.

1933–34 Considerable rural protest against tithes.

1935 Foundation of periodical *The Catholic Worker*. Further tithe disturbances: effigy of Archbishop Lang burnt at Ashford, Kent. Archbishops' Commission on Church and State rejects Church disestablishment in England.

1936 Tithes abolished, with some state compensation. Shops (Sunday Trading Restriction) Act limits types of shops that can open on a Sunday and their hours of opening, with certain exemptions in holiday areas.

1940 Joint declaration on war aims by head of Roman Catholic Church in Britain, Archbishops of Canterbury and York, and moderator of Free Church Council.

1941 Church of England's Malvern conference tries in vain to revive fortunes of Church's social radical wing.

1942 Establishment of British Council of Churches, a significant move in quest for Christian unity. William Temple, Archbishop of York, publishes *Christianity and the Social Order*, stressing need for Church to play a leading role in formation of social and economic policy; it sells over 100 000 copies. Later in the year he becomes Archbishop of Canterbury.

1944 Temple's death marks end of dominance of social radicalism in leadership of the Church of England. Anglicans and Nonconformists accept the Butler Education Act and its provisions for church schools and religious education.

Archbishops of Canterbury

1903–28	Randall Davidson
1928–42	Cosmo Lang
1942–4	William Temple
1944–61	Geoffrey Fisher

Archbishops of Westminster (heads of the Roman Catholic Church)

1903–35	Francis Bourne (Cardinal 1910)
1935–43	Arthur Hinsley (Cardinal 1937)
1943–56	Bernard Griffin (Cardinal 1946)

Estimated Roman Catholic population

1913	2 339 000
1916	2 433 000
1922	2 531 000
1931	2 813 000
1935	2 933 000
1939	2 990 000
1943	2 956 000
1947	3 122 000

Source: R Currie, A Gilbert and L Horsley, *Churches and Churchgoers* (1977), p 153

Episcopal churches: communicants

	Church of England	Church in Wales	Church in Scotland
1914	2 226 000	155 000	146 000
1919	2 153 000	159 000	144 000
1924	2 315 000	171 000	145 000
1929	2 304 000	187 000	135 000
1934	2 319 000	196 000	130 000
1939	2 245 000	n/a	124 000
1944	n/a	n/a	114 000
1947	1 728 000	n/a	108 000

Source: R Currie, A Gilbert and L Horsley, *Churches and Churchgoers* (1977), pp 128–9

Presbyterian churches: members and communicants

	Church of Scotland	United Free Church of Scotland	Presbyterian Church in England
1914	718 000	512 000	88 000
1919	728 000	528 000	84 000
1924	760 000	534 000	85 000
1929	1 284 000	13 000a	83 000
1934	1 290 000	21 000	82 000
1939	1 285 000	23 000	78 000
1944	1 264 000	23 000	68 000
1947	1 256 000	24 000	66 000

Note

a The United Free Church united with the Church of Scotland in 1928, leaving a small rump

Source: R Currie, A Gilbert and L Horsley, *Churches and Churchgoers* (1977), pp 134–5

Methodist churches: members (000s)

	England				Wales	Scotland	Total
	Wesleyan	Primitive	United Methodist		Wales	Scotland	Total
1914	432	204	143		39	9	827
1919	416	200	139		39	9	803
1924	431	200	140		42	10	823
1929	445	201	141		42	11	840
1934				763	52	13	828
1939				738	50	13	801
1944				693	48	14	755
1947				681	47	13	741

Source: R Currie, A Gilbert and L Horsley, *Churches and Churchgoers* (1977), pp 143–4

Other Non-conformist churches: members

	Baptists	Congregationalists	Welsh Presbyterians[a]
1914	412 000	489 000	185 000
1919	402 000	n/a	188 000
1924	410 000	n/a	189 000
1929	403 000	490 000	186 000
1934	399 000	480 000	182 000
1939	381 000	456 000	177 000
1944	364 000	n/a	174 000
1947	347 000	408 000	167 000

Note
a   Known as Welsh Calvinistic Methodists Connexion until 1933

Source: R Currie, A Gilbert and L Horsley, *Churches and Churchgoers* (1977), p 150

Economic history

1. Trade

Chronology of legislation and principal events

1914 On the outbreak of war government takes power to restrict export of any article and to seize any article being 'unreasonably withheld' from the market; and trading with the enemy is banned.

1915 A tariff of 33.3 per cent is imposed on all luxury imports, eg cars ('McKenna Duties').

1920 Overseas Trade Act allows the Board of Trade to offer credits and insurance to industry in order to help re-establish British overseas markets. Import of all synthetic dyestuffs is banned, to protect the infant British dye industry.

1921 Safeguarding of Industries Act imposes duties of 33.3 per cent on imports of goods, like wireless equipment, optical products and chemicals, which are competing with British 'new' industries.

1921 Trade Facilities Act allows the Treasury to make loans to exporting industries to promote employment.

1924 Snowden abolishes the McKenna Duties.

1925 Churchill reimposes the McKenna Duties. Safeguarding of Industries Act imposes a 33.3 per cent tariff on imports of lace, gloves, cutlery and gas mantles to protect British industry from dumping; the duties are extended to minor industries like pottery (1927) and buttons (1928), but requests from major industries like iron and steel for protection are rejected.

1927 Cinematograph Films Act states that a certain quota of films exhibited must be British-made.

1929–31 Second Labour government attempts to negotiate an international tariff truce, but with little success.

1931 Temporary legislation permits the imposition of emergency tariffs of up to 100 per cent on goods being imported in 'abnormal quantities' with a view to beating the expected introduction of permanent import duties.

1932 Import Duties Act imposes a general system of protection for the first time since the mid-nineteenth century: (a) a general tariff of 10 per cent was imposed on imports; (b) imports already covered by duties remained at 33.3 per cent; (c) imports like food and raw materials were on the 'free list', with no tariff being charged; (d) duties were not to be imposed on the products of the Dominions or colonies; (e) an Import Duties Advisory Council (IDAC) was set up as an autonomous body to monitor and advise on tariff levels.

Apr.   On the recommendation of IDAC, the general tariff was raised to 20 per cent.

Jun.   Special duties imposed on imports from the Irish Free State after its refusal to pay annuities due to Britain.

Sep.   Ottawa Agreements Act, following the imperial conference, commits Britain to preserving and in some cases extending the preferences given to Dominion products, while the Dominions give preferential tariff rates to British exports.

1933 Temporary ban on imports from the USSR following the arrest of British engineers working there.

1934 Ban on imports of synthetic dyestuffs extended.

1937 Duties of 10–20 per cent imposed on imports of beef and veal products from outside the Empire.

1938 Essential Commodities Reserves Act allows government to stockpile essential war items.

1939 Government takes full power to control all British imports and exports; bans trading with the enemy; and transfers the IDAC to the Treasury and the Board of Trade.

Geographical distribution of total imports (value)

	British Empire		Foreign Countries			
(%)	Total	Total	USA	Germany	France	Argentina
1913	24.9	75.1	18.4	10.5	6.0	5.5
1918	32.1	67.9	39.2	0.6	2.7	4.8
1923	29.7	70.3	19.2	3.2	5.3	5.9
1928	30.4	68.6	15.8	5.3	5.1	6.4
1933	36.9	63.1	11.2	4.4	2.8	6.2
1938	40.4	59.6	12.8	3.3	2.6	4.2
1943	38.9	61.1	43.4	—	—	4.7
1948	48.8	51.2	17.5	0.5	1.1	5.2

Sources: Calculated from *Statistical Abstract* 70 (1927), pp 282–5; 80 (1937), pp 354–7; 84 (1947), p 183

Geographical distribution of total exports (% value)

	British Empire	Foreign Countries				
	Total	Total	USA	Germany	France	Argentina
1913	37.2	62.8	5.6	7.7	5.5	4.3
1918	35.6	64.4	4.7	—	26.1	3.5
1923	39.2	60.8	7.8	5.6	6.4	3.7
1928	45.3	54.7	6.4	5.7	3.5	4.3
1933	44.4	55.6	5.2	4.0	4.9	3.6
1938	49.9	50.1	4.4	4.4	3.2	4.1
1943	63.9	36.1	8.4	—	—	4.1
1946	49.3	50.7	3.9	2.0	3.8	2.2

Sources: Calculated from *Statistical Abstract* 70 (1927), pp 290–3; 80 (1937), pp 362–5; 84 (1947), p 184

Balance of visible trade (value £ million)

	Retained imports	Exports	Visible trade balance
1913	659.1	525.3	−133.8
1918	1 285.3	501.4	−783.9
1923	977.7	767.3	−210.4
1928	1 075.3	723.6	−603.3
1933	625.9	367.9	−258.0
1938	858.0	471.0	−387.0
1943	1 228.0	234.0	−994.0
1946	1 247.0	912.0	−335.0

Sources: Calculated from *Statistical Abstract* 70 (1927), pp 300–1; 80 (1937), pp 372–3; 84 (1947), 178

2. Prices and wages

Chronology of legislation and principal events

1914 Board of Trade given power to seize foodstuffs being 'unreasonably' kept from the market, to prevent profiteering.

1915 Price of coal brought under state regulation.

1918 Defence of the Realm (Food Profits) Act attempts to outlaw overcharging for food. Wages (Temporary Regulation) Act, passed in November, sets minimum wage rates for six months; renewed 1919.

1919 Profiteering Act increases Board of Trade's powers to prevent overcharging for six months after Armistice; ultimately extended until May 1921.

1924 Legislation sets up wages committees and a national wages board with powers to set minimum wage rates in agriculture.

1931 National government cuts salaries of all public servants by 10 per cent, and following devaluation passes legislation to safeguard against unreasonable price increases for six months.

1934 Public servants' salaries restored to their 1931 level.

1938 Legislation sets up central and area wages boards and provides for the establishment of minimum wage rates in road haulage. Holidays with Pay Act allows trade boards and agricultural wages committees to declare a week's annual paid holiday in the industries they covered.

1939 Extensive price controls reintroduced on outbreak of war.

1940 New legal national minimum wage set for agricultural workers.

1941 Goods and Services (Price Control) Act gives government wide-ranging powers to fix maximum prices for goods and services.

1943 Catering Wages Act sets up a permanent Catering Commission to review and police wages and conditions in the industry.

1945 Wages Councils Act replaces the old trade boards with more powerful wages councils, able to set and enforce minimum wages, etc.

Average annual earnings (£)

	1913–14	1922–4	1935–6	1955–6
Men				
Higher professions	328	582	634	1 541
Lower professions	155	320	308	610
Managers, etc	200	480	440	1 480
Clerks	99	182	192	523
Foremen	123	268	273	784
Manual: skilled	106	180	195	622
Semi-skilled	69	126	134	469
Unskilled	63	128	129	435
Average	94	180	186	634
Women				
Higher professions	—	—	—	1 156
Lower professions	89	214	211	438
Managers, etc	80	160	168	800
Clerks	45	106	99	317
Forewomen	57	154	156	477
Manual: skilled	44	87	86	317
Semi-skilled	50	98	100	269
Unskilled	28	73	73	227
Average	50	103	104	319
Men and women				
Average	81	157	162	531

Source: G Routh, *Occupation and Pay in Great Britain 1906–79* (1980), pp 120–1

Wages of manual workers and cost of living

Average for 1906–10 = 100	Wage rates	Cost of living
1913	106	108
1918	185–91	216
1923	208	184
1928	207	175
1933	196	148
1938	218	166
1943	300	237
1946	353	249

Source: A H Halsey (ed) *British Social Trends since 1900* (2nd edn, 1988), pp 180–2

Consumers' expenditure (%)

	Food	Alcoholic drink	Tobacco	Rent, etc	Fuel/ light	Clothing	Household durables	Transport
1913	33.7	8.5	1.9	11.2	3.8	10.2	3.7	6.0
1918	38.7	7.1	2.4	7.5	4.1	11.1	4.3	4.7
1923	34.2	8.8	2.9	9.2	4.0	10.8	5.1	6.7
1928	32.8	7.7	3.3	9.5	3.8	10.8	5.4	7.3
1933	29.9	6.9	3.8	11.3	4.2	9.8	5.8	7.3
1938	29.2	6.6	3.9	11.0	4.2	9.8	5.9	7.7
1943	28.8	12.6	9.5	9.9	4.6	8.5	2.9	5.6
1946	28.5	10.1	9.3	7.4	3.9	11.0	5.8	6.5

Note
The figures do not total 100% because 'Other goods and services' has been excluded

Source: Calculated from B R Mitchell and P Deane, *Abstract of British Historical Statistics* (1962), pp 370–1

3. Employment and unemployment

Chronology of legislation and principal events

1916 Unemployment insurance extended to munitions workers, making a total of 4 million people in the scheme.

1920 Unemployment insurance extended to virtually all industrial manual workers, covering a total of 12 million people.

1921 Unemployment Insurance Acts allow unemployment insurance fund to borrow £10 million (and later £20 million) because of exceptionally high unemployment. Introduction of 'uncovenanted' (later known as 'transitional') benefit, whereby unemployed workers who have exhausted their right to insurance benefit can claim further periods of benefit. A clause stating that recipients of benefit must prove that they are 'genuinely seeking work' is introduced. Allowances of 5s (25p) for the claimant's spouse and 1s (5p) for each child under 14 are set up.

1922 Benefits and contributions increased; borrowing power raised to £30 million.

1924 Labour government increases benefits and abolishes 'genuinely seeking work' clause.

1927 Following Blanesburgh Report, benefits are cut and 'genuinely seeking work' clause is reintroduced.

1928 Borrowing power increased to £40 million.

1929 Labour abolishes 'genuinely seeking work' clause and liberalizes entitlement to benefits.

1930 Fund's borrowing power increased to £50 million, then £60 million and later £70 million in face of soaring unemployment. Royal Commission on Unemployment Insurance set up under Judge Holman Gregory to suggest reforms to make the scheme more efficient and cut fund's deficit.

1931 Fund's borrowing powers increased to £90 million and later £115 million. The Holman Gregory commission's interim report recommends increased contributions, benefit cuts of around 12 per cent, the removal of 'anomalies' such as claims by married women who did not really want work and by casual workers, and the ending of transitional benefit, in order to restore the fund to an insurance basis. The Labour government largely ignores this, except that the Unemployment Insurance (No. 3) ('Anomalies') Act removes benefit entitlement from various people including most married women. The May Report recommends increased contributions and a cut of 20 per cent in benefits; in August, the Labour cabinet collapses when it fails to reach agreement on a 10 per cent cut in unemployment benefit. The National government cuts benefits by 10 per cent and increases contributions, and the administration of transitional benefit is passed to local public assistance committees, which can set their own rates, subject to a means test for applicants.

1932 Borrowing by the fund reaches the £115 million limit; henceforth deficits are funded directly from the Exchequer.

1934 Unemployment Act: Part I restores the 1931 cuts; brings 14 to 16 year-olds into the insurance scheme; and sets up an Unemployment Insurance Statutory Committee (UISC) to manage the insurance fund (which should now be self-supporting) and recommend changes in benefit and contribution rates. Part II sets up an Unemployment Assistance Board (UAB) to administer transitional benefit (renamed 'unemployment assistance'); national scales will replace local ones; and, like the UISC, the UAB is to be free from day-to-day government control.

1935 When the new national UAB rates come into effect, it is found in many areas that they are lower than the old local rates, and a great protest movement springs up; the UAB tries to ride out the storm but the government is shaken and allows Public Assistance Committees (PACs) to pay whichever of the old or new rates was higher, in effect destroying the UAB's credibility as an independent body.

1936 Unemployment insurance scheme extended to agricultural labourers at lower rates of benefit and contribution.

1938 Unemployment insurance scheme extended to certain types of domestic servants at lower rates of benefit and contribution.

1941 Determination of Needs Act abolishes the household means test: benefits are now to be assessed on the basis of personal need alone. The unemployment assistance fund is abolished.

1944 Reinstatement in Civil Employment Act obliges employers to reinstate former employees who have been serving in the war. Ministry of National Insurance set up, and takes over responsibility for unemployment insurance and assistance from Ministry of Labour. White Paper on Employment commits government to maintenance of a 'high and stable' level of employment.

Major occupational groups

(% of total occupied population)	1911	1921	1931	1951
Employers/proprietors	6.7	6.8	6.7	5.0
Managers	3.4	3.6	3.7	5.5
Higher professionals	1.0	1.0	1.1	1.9
Lower professionals/technicians	3.1	3.5	3.5	4.7
Forepersons/inspectors	1.3	1.4	1.5	2.6
Clerical and related workers	4.5	6.5	6.7	10.4
Sales employees	5.4	5.1	6.5	5.7
Manual workers	74.6	72.0	70.3	64.2

Source: A H Halsey (ed) *British Social Trends since 1900* (2nd edn, 1988), p 164

Occupational groups by industry

(% of occupied workforce) Industry		Census year		
	1911	1921	1931	1951
Agriculture	8.4	7.3	6.1	5.0
Mining	6.3	6.9	5.7	3.8
Engineering & shipbuilding	4.9	6.4	5.3	8.0
Vehicles	1.6	2.0	2.0	4.5
Textiles	7.6	6.9	6.5	4.4
Clothing	6.5	4.6	4.3	3.2
Building	5.3	4.2	5.5	6.4
Transport & communication	7.9	8.3	8.2	7.7
Distributive trades	11.9	11.9	13.2	12.1
Public administration & defence	3.9	5.3	4.9	7.7
Professional services	4.4	4.7	5.2	6.9
Other	31.3	31.5	33.1	30.3

Includes employers, self-employed and unemployed people

Source: G Routh, *Occupation and Pay in Great Britain 1906–79* (1980), p 42

Manual workers' hours of work

	1900	1910	1920	1930	1938	1946
Normal weekly hours	54	54	46.9	47.3	47.2	46.8

Source: A H Halsey (ed) *British Social Trends since 1900* (2nd edn, 1988), p 178

Unemployment figures

	Percentage	Number registered unemployed (Insured and uninsured)	
	(Insured only) (yearly average)	January	July
1913	3.6	n/a	n/a
1914	4.2	n/a	n/a
1915	1.2	n/a	n/a
1916	0.6	n/a	n/a
1917	0.7	n/a	n/a
1918	0.8	n/a	n/a
1919	n/a	n/a	n/a
1920	3.9	n/a	n/a
1921	16.9	n/a	n/a
1922	14.3	n/a	n/a
1923	11.7	1 460 400	1 234 500
1924	10.3	1 322 500	1 262 300
1925	11.3	1 287 400	1 664 100
1926	12.5	1 262 400	1 054 500
1927	9.7	1 375 400	1 054 500
1928	10.8	1 199 100	1 353 800
1929	10.4	1 433 900	1 188 200
1930	16.1	1 533 700	2 071 900
1931	21.3	2 671 200	2 783 200
1932	22.1	2 793 700	2 888 600
1933	19.9	2 979 400	2 507 200
1934	16.7	2 457 200	2 185 100
1935	15.5	2 397 100	2 045 400
1936	13.1	2 230 000	1 717 100
1937	10.8	1 766 400	1 445 300
1938	12.9	1 927 000	1 875 100
1939	9.3	2 133 800	1 326 100
1940	6.0	1 602 600	906 500
1941	2.2	764 300	315 900
1942	0.8	224 700	124 500
1943	0.6	121 000[a]	90 600[b]
1944	0.5	96 300[a]	77 900[b]
1945	1.3	122 200[a]	131 000[b]
1946	2.5	374 400	395 500

Notes
a   Figure for first quarter of year
b   Figure for third quarter of year

Source: Department of Employment and Productivity, *British Labour Statistics: Historical Abstract 1886–1968* (1971), pp 306–11

4. Agriculture

Chronology of legislation and principal events

1916 Ministry of Food set up as a wartime measure (abolished 1921).

1917 Corn Production Act guarantees minimum prices for wheat and oats; appoints a wages board to operate a new minimum wage in agriculture; and gives Board of Agriculture power to ensure that all land is properly cultivated.

1918–21 Massive land sales, mainly with breaking up of large estates and their sale to tenant farmers: about one-quarter of all land changes hands, largest permanent transfer since sixteenth century.

1919 Forestry Commission established to promote afforestation and timber production. Land Settlement Act and Land Settlement (Scotland) Act encourage local authorities to provide land for people to take up farming, and also to provide allotments in urban areas. Ministry of Agriculture and Fisheries replaces old Board of Agriculture.

1921 Corn Production Act 1917 repealed, so abolishing guaranteed prices and minimum wages; establishment of voluntary joint councils of workers and employers to regulate wages and conditions is permitted.

1923 Tenant farmers given greater security of tenure. Agricultural Credits Act makes public money available for loans to farmers.

1924 Agricultural Wages (Regulation) Act sets up wages committees and a national wages board with powers to set a minimum wage.

1925 British Sugar (Subsidy) Act guarantees a tapering ten-year subsidy to British sugar-beet producers, provided manufacturers pay farmers a set minimum price, buy at least 75 per cent of their machinery from British firms, and pay 'fair wages' to their workers. Agricultural Returns Act increases state's power to collect statistics on all aspects of farming.

1926 Small Holdings and Allotments Act orders county councils to provide smallholdings for people wanting to settle on the land, provided that it can be done economically, or if the government gives special consent.

1928 Agricultural Mortgage Corporation set up with state funding to grant farmers improvement credits and mortgages on agricultural land.

1929 All agricultural land and buildings given exemption from rates.

1931 Sugar beet subsidy increased. Agricultural Land (Utilisation) Act aims to stimulate resettlement on the land and cut unemployment by providing subsidies to jobless people and ex-servicemen to set up smallholdings. Agricultural Marketing Act allows producers to form bodies to regulate the marketing of their products, with a view to obtaining higher prices. Horticultural Products (Emergency Customs Duties) Act allows temporary tariffs of up to 100 per cent to be imposed on imports of fruit, vegetables, flowers and plants.

1932 Import Duties Act leaves most agricultural products free of duties, although horticultural products are covered and protection is soon extended to oats and barley. Wheat Act gives producers a guaranteed minimum price, underwritten by government.

1933 Agricultural Marketing Act gives Board of Trade power to restrict imports of agricultural products covered by marketing schemes: bacon, pork and potato imports are regulated as a result. Fish imports restricted. Milk marketing boards for England, Scotland and Wales set up.

1934 Potato marketing board set up. Sugar subsidy extended (and again in 1935). Milk Act gives a guaranteed price for milk to be used in manufacture; extended 1936 and 1937. Cattle Industry (Emergency Provisions) Act sets up a cattle fund with state money; extended 1937.

1935 Legislation passed to reorganize the herring industry.

1936 Agricultural labourers enter unemployment insurance scheme. Legislation sets up the British Sugar Corporation Ltd, as an amalgamation of UK sugar factories, overseen by a Sugar Commission.

1937 Tariffs of 10–20 per cent imposed on imports of beef and veal products from outside the Empire. Agriculture Act extends subsidies and guaranteed prices to oats and barley production.

1938 Herring industry further reorganized, and a grant of £250 000 is given for new boats. Bacon Industry Act sets up a new, improved marketing scheme and gives a three-year subsidy to bacon producers.

1939 Agricultural Development Act further guarantees oats and barley subsidies; sheep subsidies are also extended; and encouragement is given to ploughing up pasture for arable use, in anticipation of wartime food supply problems.

1940 Agricultural subsidies generally increased. New legal national minimum wage set for farm labourers.

Production of crops (000s tons)

	Wheat	Barley	Oats	Potatoes	Sugar beet
1910	1 502	1 339	2 161	3 477	—
1915	1 961	986	2 168	3 830	—
1920	1 515	1 391	2 215	4 388	—
1925	1 414	1 153	2 095	4 209	428
1930	1 127	832	1 988	3 603	3 049
1935	1 743	732	1 819	3 765	3 346
1940	1 628	1 089	2 514	5 375	3 120
1945	2 174	2 096	2 862	8 702	3 783

Source: Ministry of Agriculture, Fisheries and Food, *A Century of Agricultural Statistics: Great Britain 1866–1966* (1968), pp 108–16

Corn prices

(Average price per cwt in England and Wales)

	Wheat		Barley		Oats	
	s	d	s	d	s	d
1913	7	5	7	8	7	9
1918	17	0	16	6	17	9
1923	9	10	9	5	9	7
1928	10	0	11	0	10	5
1933	5	4	7	11	5	7
1938	6	9	10	2	7	7
1943	16	3	31	5	15	8
1946	14	10	24	3	16	3

Source: Ministry of Agriculture, Fisheries and Food, *A Century of Agricultural Statistics: Great Britain 1866–1966* (1968), p 82

Domestic tractor production

	Tractors produced
1931	4 000
1933	3 000
1935	9 000
1937	18 000
1939	10 000
1945	18 000

Source: G C Allen, *British Industries and their Organization* (5th edn, 1970), p 177

5. Industry

Chronology of legislation and principal events

1915
Munitions of War Act lays down strict regulations for factories, etc, employed in producing war materials, including compulsory arbitration of industrial disputes, leaving certificates (whereby workers must have the permission of their employer to seek another job), and dilution; by November almost 1.2 million people are working in 'controlled' establishments. Imposition of McKenna Duties of 33.3 per cent on 'luxury' imports including cars.

1916
Munitions of War (Amendment) Act widens number of factories to which the 1915 Act applies.

1919
Sankey Commission on coal is appointed, and reports: a majority favours nationalization, but the government does not act. Legislation restores pre-war trade practices and restrictions in industry. Coal Mines Act cuts working day from eight hours to seven. Industrial Courts Act sets up a tribunal to which disputes can be referred if both parties so wish: it is purely voluntary. The electricity supply industry is reorganized by legislation under an overseeing board of Electricity Commissioners appointed by the government.

1920
Mining Industry Act establishes, under the Board of Trade, a Mines Department with its own minister and with power to regulate prices and exports; a national board is to be set up to oversee the industry, with area boards and district and pit committees, but these come to very little.

1921
The coal mines are returned to private control as from 31 March. Safeguarding of Industries Act imposes protective duties of 33.3 per cent in favour of growing industries like chemicals, etc.

1924
McKenna Duties abolished by Snowden.

1925
Safeguarding of Industries (Customs Duties) Act imposes duties of

33.3 per cent on imports of lace, gloves, cutlery and gas mantles; larger industries are refused protection.

Apr. Return to gold standard raises the price of British exports: coal owners demand wage cuts.

Jul. Government announces a nine-month subsidy to preserve mining wage levels and sets up the Samuel Commission to report on the industry. McKenna Duties reimposed.

1926

Mar. Samuel Report suggests the nationalization of coal royalties, encouragement of voluntary amalgamations, greater government support for research, and improved pit facilities (eg pit-head baths), but also an immediate cut in wages.

May–Dec. Mining lockout.

Jul. Coal Mines Act restores the eight-hour day; Mining Industry Act tries to back up the Samuel Report by giving government support to voluntary amalgamations of coal companies. Electricity (Supply) Act appoints an eight-strong Central Electricity Board to control the supply of electricity on behalf of the state.

1928–9

Mond–Turner talks: discussion of industrial rationalization between employers and TUC.

1929

Report of the Balfour Committee on Industry and Trade after five years of work produces a wide-ranging survey but little is done to implement its recommendations.

1930

Coal Mines Act, the major piece of interwar mining legislation: Part I sets up a cartel scheme, with a central council to allocate production quotas between seventeen areas, which in turn will allocate quotas to each pit; Part II sets up a Coal Mines Reorganization Commission to encourage amalgamations and rationalization; the working day is cut from 8 to $7\frac{1}{2}$ hours. Formation of Bankers' Industrial Development Company under Montagu Norman to help finance rationalization of industry. Formation of National Shipbuilders' Security Ltd to buy up and close down excess capacity in the industry.

1931

Jun. Report of Macmillan Committee on Finance and Industry.

Sep. Departure from gold standard reduces price of British exports.

1932

Import Duties Act imposes a general tariff on manufactured imports, so protecting British industry.

1934

North Atlantic Shipping Act provides a maximum of £9.5 million for the construction of large vessels for the North Atlantic shipping trade, and for the amalgamation of companies. Petroleum (Production) Act nationalizes the mineral rights to oil and gas in the UK.

1936

Cotton Spinning Industry Act attempts to 'rationalize' industry by setting up a Spindles Board to buy up and scrap excess capacity in spindles; scheme financed by a levy on the industry.

1937

Coal (Registration of Ownership) Act sets up a register of ownership of mineral rights in mining, a prelude to Coal Act 1938.

1938

Coal Act nationalizes coal royalties; they, and the reorganization powers of the old Coal Mines Reorganization Commission, are put under the control of a new Coal Commission.

1939

Cotton Industry (Reorganisation) Act introduces price-fixing and quotas for production, but is suspended on the outbreak of war.

1940

Report of the Royal Commission on the Distribution of the Industrial Population ('Barlow Report') recommends the dispersal of industry, including controls on where companies should be allowed to locate new enterprises, etc; it is to form the basis of much of post-war regional policy.

1942

Restoration of Pre-War Practices Act promises that this will take place in industry as soon as possible after the war.

1943

Hydro-Electric Development (Scotland) Act establishes a board with powers to develop hydro-electric projects, particularly in supplying areas hitherto isolated from electricity supply.

Coal industry: employment and production

	Employment	Output (million tons)
1913	1 127 000	287
1924	1 230 000	267
1928	952 000	238
1933	797 000	208
1938	782 000	227
1943	708 000	195
1946	697 000	181

Source: G C Allen, *British Industries and their
Organization* (5th edn, 1970), pp 72–3

Iron and steel production

(million tons)	Pig iron	Steel
1913	10.26	7.66
1923	7.44	8.48
1928	6.61	8.52
1933	4.14	7.02
1938	6.76	10.40
1943	n/a	13.03
1946	7.76	12.70

Source: G C Allen, *British Industries and their
Organization* (5th edn, 1970), pp 110–11

Motor vehicle production

	Passenger cars	Commercial vehicles
1913	34 000	
1918	n/a	n/a
1923	71 000	24 000
1929	182 000	57 000
1933	221 000	66 000
1938	341 000	104 000
1945	17 000	122 000
1946	219 000	146 000

Source: G C Allen, *British Industries and their
Organization* (5th edn, 1970), p 177

6. Labour and trade unions

Chronology of legislation and principal events

1914
Formation of War Emergency Workers' National Committee.

1915
Mar. Treasury Agreement: Lloyd George persuades unions to accept a considerable measure of dilution and suspension of certain established trade practices.
May This is strengthened by the Munitions of War Act.
Jul. A strike of 200 000 miners in south Wales for more pay is declared illegal, but miners win most of their demands.

1915–17
Militant shop stewards in Clydeside, Sheffield and other engineering centres agitate strongly against suspension of established practices.

1916
Introduction of trade cards scheme: unions are to determine which workers are 'essential' and so exempt from military service.

1917
Trade cards scheme abolished. Trade Union (Amalgamation) Act makes union amalgamations easier: they now require only a 20 per cent majority in a ballot of the members involved. TUC gives its parliamentary committee greater power to speak on foreign affairs, and increases its resources. Whitley Report on Relations of Employers and Employed recommends the establishment of councils representing both sides of an industry to settle disputes.

1918
London police strike: Lloyd George seems to promise recognition of National Union of Police and Prison Officers (NUPPO) after war. TUC sets up an international bureau.

1919
Revival of pre-war Triple Alliance of miners, railwaymen and transport workers, to help each other in industrial disputes. Restoration of Pre-War Practices Act compels employers to accept return of trade practices and restrictions suspended in wartime.
Aug. Police strikes in London, Liverpool and Birmingham defeated; NUPPO crushed.

Sep. Railway strike; settled on union's terms. Industrial Courts Act sets up a permanent arbitration tribunal to which disputes can be referred by parties concerned, but government has no power to compel this.

1920

Ernest Bevin successfully puts case for an increase in dockers' pay to the Shaw Inquiry, earning the nickname 'the Dockers' KC'.
May Dockers refuse to load the *Jolly George* with arms for use by Poland against Russia.
Aug. Council of Action, representing all sides of the Labour movement, formed to threaten a general strike if British involvement in Russo-Polish War does not cease. Collapse of post-war boom: great increase in unemployment and weakening of unions' position.
Oct. Miners' strike: ends inconclusively.

1921

Mar. Start of mining lockout to enforce pay cuts; miners call on Triple Alliance to take sympathetic action.
15 Apr. 'Black Friday' as railwaymen and transport workers refuse to help miners.
Jul. Miners return to work on employers' terms. TUC parliamentary committee replaced by a larger and more powerful general council. Combination of the Amalgamated Society of Engineers and a number of smaller organizations to form Amalgamated Engineering Union.

1922

Jan. Formation of Transport and General Workers' Union under Bevin.
Mar.–Jun. National engineering lockout: ends in victory for employers.

1924

First Labour government plans to use troops in event of dock and tram strikes. National Union of General and Municipal Workers formed from a number of smaller organizations.

1925

Mar. Baldwin rejects a Conservative back-bench proposal to replace 'contracting out' of the trade union political levy with 'contracting in'.
31 Jul. 'Red Friday': faced with threat of a national mining strike supported by an embargo on transportation of coal, government grants a nine-month subsidy to the coal industry to prevent pay cuts.

1926

May–Dec. National mining lockout: ends with miners returning to work for lower wages and longer hours.
4–12 May General Strike: in support of miners, TUC calls out its members in transport, railways, printing, heavy industry, and power

supply, but once it becomes clear the government is not going to back down, the TUC seeks to end the Strike, and it surrenders unconditionally after nine days.

Nov. George Spencer, right-wing Labour MP, forms a breakaway mining union which mainly prospers in Nottinghamshire. Amalgamated Engineering Union (AEU) admits large numbers of semi-skilled workers for first time. Dissolution of joint TUC–Labour party departments (eg Research, Press and Publicity).

1927
Trade Disputes and Trade Union Act declares sympathetic strikes and lockouts, and the recent General Strike, illegal; outlaws 'intimidation' of non-strikers; replaces 'contracting out' of the trade union political levy with 'contracting in'; forbids civil service unions from affiliating to outside organizations like the TUC; and bans closed shops.

1928
Transport & General Workers' Union (TGWU) absorbs the Workers' Union.

1928–9
Mond–Turner talks between TUC and a group of large employers, although largely inconclusive, suggest a new, more conciliatory tendency in industrial relations.

1929
TUC sets up an economic committee; Bevin becomes a member of the Macmillan Committee on Finance and Industry.

1929–31
Bad and worsening relations between unions and second Labour government.

1930
Series of textile disputes results in wage cuts. Bevin and Citrine become members of the economic advisory council.

1931
Apr. Collapse of Labour government's attempts to repeal 1927 Trade Disputes Act.

Aug. TUC opposition to cuts plays a significant role in government's collapse.

Sep. TUC votes to reconstitute National Joint Council, to give it more control over the Labour party (renamed National Council of Labour, 1934).

1933
Formation of Communist-led London Busmen's Rank-and-File Committee within TGWU.

1935
Arthur Pugh (steel workers' leader) and Citrine knighted.

1937
TGWU crushes London busmen's movement, expelling its leaders. A lengthy and bitter miners' strike at Harworth colliery (Notts) leads government to promote reunification of Spencer union with official Nottinghamshire Miners' Association.

1939
TUC's Bridlington Agreement: no union will attempt to establish itself in a workplace where at least half the workforce is already in another union. Control of Employment Act attempts to restrict the movement of skilled workers between firms. Chamberlain tells TUC that reform of trade union law must depend on the unions' conduct during wartime.

1940
Bevin becomes Minister of Labour and National Service with unprecedented powers: (a) Defence Regulation 58A gives him considerable power over the control of labour; (b) Order 1305 bans strikes and lockouts and makes disputes subject to compulsory and binding arbitration; (c) Restriction of Engagement Order prohibits 'poaching' of skilled workers by one firm from another. Agreement on wartime dilution in engineering is reached.

1941
Mar. Essential Work (General Provisions) Order compels all skilled workers to register and be prepared to move to more essential work as required.
Jun. German invasion of USSR places Communist party firmly behind British war effort.

1942
Restoration of Pre-War Practices Act passed to stress that wartime changes in working conditions are temporary.

1944
A series of unofficial mining strikes culminates in the issuing of Defence Regulation 1AA, making it an offence to incite or start a stoppage of essential work.

1945
Miners' Federation of Great Britain becomes the more centralized National Union of Mineworkers.

1946
Repeal of the 1927 Trade Disputes Act.

General secretaries of the TUC

1911–23	Charles Bowerman
1923–5	Fred Bramley
1925–6	Walter Citrine (acting)
1926–46	Walter Citrine

Industrial disputes and unionization

	Strikes	Working days lost	Union membership	Union density (%)
1913	1 459	9 804 000	4 135 000	23.1
1914	972	9 878 000	4 145 000	23.0
1915	672	2 953 000	4 359 000	24.1
1916	532	2 446 000	4 644 000	25.6
1917	730	5 647 000	5 499 000	30.2
1918	1 116	5 875 000	6 533 000	35.7
1919	1 352	34 969 000	7 927 000	43.1
1920	1 607	26 568 000	8 348 000	45.2
1921	763	85 872 000	6 633 000	35.8
1922	576	19 850 000	5 625 000	31.6
1923	628	10 672 000	5 429 000	30.2
1924	716	8 424 000	5 544 000	30.6
1925	603	7 952 000	5 506 000	30.1
1926	323	162 233 000	5 219 000	28.3
1927	308	1 174 000	4 919 000	26.4
1928	302	1 388 000	4 806 000	25.6
1929	431	8 287 000	4 858 000	25.7
1930	422	4 399 000	4 842 000	25.4
1931	420	6 983 000	4 624 000	24.0
1932	389	6 488 000	4 444 000	23.0
1933	357	1 072 000	4 392 000	22.6
1934	471	959 000	4 590 000	23.5
1935	553	1 955 000	4 867 000	24.9
1936	818	1 829 000	5 295 000	26.9
1937	1 129	3 418 000	5 842 000	29.6
1938	875	1 334 000	6 053 000	30.5
1939	940	1 356 000	6 298 000	31.6
1940	922	940 000	6 613 000	33.1
1941	1 251	1 079 000	7 165 000	35.7
1942	1 303	1 527 000	7 866 000	39.0
1943	1 785	1 808 000	8 174 000	40.4
1944	2 194	3 714 000	8 087 000	39.8
1945	2 293	2 835 000	7 875 000	38.6
1946	2 205	2 158 000	8 803 000	43.0

Source: J E Cronin, *Labour and Society in Britain 1918–1979* (1983), pp 241–2

7. Finance and taxation

Chronology of legislation and principal events
1914
Aug.   War Loan Act increases Treasury's borrowing powers for war purposes. Currency and Bank Notes (Amendment) Act allows Bank of England to print money regardless of gold stocks and effectively takes Britain off gold standard.
Nov.   Finance (Session 2) Act almost doubles income tax and super tax, and increases tea and beer duties; a predicted deficit of £321 million is to be covered by a war loan issue of £350 million at 3.5 per cent.

1915
Jun.   War Loan Act borrows a further £587 million at 4.5 per cent.
Oct.   American Loan Act allows the Treasury, in conjunction with France, to borrow up to $500 million in the USA.
Dec.   Finance (No. 2) Act attempts to put government finances on a full war footing, increasing taxes and reducing the income tax threshold to £130, increasing indirect taxes by up to 100 per cent, imposing tariffs (the 'McKenna Duties') of 33.3 per cent on 'luxury' imports like cars, and imposing excess profits duty (EPD) at the rate of 50 per cent.

1916
Feb.   First issue of war savings certificates to attract money from small investors.
Apr.   New taxes imposed on railway tickets, etc. Finance Act further increases direct and indirect taxation.
Dec.   War Loan Act borrows £966 million at 5 per cent.

1917
Aug.   Finance Act increases indirect taxes and raises EPD from 60 to 80 per cent. War Loan Act borrows £250 million.

1918
Jul.   Finance Act increases income tax, super tax and many indirect taxes; War Loan Act borrows £250 million.

1919
Mar.   Britain formally leaves the gold standard for a specified period of six years.

Aug. Finance Act increases income tax and death duties, cuts EPD from 80 to 40 per cent, and introduces limited imperial preference, cutting McKenna Duties by one-third for Empire products.
Jun. War Loan Act raises a further £250 million.
Nov. Government announces intention to return to gold standard, as recommended by Cunliffe Committee.

1920
Aug. Finance Act budgets for a large surplus: super tax and some indirect taxes are increased, EPD goes up to 60 per cent, a new corporation profits tax of 5 per cent is imposed, the road fund is established and land taxes are abolished.

1921
Aug. Finance Act abolishes EPD but fails to cut expenditure to the satisfaction of 'Anti-Waste' campaigners.

1922
Jul. Finance Act cuts expenditure by 15 per cent; some indirect taxes and income tax are cut.

1923
Jul. Finance Act cuts spending; income tax and corporation profits tax are also reduced, the latter to 2.5 per cent.

1924
Aug. Finance Act cuts indirect taxes on beverages and sugar, in line with Snowden's aim of the 'free breakfast table', and abolishes McKenna Duties and corporation profits tax.

1925
Apr. Britain returns to gold standard at the pre-war parity. Finance Act increases death duties, cuts income tax and supertax, reimposes McKenna Duties, and increases preferences on some Empire goods.

1926
Jul. Finance Act extends McKenna Duties to commercial vehicles, raises motor vehicle duties and imposes a new betting tax.

1927
Jul. Finance Act increases indirect taxes, extends McKenna Duties to tyres, and imposes safeguarding duties on pottery.

1928
Aug. Finance Act increases income tax relief for children, cuts sugar duties, and provides for central government block grants to compensate local authorities for derating.

1929
May Finance Act repeals tea and betting duties.

1930

Aug. Finance Act increases income tax, super tax, death duties and some indirect taxes; it allows safeguarding duties on lace, cutlery, gloves and gas mantles to expire.

1931

Feb. Appointment of the May Committee on National Expenditure to recommend ways of balancing the budget.

May Start of European financial crisis; by June the pound is under pressure.

Jul. Finance Act increases some indirect taxes, and prepares for a land tax of 1d (0.5p) in the £ from 1933–4. May Report predicts a deficit of £120 million for 1932–3 and recommends spending cuts of £96 million and increased taxation of £24 million. Run on the pound intensifies.

Aug. Labour cabinet breaks up after failing to reach agreement on spending cuts; National government formed.

Sep. Britain leaves gold standard after renewed run on sterling. National Economy Act cuts public salaries and benefits by 10 per cent. Finance (No. 2) Act increases income tax, super tax and a range of indirect taxes.

1932

Jun. Finance Act sets up exchange equalization account to manage exchange rates and reimposes tea duties.

1933

Jun. Finance Act increases road duties on heavier goods vehicles, and cuts beer duty.

1934

Jul. Finance Act cuts income tax and restores the 1931 salary cuts.

1935

July Finance Act raises income tax allowances and thresholds, cuts entertainments duty, and increases duty on diesel fuel.

1936

Jul. Finance Act increases income tax, though it also increases allowances.

1937

Mar. Defence Loans Act allows government to borrow up to £400 million at 3 per cent for defence purposes.

Jul. Finance Act increases income tax and imposes a new tax, the national defence contribution, on profits arising from increased public spending on defence.

1938
Jul. Finance Act increases income tax and some indirect taxes.

1939
Mar. Defence Loans Act increases borrowing powers to £800 million.
Jul. Finance Act increases super tax and death duties, plus some indirect taxes.
Oct. Finance (No. 2) Act increases super tax, death duties and income tax, while reducing allowances; imposes a new excess profits tax (EPT) of 60 per cent; and increases indirect taxes.
Nov. National Loans Act further extends Treasury's borrowing powers; similar measures follow in every year of war.

1940
Jun. Finance Act increases income tax, EPT (to 100 per cent) and super tax; a new purchase tax is introduced to raise revenue and restrict domestic expenditure; indirect taxes are increased.
Aug. Finance (No. 2) Act increases income tax, super tax and death duties; reforms purchase tax into three bands, 0 per cent for essentials like food, 16.6 per cent for less basic necessities, like furniture, and 33.3 per cent for luxuries.

1941
Jul. Finance Act marks a new Keynesian approach in aiming to use the budget as a market regulator for the first time; government undertakes to subsidize prices of all essential goods and services, to counter inflation; super tax is increased; and income tax is raised, while thresholds and allowances are reduced to bring 4 million more people into the tax net.

1942
Jun. Finance Act increases indirect taxes and doubles purchase tax on luxuries.

1943
Jul. Finance Act increases indirect taxes.
Nov. Income Tax (Employments) Act revolutionizes tax system by compelling employers to deduct income tax directly from their employees' salaries and wages ('Pay As You Earn'): scheme comes into operation in April 1944.

Standard rate of income tax

	Rate in £				Rate in £		
	s	d	%		s	d	%
1914	1	2	6	1932	5	0	25
1915	1	8	8.5	1934	4	6	22.5
1916	3	0	15	1936	4	9	24
1917	5	0	25	1938	5	0	25
1919	6	0	30	1939	5	6	27.5
1923	5	0	25	1940	7	0	35
1924	4	6	22.5	1941	8	6	42.5
1926	4	0	20	1942	10	0	50
1931	4	6	22.5	1947	9	0	45

Bank rate

		(%)			(%)
1914	30 July	4	1929	7 Feb.	5.5
	31 July	8		26 Sept.	6.5
	1 Aug.	10		31 Oct.	6
	7 Aug.	6		21 Nov.	5.5
	8 Aug.	5		12 Dec.	5
1916	10 July	8	1930	6 Feb.	4.5
1917	18 Jan.	5.5		6 Mar.	4
	5 Apr.	5		20 Mar.	3.5
1919	6 Nov.	6		1 May	3
1920	15 Apr.	7	1931	14 May	2.5
1921	29 Apr.	6.5		23 July	3.5
	23 June	6		30 July	4.5
	21 July	5.5		21 Sept.	6
	3 Nov.	5	1932	18 Feb.	5
1922	17 Feb.	4.5		10 Mar.	4
	13 Apr.	4		17 Mar.	3.5
	15 June	3.5		21 Apr.	3
	13 July	3		12 May	2.5
1923	5 July	4		30 June	2
1925	5 Mar.	5	1939	24 Aug.	4
	6 Aug.	4.5		28 Sept.	3
	1 Oct.	4		26 Oct.	2
	3 Dec.	5	1951	8 Nov.	4
1927	21 Apr.	4.5			

Sources: *Statistical Abstract* 70
(1927), p 177; 80 (1937), p 233

National debt: gross liabilities of the state

	(£ million)
1913	711.3
1918	5 921.1
1923	7 812.6
1928	7 631.0
1933	7 859.7
1938	8 149.0
1943	15 973.7
1946	23 773.9

Sources: *Statistical Abstract*
70 (1927), p 116; 80 (1937),
p 164; 84 (1947), p 219

National accounts (£ 000s)

	Revenue	Expenditure	Surplus/deficit	
1913/14	198 243	197 493	+	750
1914/15	226 694	560 474	−	333 780
1915/16	336 767	1 559 158	−	1 222 391
1916/17	573 428	2 198 113	−	1 624 685
1917/18	707 235	2 696 221	−	1 988 986
1918/19	889 021	2 579 301	−	1 690 280
1919/20	1 339 571	1 665 773	−	326 202
1920/21	1 425 985	1 195 428	+	230 557
1921/22	1 124 880	1 079 187	+	45 693
1922/23	914 012	812 496	+	101 516
1923/24	837 169	788 840	+	48 329
1924/25	799 436	795 777	+	3 659
1925/26	812 062	826 100	−	14 038
1926/27	805 701	842 395	−	36 694
1927/28	842 824	838 585	+	4 239
1928/29	836 435	818 041	+	18 394
1929/30	814 971	829 494	−	14 523
1930/31	857 761	881 037	−	23 276
1931/32	851 482	851 118	+	364
1932/33	827 031	859 310	−	32 279
1933/34	809 379	778 231	+	31 148
1934/35	804 629	797 067	+	7 562
1935/36	844 775	841 834	+	2 941
1936/37	896 596	902 193	−	5 597
1937/38	948 700	919 900	+	28 800

National accounts (£ 000s) (cont.)

	Revenue	Expenditure	Surplus/deficit
1938/39	1 006 200	1 018 900	– 12 700
1939/40	1 132 200	1 408 200	– 276 000
1940/41	1 495 300	3 970 700	– 2 475 400
1941/42	2 174 600	4 876 300	– 2 704 700
1942/43	2 922 400	5 739 900	– 2 817 500
1943/44	3 149 200	5 909 300	– 2 760 100
1944/45	3 354 700	6 179 500	– 2 824 800
1945/46	3 401 200	5 601 100	– 2 199 900

Sources: B Mallet and C O George, *British Budgets 1913–14 to 1920–21* (London, 1929), pp 286–307; idem, *British Budgets 1921–22 to 1932–33* (London, 1933), pp 425–53; *Statistical Abstract* 81 (1938), p 169; 84 (1947), pp 213, 215

8. Transport and communications

Chronology of legislation and principal events

1914   Railways taken into public control on outbreak of war.

1919   Alcock and Brown fly the Atlantic. Air Navigation Act permits civil aviation in Britain for first time. Ministry of Transport established with power over railways, roads and canals.

1920   Road Fund set up to receive new vehicle excise duties.

1921   Railways Act returns railways to private ownership, but grouped into four large regional companies: Southern, Great Western, London, Midland and Scottish, and London and North-Eastern.

1924   London Traffic Act limits number of roads over which buses can run, and imposes strict timetables and safety standards.

1925   Local authorities given increased powers to carry out road improvements on safety grounds.

1928   Liberal Industrial Inquiry proposes the construction of a national network of new trunk roads between major towns.

1930   Air Transport (Subsidy Agreements) Act gives subsidies of up to £1 million a year to airlines. Road Traffic Act appoints thirteen Area Traffic Commissioners with full powers to license public service vehicles, and establishes guidelines as to drivers' wages.

1933   London Passenger Transport Act takes the capital's public transport into public ownership: the minister is to appoint a London Passenger Transport Board to control and coordinate all bus, tube and tram services. Road and Rail Traffic Act strengthens the wages clause of the Road Traffic Act 1930, introduces licensing for the carriage of goods, sets rigorous standards for commercial vehicles and deregulates rail freight charges.

1934   Road Traffic Act introduces a 30 mph speed limit in built-up areas and a compulsory driving test, and allows local authorities to create pedestrian crossings on roads.

1935   Railways (Agreement) Act guarantees low-interest improvement loans to the railways.

1936 Air Navigation Act makes the Secretary of State for Air responsible for civil aviation, and increases local authorities' powers to build aerodromes. Trunk Roads Act transfers responsibility for 4 500 miles of major roads from local authorities to Ministry of Transport, to ensure greater coordination and standardization.

1938 Air Navigation (Financial Provisions) Act doubles state subsidies to airlines to £3 million, and introduces a stricter system of airline licensing. Road Haulage Wages Act sets up central and area wages boards and gives the industrial court power to fix statutory wage levels.

1939 Imperial Airways and British Airways amalgamated into a state-owned British Overseas Airways Corporation. Railways taken under state control on outbreak of war. Petrol rationing introduced.

1942 Private cars lose petrol ration entirely.

Railways: passengers and freight carriage

	Passengers (million)	Freight (million tons)
1913	1 199	364
1919	1 523	305
1923	1 236	343
1928	847	306
1933	799	251
1938	850	266
1943	1 037	301
1946	901	262

Sources: Calculated from *Statistical Abstract* 70
(1927), pp 254–5; 80 (1937), pp 324–5; 84
(1947), p 202

Motor vehicles in use

	Private cars	Total
1914	132 000	389 000
1923	384 000	1 132 000
1928	877 000	2 027 000
1933	1 196 000	2 272 000
1938	1 944 000	3 094 000
1943	718 000	1 544 000
1946	1 770 000	3 113 000

Sources: *Statistical Abstract* 70 (1927), p 248; 80
(1937), pp 316–17; 84 (1947), p 198

Civil aviation

	Passenger miles flown
1925	3 million
1930	6 million
1938	53 million
1950	794 million

Source: G C Allen, *British Industries
and their Organization* (5th edn,
1970), p 191

Foreign affairs, defence and the Empire

1. The armed forces and defence

Chronology of legislation and major developments

1914
Defence of the Realm Act gives government sweeping powers to rule by decree during wartime. Start of mass recruiting campaign for Army.

1916
Jan.   Military Service Act makes liable for conscription to the armed forces all single men, and widowers without dependants, between the ages of 18 and 41; exemption is allowed for essential war workers and conscientious objectors, subject to the approval of local tribunals set up by the Act.

Apr.   Air Board set up under Lord Curzon to coordinate air services and oversee air policy.

May   Military Service (Session 2) Act conscripts married men and remaining widowers between the ages of 18 and 41.

1917
Royal Naval Air Service and Royal Flying Corps amalgamate to form the Royal Air Force (RAF), independent of Army and Navy.

1918
Feb   Military Service Act gives the director-general of National Service absolute power to withdraw employment exemptions and to force men into the armed forces.

Apr.   Military Service (No. 2) Act extends the maximum age of conscription to 51.

1919
Introduction of the 'Ten Year Rule' whereby British defence planners were to work on the assumption that Britain would not be involved in war with another major power for ten years.

1921
Territorial army reorganized.

1922
Washington Naval Treaty restricts British naval building. Britain plans building of naval base at Singapore. Government decides to preserve the independence of the RAF.

1923

Scheme for the expansion of the RAF to 17 fighter and 35 bomber squadrons agreed.

1924

Government starts planning air raid precautions but stops work on Singapore naval base.

1925

Government postpones fulfilment of RAF expansion plan until 1935–6.

1926

Work resumes on Singapore naval base.

1928

Ten Year Rule reaffirmed on a rolling basis.

1929

Work stops on Singapore naval base.

1930

London Naval Treaty further restricts new naval building. Fulfilment of 1923 RAF expansion plan put back to 1938.

1931

'Invergordon Mutiny' as naval ratings protest against proposed pay cuts; the threat of further unrest convinces National government to restrict pay cuts to a maximum of 10 per cent.

1932

Abandonment of the Ten Year Rule; work on the Singapore naval base resumes.

1934

Development of radar started.

1935

White Paper, *Statement Relating to Defence*, signals the start of rearmament. First flight of Hurricane fighter prototype.

1936

First flight of the Spitfire fighter.

1937

Dec.   Air-Raid Precautions Act requires local authorities to prepare and submit schemes for civil defence in the event of air raids, and to cooperate with arrangements to evacuate the civilian population from the major centres in the event of war; central government is to meet 60–75 per cent of the cost. Chiefs of Staff warn that Britain could not fight successfully against Germany, Italy and Japan at once, and that steps must be taken to reduce the number of potential enemies and to gain allies.

1939
Jan. Chiefs of Staff state that a fleet could be sent to the Far East only if European conditions allowed, effectively abandoning the area to the Japanese.
May Military Training Act conscripts men aged 20 and 21 to the armed forces.
Jul. Civil Defence Act extends local authorities' powers to requisition buildings for air raid purposes, and reaffirms their duty to help with evacuation.
Sep. National Service (Armed Forces) Act allows conscription of men aged 18 to 41 as necessary.

1940
May Setting up of the Local Defence Volunteers (Home Guard).

1941
Apr. National Service Act makes all citizens liable for national service, military or civilian.
Dec. National Service (No. 2) Act extends maximum age for conscription from 41 to 50.

1944
Reinstatement in Civil Employment Act obliges the former employers of those on national service to reappoint them to their former jobs on demobilization.

Chiefs of the Imperial General Staff

1912–14	Sir John French
1914	Sir Charles Douglas
1914–15	Sir J Wolfe-Murray
1915	Sir Archibald Murray
1915–18	Sir William Robertson
1918–22	Sir Henry Wilson
1922–6	Earl of Cavan
1926–33	Sir George Milne
1933–6	Sir Archibald Montgomery-Massingberd
1936–7	Sir Cyril Deverell
1937–9	Viscount Gort
1939–40	Lord Ironside
1940–1	Sir John Dill
1941–6	Sir Alan Brooke (Viscount Alanbrooke)

First Sea Lords

1914–15	Lord Fisher
1915–16	Sir Henry Jackson
1916–17	Sir John Jellicoe
1917–19	Sir Rosslyn Wemyss
1919–27	Earl Beatty
1927–30	Sir C Madden
1930–3	Sir F Field
1933–8	Lord Chatfield
1938–9	Sir R Backhouse
1939–43	Sir Dudley Pound
1943–6	Sir Andrew Cunningham

Chiefs of Air Staff

1918	Sir Hugh Trenchard
1918–19	Sir Frederick Sykes
1919–30	Sir Hugh Trenchard
1930–3	Sir John Salmond
1933	Sir G Salmond
1933–7	Sir Edward Ellington
1937–40	Sir Cyril Newall
1940–6	Sir Charles Portal

Armed forces: personnel

	Army	Navy	Air Force
1913	247 000	139 000	—
1914	1 327 000	201 000	—
1915	2 476 000	251 000	—
1916	3 344 000	328 000	—
1917	3 883 000	368 000	n/a
1918	3 838 000	407 000	n/a
1919	1 064 000	268 000	n/a
1924	207 000	99 000	31 000
1929	194 000	100 000	31 000
1934	195 000	91 000	31 000
1939	241 000	129 000	113 000
1940	1 656 000	276 000	291 000
1941	2 221 000	405 000	665 000
1942	2 468 000	507 000	840 000
1943	2 692 000	671 000	973 000
1944	2 742 000	790 000	1 011 000
1945	2 931 000	789 000	963 000
1946	1 129 000	350 000	439 000

Sources: *Statistical Abstracts* 70 (1927), pp 102–4; 80 (1937), pp 150–2; 84 (1947), p 102

Armed forces: expenditure (£ million)

	Army	Navy	Air Force	Votes of credit	Total
1913/14	28	49	—		77
1914/15	29	52	—	357	438
1915/16				1 400	1 400
1916/17				1 974	1 974
1917/18				2 403	2 403
1918/19				2 198	2 198
1919/20	395	157	53	87	692
1924/5	45	56	14	—	115
1929/30	41	56	17	—	114
1934/5	40	57	18	—	115
1939/40	82	69	67	409	627
1940/1				3 220	3 220
1941/2				4 085	4 085
1942/3				4 840	4 840
1943/4				4 950	4 950
1944/5				5 125	5 125
1945/6				4 410	4 410
1946/7	717	267	256	—	1 240

Note
During the wars, separate service votes were replaced by votes of credit to cover all military, naval and Air Force activities.

Sources: *Statistical Abstracts* 70 (1927), pp 110–11; 80 (1937), pp 158–9; 84 (1947), p 215

2. The First World War

1914

4 Aug.	Following German invasion of Belgium, Britain declares war on Germany.
5 Aug.	Kitchener becomes Secretary of State for War.
19 Aug.	British Expeditionary Force (BEF), having been sent to France, concentrates on French left at Maubere.
23 Aug.	Battle of Mons: first contact between British and German troops; British fall back, but hold German advance at river Marne.
28 Aug.	British cruisers raid Heligoland Bight and sink three German ships.
5–12 Sep.	Battle of the Marne ends in stalemate.
22 Sep.	First British air raids on German airfields.
5 Nov.	Britain and France declare war on Turkey; British annex Cyprus, which they have occupied since 1878.
Nov./Dec.	Series of coastal raids by German ships on British towns, eg Yarmouth, Hartlepool, Scarborough.
8 Dec.	Battle of the Falkland Islands: a small force of German cruiser raiders is destroyed by British fleet.
18 Dec.	Britain declares a protectorate over Egypt.
21 Dec.	First German air raid on Britain (Dover).

1915

By the start of the year the lines on the Western Front were set, with a line of trenches stretching from the English Channel to Switzerland. While most of Britain's military commanders believed it was only in the west that the war could be won, the stalemate led people like Churchill and Lloyd George to wonder whether a new front in the east might produce dramatic results.

19 Jan.	First German airship raid on Britain: there are to be 19 raids in 1915 and 41 in 1916.
24 Jan.	Inconclusive naval clash between British and German fleets off Dogger Bank.

19 Feb.	British naval action against Dardanelles Straits (Turkey) commences.
Mar.	Intensification of naval blockade of Germany.
10–13 Mar.	British offensive at Neuve Chapelle produces a few short advances through German lines.
18 Mar.	British ships try and fail to force Dardanelles.
22 Apr.–	Second battle of Ypres: German use of poison
25 May	gas frustrates Allied hopes of an advance.
25 Apr.	Landing of British, French and Australian forces at Gallipoli (Dardanelles): several months of fighting follow, but against strong defences little headway can be made.
7 May	The liner *Lusitania* is sunk by a German U-boat off Ireland; among the dead (over 1 000) are many Americans.
23 May	Italy enters the war on the Allied side following the treaty of London (26 Apr.).
6 Aug.	Allied landing at Suvla (Turkey); again, little headway made.
1 Sep.	Germans end U-boat campaign against liners.
25 Sep.–15 Oct.	Third battle of Artois: British use poison gas for first time but fail to consolidate early gains.
19 Dec.	Sir Douglas Haig succeeds Sir John French as British commander-in-chief on Western Front.
19 Dec.–	British forces withdraw from Gallipoli; the
9 Jan. 1916	Straits remained closed and Russia largely isolated from Allied supplies.

1916

By the start of the year it seemed that the Western Front was the only place that the war could be won. The eastern campaign had failed to open up a second, more vulnerable front, and under Haig the Westerners were clearly in control. Shortages of men led to the introduction of conscription (**Jan.**). It was clear that there would be no early end to the war.

Feb.–Jun.	Massive French losses at Verdun place increased strain on British.
21 Feb.	Germany resumes unrestricted U-boat warfare.
24–5 Apr.	German naval raids on Yarmouth and Lowestoft.
9 May	Sykes–Picot agreement: Britain and France agree to divide Turkish territory in the Middle East between themselves after the war.
10 May	After loss of more American lives, Germans call off unrestricted U-boat warfare.

31 May–1 Jun.	Battle of Jutland, the major naval engagement of the war: the Germans sink two ships in the North Sea, and the British, under Jellicoe and Beatty, respond by trying to trap the German fleet, but it escapes: each side loses six ships. The British tonnage loss is almost twice that of the Germans, but the German High Seas Fleet rarely ventures out of port again.
1 Jul.–18 Nov.	Battle of the Somme: Haig's major effort for the year, aiming to capture territory and take pressure off struggling French. Britain loses 60 000 men on the first day, and 400 000 overall, and makes maximum gains of 7 miles. The battle sees the first British use of tanks (15 Sep.).
28 Nov.	First German aeroplane raid on London.

1917

As opposed to the stalemate of 1916, 1917 did bring significant developments. Russia was crumbling by the end of 1916: two revolutions in 1917 took it out of the war. But in the USA Wilson had been re-elected President in **November 1916** and so could afford to take a more belligerent line with the Germans. In Britain, the replacement of Asquith as Prime Minister by Lloyd George (**Dec. 1916**) suggested a more vigorous prosecution of the war effort. But there were no easy victories, it would be a hard year, and on the home front British morale was probably lower and less behind the war effort than at any other time.

11 Mar.	British forces occupy Baghdad.
Apr.	German U-Boat campaign reaches a climax, with 875 000 tons of shipping destroyed, more than half of it British. Britain finally introduces a convoy system to counter the threat, and U-boat effectiveness falls significantly.
6 Apr.	USA declares war on Germany.
9 Apr.–4 May	Battle of Arras: the British advance after making a gas attack, and Canadian troops take Vimy Ridge, but the early promise is not upheld and the maximum gain is 4 miles.
16–20 Apr.	Offensive planned by French commander-in-chief, Nivelle, fails and he is dismissed; this gives Haig more freedom to pursue his own line.
7–14 Jun.	Battle of Messines: minor British advances.

31 Jul.–10 Nov.	Third battle of Ypres (Passchendaele): Haig's major offensive of the year produces no real breakthrough, with no gain exceeding 5 miles, and that producing a difficult salient for Britain to defend; 400 000 troops are lost.
3–4 Nov.	British troops have to be rushed to Italy to prevent the collapse of the Italian forces fighting there.
20 Nov.–3 Dec.	Battle of Cambrai sees the first major tank offensive, but early British gains cannot be consolidated.
27 Nov.	Supreme Allied War Council set up to coordinate military action.
3 Dec.	Opening of Russo-German peace conference at Brest-Litovsk; treaty signed (**3 March 1918**) taking Russia out of the war.
9 Dec.	British, under Allenby, take Jerusalem.

1918

By the start of 1918 matters were still very unclear. Against the loss of Russia, which it was feared would free German troops for the west, had to be placed the intervention of the USA, with its massive resources but still not providing great numbers of troops in Europe. At home, the breaking of the stalemate in **March 1918** considerably improved morale, but at the start of the year few would have predicted an Allied victory in 1918.

5 Jan.	Lloyd George outlines extensive British war aims.
8 Jan.	President Wilson outlines his 'Fourteen Points' which would be the basis for a peace settlement.
Mar.	First American troops arrive in France.
21 Mar.–5 Apr.	Ludendorff Offensive: a massive German push in the west drives the British back 40 miles and seems to threaten imminent German victory; however, the push is finally held.
14 Apr.	General Foch (France) is declared supreme commander of all Allied forces on the Western Front.
7 May	Romania surrenders to the Central Powers.
8–11 Aug.	Battle of Amiens: using tanks the British make a major breakthrough, advancing 8 miles on the first day, which causes consternation in the German High Command.

21 Aug.–3 Sep.	Second battle of the Somme and battle of Arras: British and French forces extend their attacks on the Germans.
26 Sep.–15 Oct.	Battles of the Argonne and of Ypres see general Allied advances.
29 Sep.	German High Command demands an end to the war.
30 Sep.	Surrender of Bulgaria to Allies.
Oct.	Continuing British advance in the north, retaking a number of Belgian Channel ports.
1–2 Oct.	British and Arab forces take Damascus.
30 Oct.	Surrender of Turkey.
3 Nov.	Surrender of Austria-Hungary.
11 Nov.	Surrender of Germany.

3. Second World War

1939

On the outbreak of war Britain was probably better prepared than it had been at the time of the Munich Crisis (**Sep. 1938**). However, German attention was not fixed on the west until mid-1940, and Britain and France were reluctant to fight in earnest until attacked: this period of 'Phoney War' lasted until **May 1940.**

1 Sep.	German invasion of Poland.
3 Sep.	Britain and France declare war on Germany.
29 Sep.	Surrender of Poland.
21 Nov.	Britain tightens naval blockade on Germany.
30 Nov.–	Russo-Finnish War: some feel Britain should
12 Mar. 1940	give active support to the Finns, but nothing is done; war ends with USSR making some territorial gains.

1940

The year opened with the Phoney War still in progress. Tentative diplomatic attempts to negotiate an end to the conflict came to nothing. In many ways, this was to prove Britain's most glorious year of the entire war.

16 Feb.	British naval forces enter Norwegian waters to rescue 299 prisoners of war from German ship *Altmark*; Norwegian government protests.
8 Apr.	Britain and France announce that Norwegian waters have been mined to prevent their use by German shipping.
9 Apr.	Germany invades Denmark and attacks Norway; British attempts to prevent this fail.
16–19 Apr.	British and French forces land in southern Norway.
3 May	Britain and France forced out of Norway.
8 May	Conservative opposition to Chamberlain in parliament forces him to resign as Prime Minister.
10 May	Germany invades Netherlands, Belgium and Luxembourg; British Expeditionary Force sent

	to Belgium. Churchill becomes Prime Minister. First enemy air attack on mainland.
14 May	Dutch army surrenders.
17–21 May	Germans attack deep into France, and drive to coast, separating British and Belgian forces from the French; British and Belgians forced to retreat to Dunkirk and Ostend.
26 May	King Leopold III of Belgium orders his troops to surrender, totally exposing the British.
1 Jun.	In response to an appeal from Churchill, the USA sends military supplies to Britain.
4 Jun.	Evacuation of 200 000 British and 140 000 French troops from Dunkirk; they are forced to leave behind their equipment and around 30 000 prisoners.
10 Jun.	Italy declares war on Britain and France.
22 Jun.	France surrenders; Britain severs relations with new regime and instead supports General Charles de Gaulle as head of French National Committee in London.
Jul.	German forces occupy Channel Islands.
3 Jul.	Battle of Oran: a British fleet destroys part of the French fleet at Oran, North Africa, to prevent Germans taking it.
4 Jul.	Britain seizes all French ships in its ports.
10 Jul.–15 Sep.	Battle of Britain: German *Luftwaffe* tries to gain air superiority in readiness for invasion, but fails.
6–19 Aug.	Italy conquers British Somaliland in East Africa.
8 Aug.	German bombers launch a campaign against British airfields and military targets.
9 Aug.	British garrisons withdraw from north China.
15 Aug.	British air raids on German cities including Berlin.
17 Aug.	Germany announces a total blockade of Britain.
2 Sep.	Britain is given 50 old US destroyers in return for US control of British bases in Newfoundland and West Indies.
7 Sep.– 12 May 1941	The Blitz: bombing of London, major cities and, from **Jan. 1941**, major ports: much damage and many casualties.
11 Sep.	Britain bombs the French and Belgian Channel ports to upset German invasion preparations.
13–15 Sep.	Italy invades Egypt from Libya.
16 Sep.	Improved British air defences inflict heavy losses on German *Luftwaffe*.

22–5 Sep.	British fleet helps de Gaulle's Free French attack French West African port of Dakar, but they are forced to withdraw.
10 Nov.	First *Luftwaffe* raid on Coventry.
20 Nov.	Britain and USA agree partial standardization of military equipment.
8 Dec.	Start of major advance against Italians in Libya.

1941

By early 1941 Britain was probably secure from invasion, with German attentions turning eastwards. However, it was still prone to German air attack, and virtually without allies. With the U-boat campaign affecting food supplies, and a severe shortage of war materials, the British could continue to fight in North Africa but had no chance of starting an early effort to liberate Europe.

15 Jan.	British forces invade Italian-held Ethiopia and Eritrea.
22 Jan.	British forces take Tobruk (Libya).
26 Feb.	British forces take Mogadiscio, capital of Italian Somaliland.
11 Mar.	Lend-Lease Act approved, allowing USA to transfer goods to Britain without payment.
3 Apr.	Start of German counter-attack in North Africa under Rommel; British soon driven out of most of Libya.
6 Apr.	British take Addis Ababa, capital of Ethiopia; by end of year all Italian East Africa is under British control.
12 May	End of Blitz.
24–7 May	German battleship *Bismarck* sinks British battle-cruiser *Hood* in North Atlantic; she is in turn sunk by British planes and ships.
31 May	British forces in Crete evacuated.
31 May–4 Jun.	British forces occupy Iraq.
22 Jun.	Germans invade USSR. Churchill promises all possible British aid to the Soviets.
12 Jul.	British and Free French take control of Syria.
13 Jul.	Anglo-Soviet pact of mutual assistance signed.
25–9 Aug.	British and Soviet forces occupy Iran.
7 Dec.	Japanese forces attack Hong Kong and Malaya.
8 Dec.	USA declares war on Japan after attack on US naval base at Pearl Harbor, Hawaii. Germany and Italy declare war on USA.

10 Dec.	British ships *Prince of Wales* and *Repulse*, which have been sent to defend Singapore, sunk by the Japanese.
11 Dec.	Britain launches a second drive into Libya.
25 Dec.	British surrender Hong Kong to Japanese.

1942

Britain now had allies, but the situation remained unclear. Britain remained vulnerable to German air attack, and the battle of the Atlantic was putting food supplies in jeopardy. While the campaign in North Africa continued to ebb and flow, Britain was in no position to think of liberating Europe and was being crushed in the Far East by the Japanese.

15 Feb.	Japanese capture Singapore.
7 Mar.	Japanese occupy Burma.
27 May	Start of second Axis drive on Egypt.
24 Apr.–Jul.	'Baedecker Raids': as reprisal for British raids on historic German towns, Germans launch a series of raids on ancient British cities like Exeter, Bath, Norwich and York.
21 Jun.	Fall of Tobruk to Axis powers leads to sharp decline in civilian morale and much criticism of Churchill Coalition.
23 Oct.	Start of British counter-offensive in North Africa with victory in battle of El Alamein.
4 Nov.	Rommel begins to retreat.
8 Nov.	Successful amphibious invasion of French North Africa by British and American forces.
12 Nov.	Final Axis forces pushed out of Egypt.

1943

By early 1943 Britain's military position was improving, and its prospects in North Africa were very good. Despite pressure at home, no 'second front' was launched by an invasion of France, but the experience gained in amphibious landings during 1943 helped prepare for such an invasion, which was being planned from April 1943. In the east, the Soviet Union began to turn the Germans back.

24 Jan.	British occupy Tripoli (Libya).
2 Feb.	Surrender of German forces at Stalingrad after heroic Soviet resistance begins Soviet counter-offensive in earnest and considerably improves British morale.

8–12 May.	Collapse of Axis forces in North Africa; capture of Tunis.
10 Jul.	British, American and Canadian forces invade Sicily.
25 Jul.	Italian cabinet forces Mussolini to resign; his successor, Marshal Badoglio, bans the Fascist party and opens armistice talks.
18 Aug.	Collapse of Sicilian resistance.
3 Sep.	Allied forces cross from Sicily to south Italian mainland; Allies sign armistice with Badoglio regime.
15 Sep.	Mussolini, having been rescued by German troops, declares establishment of new Fascist regime based in northern Italy; German troops occupy many major cities, including Rome.
1 Oct.	Allies enter Naples.

1944

By the start of the year it seemed that Allied victory was only a matter of time, with the battle of the Atlantic won, North Africa conquered, and Italy partly under Allied occupation. Plans for the invasion of France were well in hand. In the east, Soviet forces were moving towards the borders of Germany itself. However, Germany reorganized its war machine and continued to pose a threat to the British mainland through new types of weaponry. It would be no easy victory.

23 Jan.	Allies invade Italy south of Rome from the sea.
4 Jun.	Allies enter Rome.
6 Jun.	D-Day landings in Normandy: by the evening, 156 000 men have been landed, and the position is quickly consolidated.
27 Jun.	Allies take Cherbourg.
9 Jul.	Allies take Caen.
12 Aug.	Florence captured by Allies, but there is then stalemate in Italy as Anglo-American efforts concentrate on France.
15 Aug.	Successful amphibious landings on French Riviera.
25 Aug.	Allies take Paris.
2 Sep.	Allies take Brussels.
12 Sep.	Allied forces penetrate into German territory, but are then held back by solid German defences.
24 Oct.	Aachen becomes first German city to fall to Allies.

16–25 Dec.	Battle of the Bulge: Germans make early gains in an Ardennes counter-offensive which aims to roll the Allied forces back to the coast, but they are held.

1945

The end of the war with Germany was now clearly in sight: the Allies had not been dislodged from France, and in the east the Soviet forces had advanced through much of eastern Europe. The position in the Far East was much less clear, with the Japanese defending their island gains tenaciously.

17 Jan	Soviet forces take Warsaw.
7 Mar.	US forces cross the Rhine at Remagen.
28 Apr.	Mussolini captured and killed by Italian partisans.
29 Apr.–1 May	German forces in Italy surrender.
30 Apr.	Suicide of Hitler in his Berlin bunker.
7 May	Germany surrenders unconditionally.
8 May	VE (Victory in Europe) Day.
6 Aug.	Atomic bomb dropped on the major Japanese city of Hiroshima: many deaths and much devastation.
9 Aug.	Second atomic bomb attack, on Nagasaki.
14 Aug.	Japanese government offers to surrender.
2 Sep.	Japanese formally surrender: VJ (Victory over Japan) Day proclaimed.

4. Major treaties

1914

5 Sep.   Declaration of London: Britain, France and Russia
agree not to make separate peace with Germany.

1915

4 Mar.–   Secret Agreements between Russia, France and
10 Apr.   Britain: Russia to gain Constantinople and the Straits
after war; Britain, in return, gains concessions in
Asiatic Turkey and Persia.

26 Apr.   Treaty of London: Italy agrees to join *Entente*
powers in war in return for post-war gains at
expense of Austria-Hungary and Turkish Empire in
Asia, plus compensation for Anglo-French gains at
expense of Germany's colonies.

1916

24 Apr.– Sykes–Picot Agreement: Britain, France and Russia
23 Oct.   agree to creation of British and French spheres
of interest in Turkish Empire in Asia, with France
being allotted Syria and Britain, Mesopotamia.
Russia is to be allowed to annex Turkish Armenia
and Kurdistan.

1917

2 Nov.   The Balfour Declaration: Britain declares support
for a Jewish homeland in Palestine subject to recognition of rights of non-Jewish communities.

1919

28 Jun.   Treaty of Versailles with Germany: declares German
responsibility for war and commits Germany to
payment of reparations to the allies. Alsace-Lorraine
returns to France, and territory is also ceded to
Poland, Czechoslovakia, Belgium and Denmark.
Rhineland is to be demilitarized, and occupied by
the allies for fifteen years. All German colonies

are placed under control of League of Nations as 'mandated' territories, which are then administered by the victorious allies. The Army is limited to 100 000, conscription is prohibited and German use of tanks and aircraft is outlawed.

28 Jun. Treaty with Poland on protection of minorities: all non-Polish peoples are to be equal with the Poles, and to be allowed to carry on their own traditions, languages and cultures.

10 Sep. Treaty of St Germain-en-Laye with Austria: Austria cedes territory to Poland, Czechoslovakia, Romania, Yugoslavia and Italy; Hungary becomes a separate state. Union of Austria and Germany forbidden. Austria's army is reduced to 30 000. It is made liable for reparations.

27 Nov. Treaty of Neuilly with Bulgaria: territory ceded to Romania, Greece and Yugoslavia. Bulgaria's army limited to 33 000. It is made liable for reparations.

1920

4 Jun. Treaty of Trianon with Hungary: reduces Hungary to one third of its pre-war size, with territory ceded to Romania, Yugoslavia, Czechoslovakia, Italy, Austria and Poland. Its army is limited to 35 000 men. It is made liable for reparations.

10 Aug. Treaty of Sevres with Turkey: in Europe, Turkey loses Thrace and most of its Aegean islands to Greece; the Straits are demilitarized and opened to merchant shipping, although staying under nominal Turkish control. Parts of mainland Turkey around Smyrna (Izmir) are to be administered by Greece for five years followed by a plebiscite. In Asia, Armenia is granted independence and Kurdistan autonomy, while France takes over Syria, Britain takes over Palestine and Mesopotamia, and the Arabian peninsula gains independence as the Kingdom of Hejaz. Treaty is never ratified due to Turkish revolution under Mustafa Kemal.

1921

16 Mar. Anglo-Soviet Trade Agreement: Britain grants *de facto* recognition to Soviet Russia to facilitate resumption of trade between the two countries. Both sides agree not to carry on propaganda against the other, while Russia accepts in principle its liability for Tsarist Russia's unpaid debts to Britain.

13 Dec. Washington Four-Power Treaty: Britain, France, Japan and USA agree not to strengthen their island possessions in the Pacific, and to confer in event of threats from another power.

1922

6 Feb. Washington Nine-Power Treaty: Britain, France, Italy, Japan, USA, Netherlands, Belgium and Portugal agree with China not to extend their existing territorial rights there.

6 Feb. Washington Naval Treaty: Britain, USA, Japan, France and Italy agree to limit tonnage of their largest ships (mainly battleships) in ratio 5 : 5 : 3 : 1.7 : 1.7, and declare a ten-year 'holiday' on capital ship construction.

1923

24 Jul. Treaty of Lausanne with Turkey: Turkey surrenders non-Turkish parts of Ottoman Empire, but regains its 1914 territories in Europe, though Greece retains most of the Aegean islands. British sovereignty over Cyprus confirmed. Turkey retains all of mainland Asiatic Turkey. Straits demilitarized.

1924

9 Aug. Dawes Plan: sets out a payment plan for German reparations, rising to 2 500 million Reichsmarks a year.

1925

16 Oct. Locarno Treaties: France, Germany and Belgium agree to the inviolability of Germany's western frontier: guaranteed by Britain and Italy.

1928

27 Aug. Kellogg-Briand Pact: Britain, France, Germany, Italy, Japan and USA renounce use of war as instrument of policy.

1929

31 Aug. Young Plan: scales down Germany's annual reparations payments to 1 900 million Reichsmarks; final

payments to amount to about one-third of the total
set in 1921.

1930

22 Apr. London Naval Treaty: building of ships other than
capital ships covered in 1922 Washington Naval
Treaty to be suspended for six years. Only Britain,
Japan and USA ratify it, as France and Italy cannot
reach agreement.

1932

June–July Lausanne Conference: reduces German reparations
to a nominal sum.

1933

7 Jun. Four-Power Pact: Mussolini's proposal for a pact
between Britain, France, Italy and Germany to revise
peace treaties is signed only after France has secured
considerable changes, and it is never ratified.

1935

14 Apr. Stresa Front: Britain, France and Italy meet and
condemn Germany's unilateral repudiation of its
obligations under the Treaty of Versailles. Possible
basis of united front against Germany but Anglo-
French goodwill is seriously damaged two months
later by Anglo-German Naval Agreement.

18 Jun. Anglo-German Naval Agreement: limits German
navy to 35 per cent of the British; within that total
limit, submarines could be 45 per cent of the British,
or equality in event of a threat from USSR. (Treaty
denounced by Hitler, **April 1939**.)

1936

25 Mar. London Naval Treaty: Britain, France and USA
agree to consult each other on naval matters.

7 Aug. Non-Intervention Treaty: Britain, France, Germany,
Italy and USSR accept a policy of neutrality and
non-intervention in Spanish Civil War, which broke
out in **July 1936**; it is abrogated by all except Britain
and France.

1937

2 Jan. Anglo-Italian 'Gentleman's Agreement': Britain and Italy agree to maintain Mediterranean status quo.

14 Sep. Nyon Agreement: following attacks by 'pirate' (Italian) submarines on neutral ships, including British ones, Mediterranean and Black Sea powers agree to defend neutral shipping by sinking suspicious submarines on sight.

1938

29 Sep. Munich Agreement: Britain, France, Germany and Italy agree on stages for German occupation of Sudetenland (German-speaking area of Czechoslovakia) between 1 and 10 October, and also give a conditional guarantee to remainder of Czechoslovakia after settlement of territorial claims of Hungary and Poland. (Abrogated by the German occupation of Bohemia and Moravia in **March 1939.**)

30 Sep. Anglo-German Declaration: Chamberlain and Hitler state that they believed their peoples never again wanted to be at war with one another, and also pledge to resolve remaining disputes in Europe peaceably.

1939

31 Mar. Guarantee to Poland: Britain and France declare support for Poland in event of a threat to its independence.

13 Apr. Guarantee to Romania and Greece: Britain and France declare that they would support them against external threats.

25 Aug. Anglo-Polish Mutual Assistance Agreement: Britain and Poland pledge to support each other in event of attack by a third country.

19 Oct. Anglo-Franco-Turkish Mutual Assistance Treaty: Britain and France agree with Turkey on mutual support in event of war in Mediterranean; Turkey agrees to observe at least benevolent neutrality in any conflict involving Britain and France.

1940

2 Sep. Anglo-American Destroyer-Naval Base Agreement: USA gives Britain 50 First World War destroyers in return for leases on British naval bases in the British western Atlantic islands, the Caribbean and British Guiana.

1941

11 Mar.   Lend-Lease Act: USA offers material assistance to countries whose defence the President deems necessary for defence of USA, such as Britain.

1941

14 Aug.   Atlantic Charter: Britain and USA pledge themselves to preserve world freedom, including the right to be free from foreign aggression and to national self-determination.

1942

1 Jan.   United Nations Declaration: Britain, China, USSR and USA, plus other members of the 'United Nations' agree not to make a separate peace.

29 Jan.   Anglo-Soviet-Iranian Alliance Treaty: Iran promises Britain and USSR help to defend it from aggression; Britain and USSR pledge respect for Iranian independence and to withdraw within six months of the end of the war.

23 Feb.   Anglo-American Mutual Aid Agreement: confirms 'Lend-Lease' terms and pledges both countries to work for reduction of trade barriers after war.

26 May   Anglo-Soviet Alliance: to last for twenty years, with a repeated assurance against making separate peace agreements and for mutual aid, and pledging themselves against territorial expansion.

1945

11 Feb.   Yalta Agreement: Britain, USSR and USA agree to partition Germany into zones of occupation after war, to destroy German militarism and Nazi party, to try war criminals, and to have post-war meetings of foreign secretaries on a regular basis. Plans made for formal establishment of United Nations.

26 Jun.   United Nations Charter signed: establishes United Nations Organization, comprising a General Assembly (including all member states); a Security Council (including Britain, China, France, USSR and USA as permanent members plus lesser powers elected by the General Assembly): a Secretariat under an elected Secretary-General; and an International Court of Justice.

2 Aug.   Potsdam Agreement: Britain, USSR and USA agree to set up a Council of Foreign Ministers to consult regularly in peacetime; arrangements are made for the trial of war criminals; and it is agreed that reparations are to be taken from the zones of occupation by the respective occupiers.

5. Ireland

Major developments in relations

1912–14
Crisis over third Home Rule Bill; in 1914 tension mounts as Unionists and Home Rulers import arms ready for conflict.

1914
On outbreak of war John Redmond, Irish Nationalists' leader, pledges support for British war effort. A group of revolutionary leaders meets to discuss war's potential for helping insurrection in Ireland. Government of Ireland Act grants Home Rule (within UK) for whole of Ireland: an Irish parliament will control domestic affairs, while Westminster will control defence, foreign policy, land purchase, and customs and excise; the Act's operation is suspended for the duration of the war.

1916
Easter Rising of republicans in Dublin, swiftly repressed with heavy casualties; most of the leaders are executed; the most senior survivor, Eamon de Valera, is imprisoned, but soon released.

1917
Sinn Fein makes a number of by-election gains from the Nationalists, but refuses to take seats at Westminster.
Oct. De Valera is elected president of Sinn Fein.

1918
Mar. Death of Redmond; succeeded by John Dillon.
Apr. Military Service (No. 2) Act permits extension of conscription to Ireland (never carried out); Sinn Fein calls a one-day general strike in protest; it and de Valera gain further support from the Nationalists as a result; de Valera is imprisoned.
Dec. In general election, Sinn Fein wins 73 seats, the Nationalists 6, and the Unionists 26; Sinn Fein refuses to take its seats at Westminster.

1919
Jan. Irish Volunteers kill two policemen (usually seen as the start of the 'War of Independence'); Sinn Fein MPs meet as Dáil Eireann (Irish parliament) in Dublin and declare Irish independence.
Apr. De Valera elected president of Dáil Eireann.

1920

Jan. Sinn Fein wins landslide in local elections. Royal Irish Constabulary starts to enrol British volunteers, known as the 'Black and Tans', to repress the rebellion; violence continues to mount.

Aug. Restoration of Order in Ireland Act imposes virtual martial law, giving increased powers to the military commander to suppress disorder by detention of suspects without trial, trial by court martial, etc.

Nov. Escalation of IRA assassinations of policemen and suspected British agents.

Dec. Government of Ireland Act sets up two Irish parliaments, for the North and South, under Westminster suzerainty, with a Council of Ireland to discuss matters of common interest; it is accepted only in the North.

1921

Jun. George V opens Northern Ireland parliament in Belfast.

Jul. Truce signed between British Army and IRA.

Aug. Second Dáil Eireann elects delegates to negotiate agreement with Britain.

Dec. Anglo-Irish Treaty, proposing an Irish Free State (excluding Ulster) with Dominion status in the British Empire, signed in London; Britain to retain control of three 'treaty ports', while the Irish promise to continue to pay the annuities due under the Irish Land Acts, and guarantee freedom of religion. De Valera resigns in protest; succeeded as president by Arthur Griffith.

1922

Jan. Dáil Eireann accepts treaty by 64 votes to 57.

Feb. Extreme republicans reject treaty.

Jun. Irish Free State elections: pro-Treaty 58, anti-Treaty 36, others 34. Field-Marshal Sir Henry Wilson assassinated by the IRA in London. Civil war starts.

Aug. Death of Griffith and assassination of Michael Collins, leader of the pro-Treaty government; new pro-Treaty government under W T Cosgrave continues anti-republican struggle.

1923

May De Valera, for the republicans, calls off the civil war.

Sep. Irish Free State admitted to the League of Nations.

1925

Dec. Boundary Commission appointed to review border of Northern Ireland and Irish Free State ends, with no changes made.

1926

Start of UK subsidies to Northern Ireland for unemployment insurance benefits. De Valera forms new constitutional party, Fianna Fáil.

1932

Feb. Cosgrave's government defeated at general election by Fianna Fáil; de Valera Prime Minister (until 1948).

Jun. De Valera withholds the land annuities payable to the British government.

Jul. Britain responds with the Irish Free State (Special Duties) Act, which imposes tariffs of up to 100 per cent on imports from Ireland; de Valera responds with special duties on British coal.

1935

Jan. Easing of trade war with agreement over Irish cattle exports to Britain and British coal exports to Ireland.

1937

Jul. Free State adopts a new constitution, changing its name to Eire and signalling still greater independence from Britain.

1938

May Eire (Confirmation of Agreement) Act ratifies a treaty negotiated by Chamberlain and de Valera: Britain returns the three treaty ports to Eire, and agrees to waive its claim to annuities (over £100 million) in return for a lump payment of £10 million; all special duties cease and the trade war ends.

1939

Jan. The IRA demands the withdrawal of all British troops from Irish soil and starts a terror campaign on the mainland (until Mar. 1940).

Sep. De Valera declares Irish neutrality in the Second World War; this is maintained throughout the conflict.

Prime Ministers of Northern Ireland

1921–40	Sir James Craig (Lord Craigavon 1927)
1940–3	John Andrews
1943–63	Sir Basil Brooke

Prime Ministers (Taoiseachs) of Irish Free State/Eire

1922–32	William T Cosgrave
1932–48	Eamon de Valera

6. Empire

The British Empire in 1938

	Area (sq. miles)	Population (million)
United Kingdom	94 300	47.5
Eire	29 100	3.0
Canada	3 729 700	11.2
Australia	2 974 600	6.9
South Africa	473 100	10.0
Southern Rhodesia	150 300	1.4
New Zealand	103 600	1.6
Newfoundland	42 700	0.3
India	1 575 200	380.5
Colonial Empire	2 252 000	62.0
Total	11 422 600	524.4

Source: M Abrams (ed) *Britain and her Export Trade* (1946),
p 122

India: Chronology of legislation and principal events

1914
Mahatma Gandhi returns from South Africa to India.

1915
Home Rule League formed to demand greater self-government.

1916
Lucknow Pact: Muslims agree to support Hindu Congress party in return for separate Muslim constituencies in a free India.

1917
Montagu, India Secretary, says the government's policy is to gradually increase Indian participation in administration and to devolve power until India could realize 'responsible self-government . . . as an integral part of the Empire'.

1918
Montagu-Chelmsford Report suggests reforms to achieve this.

1919

Apr. Amritsar Massacre: British troops open fire on a crowd, killing 379 and injuring 1 200.

Dec. Government of India Act gives effect to the Montagu-Chelmsford Report, setting up a largely elected bicameral legislature at the centre with limited power; in the provinces, 'dyarchy' is to be implemented – while governors retain control over justice, police and finance, elected legislatures will have authority in most other areas of government.

1920

Congress, under Gandhi, rejects the reforms and starts a campaign of non-cooperation, which leads to some violence.

1922

Gandhi sentenced to six years' imprisonment (released **1924**).

1923

Tariff Board set up to protect infant Indian industries.

1926

Reading, in his declaration on 'paramountcy', asserts the supremacy of the Crown in India: thus states ruled by Indian princes are subordinate and owe their position to it.

1927

Indian navy put under Viceroy's control; Indian revenues are not to pay for naval operations except in defence of India itself. Statutory Commission set up, earlier than required by 1919 Act, to investigate the working of the 1919 reforms, under Sir John Simon. Boycotted by Congress as it has no Indian representatives.

1928

Congress calls for complete independence for India.

1929

'Irwin Declaration': Viceroy says Dominion status is goal of British policy in India.

1930

May Simon Report says a federation including the princely states must be set up before responsible government can be granted; this seems to many to suggest indefinite postponement.

Oct. First Round Table conference in London: princes declare willingness to join a federation if there is responsible government at the centre.

1930–1

Congress leads first civil disobedience movement, aiming to bring down British rule by nonviolent methods.

1931
Mar.   Irwin-Gandhi truce ends civil disobedience.
Oct.   Second Round Table conference makes no tangible progress.

1932
Second civil disobedience movement: Gandhi imprisoned.

1934
Gandhi is released and ends civil disobedience. Muslim League reorganized under Mohammed Ali Jinnah, seeking safeguards for minorities and greater autonomy for Muslim areas.

1935
Government of India Act provides for an Indian federation (which never in fact comes about) to comprise British India and the princely states, but leaving Viceroy responsible to London rather than to his Indianized Council, and provincial self-government by legislatures elected on a widened franchise including separate electorates for different ethno-religious groups, though provincial governors retain control over certain areas of policy and can suspend the constitution at their own discretion. Burma separated from India and granted responsible government.

1937
Feb.   Provincial elections under the 1935 Act: Congress wins control of seven of the eleven provinces; in North-West Frontier province, a Muslim coalition wins.
Jul.   Formation of seven Congress ministries, which prove generally stable and competent.

1939
Viceroy unilaterally declares India at war on the side of Britain and suspends talks with the princes for the formation of a federation. The Congress provincial ministries resign in protest.

1940
Muslim League adopts policy of a separate Muslim state, 'Pakistan'.

1940–1
Congress declares a (largely unsuccessful) civil disobedience movement.

1942
Cabinet mission under Sir Stafford Cripps offers radical new package, whereby India would become a Dominion as soon as possible after the war, with a constituent assembly elected by the provincial legislatures to negotiate a treaty with the British government; India would have the right to secede from the Commonwealth; and, to protect the position of Muslims, provinces would be able to join or leave the Dominion as they wished. Congress rejects this, demanding

141

independence for a united India; violence and arrests follow, and the political deadlock remains.

1943
Famine in Bengal: provincial government's inability to maintain food supplies in wartime, and the central government's reluctance to interfere, leads to around 2 million deaths.

1947
India partitioned into India and Pakistan, and granted independence.

Viceroys of India

1910–16	Lord Hardinge
1916–21	Lord Chelmsford
1921–6	Lord Reading
1926–31	Lord Irwin
1931–6	Lord Willingdon
1936–43	Lord Linlithgow
1943–7	Lord Wavell
1947	Lord Mountbatten

India: trade with UK as percentage of total trade (value)

	Imports	Exports
1913	76.1	24.0
1914	74.7	31.4
1915–19	56.3	30.5
1920–4	58.7	20.7
1925–9	47.7	22.0
1930–4	37.9	26.6
1935–9	31.0	31.6
1940–4	4.1	28.6
1945	19.4	25.2
1946	28.4	22.9

Source: Calculated from figures in B R Mitchell, *International Historical Statistics: Africa and Asia* (1982), pp 441, 453

Indian Empire: population

(million)	1911	1921	1931	1941	1951	1973
India	303	306	338	389	356[a]	—
Burma	12	13	15	17	—	26

Note
a The population of East Pakistan was 42 million and West Pakistan 34 million, making a total of 432 million

Source: B R Mitchell, *International Historical Statistics: Africa and Asia* (1982), pp 43, 45

Dominions and colonies: Chronology of legislation and principal events

1914
Britain's declaration of war commits whole Empire, but in South Africa a rebellion of Afrikaaners has to be crushed before it can be fully committed.

1917
Mar.   First meeting of imperial war cabinet in London, representing Britain, the Dominions and India. Smuts (South Africa) stays on as member of British war cabinet. Imperial war cabinet meets again in 1918 but does not survive into peacetime.
Mar.–May   Under Canadian and South African pressure, imperial war conference in London decides Dominions should have more say in foreign policy matters. Balfour Declaration commits Britain to a Jewish homeland in Palestine.

1919
Dominions are represented at Paris peace conference; under 'mandates' system, Britain gains Palestine, Transjordan, Iraq and Tanganyika, South Africa gains German South-West Africa and Australia gains New Guinea.

1921   British Empire reaches its maximum extent.

1922
Jan.   Southern Rhodesia accepts a draft constitution giving it limited self-government.
Feb.   Egypt granted independence, though Britain continues to have a garrison there and to control its foreign policy.
May   Empire Settlement Act guarantees £3 million a year to pay up to half the cost of resettling British citizens in the Empire; it particularly helps emigration to Australia.
Sep.   Chanak Incident: only New Zealand is prepared to offer full support to Britain in the event of war with Turkey.

1923
Imperial conference (London) agrees Dominions should be able to make international agreements without British interference.

1925
Dominions Office separated from Colonial Office.

1926
Mar.   Empire Marketing Board set up to stimulate imperial trade.
Oct.   Imperial conference (London) issues a declaration that the Dominions are equal with each other and with Britain, in free and voluntary association under the Crown.

1927
Canada elected to League of Nations Council for three years.

1929
Colonial Development Act provided regular funding for colonial development for first time, setting up a colonial development fund to receive up to £1 million a year to promote agriculture and industry in the colonies as a means of stimulating employment in Britain. Lord Beaverbrook launches his 'Empire Free Trade' campaign for an integrated imperial trading bloc.

1930
Irish Free State elected to Council of League for three years. Lord Passfield's White Paper on Palestine proposes strict restrictions on Jewish immigration there and arouses great Zionist hostility. Imperial conference (London): Bennett (Canada) proposes a system of imperial preference; Britain rejects it, but Conservatives take the opportunity to switch to protectionism.

1931
Statute of Westminster ratifies the Commonwealth agreements made at the 1926 imperial conference.

1932
Imperial conference (Ottawa) reaches agreement on imperial preference in trade. On expiry of British mandate, Iraq becomes independent and joins the League of Nations.

1933
Australia elected to League of Nations Council for three years. Empire marketing board abolished. Newfoundland loses dominion status after the collapse of its finances; a governor responsible to London is appointed (it becomes part of Canada, 1949).

1935
Dominion premiers meet in London and discuss rearmament and the naval base at Singapore.

1936
New Zealand elected to Council of League for three years.

1937
Mar. Empire Settlement Act renews 1922 Act for fifteen years.
May Imperial conference (London) reveals deep splits on defence, with Canada and South Africa especially hostile to centralized imperial defence planning.
Jul. Peel Commission recommends partition of Palestine between Jews and Arabs.

1938
Britain, Canada and the USA agree tariff reductions.

1939

May White Paper on Palestine announces an end to Jewish immigration within five years, and strict quotas in the interim, and effectively abandons the idea of partition by promising that a unitary Palestinian state will be established.

Sep. All Dominions declare war on side of Britain, though in South Africa only after the overthrow of the pro-neutrality Hertzog as premier by Smuts.

1940

Colonial Development and Welfare Act widens scope for direct assistance, providing a ten-year scheme with maximum payments of £500 000 a year for research and £5 million for other schemes; it also cancels the debts of some colonial governments.

1941

Surrender of Hong Kong to Japanese.

1942

Surrender of Singapore to Japanese.

1945

Colonial Development and Welfare Act increases total funds available to £120 million over a ten-year period.

Prime Ministers of Australia

1913–14	Sir Joseph Cook (Liberal)
1914–16	Andrew Fisher (Labour)
1916–23	William Hughes (Labour)
1923–9	S M Bruce (Nationalist)
1929–32	J H Scullin (Labour)
1932–9	J A Lyons (United Australia party)
1939–41	Robert Menzies (United Australia party)
1941–9	J Curtin (Labour)

Prime Ministers of Canada

1911–20	Sir Robert Borden (Conservative)
1920–1	Arthur Meighen (Conservative)
1921–6	W L Mackenzie King (Liberal)
1926	Arthur Meighen (Conservative)
1926–30	W L Mackenzie King (Liberal)
1930–5	R B Bennett (Conservative)
1935–48	W L Mackenzie King (Liberal)

Prime Ministers of New Zealand

1912–25	William Massey (Reform)
1925–8	M J G Coates (Reform)
1928–30	Sir Joseph Ward (Coalition)
1930–5	G W Forbes (Coalition)
1935–40	Michael Savage (Labour)
1940–5	Peter Fraser (Labour)

Prime Ministers of South Africa

1910–19	Louis Botha (National)
1919–24	Jan C Smuts (Unionist)
1924–39	J B M Hertzog (National)
1939–48	Jan C Smuts (Unionist)

Australia: trade with UK as percentage of total trade (value)

	Imports	Exports
1913	51.4	44.5
1914	50.3	44.9
1915–19	55.0	70.8
1920–4	47.1	46.6
1925–9	42.2	38.0
1930–4	37.9	36.8
1935–9	36.5	41.1
1940–4	37.0	35.2
1945	36.0	33.5
1946	41.6	27.4

Source: Based on figures in
B R Mitchell, *International Historical Statistics: The Americas and Australasia* (1983), pp 559–60, 612, 614

Canada: trade with UK as percentage of total trade (value)

	Imports	Exports
1913	21.3	47.3
1914	19.7	40.6
1915–19	11.5	50.3
1920–4	16.9	34.5
1925–9	16.3	33.0
1930–4	18.4	32.9
1935–9	18.1	39.4
1940–4	10.3	35.9
1945	7.8	29.7
1946	7.6	25.6

Source: Based on figures in
B R Mitchell, *International Historical Statistics: The Americas and Australasia* (1983), pp 543, 546, 569, 579

New Zealand: trade with UK as percentage of total trade (value)

	Imports	Exports
1913	55.8	78.3
1914	50.5	80.5
1915–19	40.3	77.8
1920–4	48.0	80.1
1925–9	46.1	74.2
1930–4	42.7	72.9
1935–9	38.1	63.8
1940–4	29.5[a]	74.7[a]
1945	36.3	72.1
1946	47.5	71.0

Note
a Based on 1940–2 only; figures for 1943–4 not available

Source: Based on figures in
B R Mitchell, *International Historical Statistics: The Americas and Australasia* (1983), pp 559–60, 613, 615

Dominions: population (000s)

	1911	1921	1931	1946
Canada	7 207	8 788	10 377	11 507
South Africa	5 973	6 927	9 558	11 416
Australia	4 455	5 436	6 630	7 579
New Zealand	1 058	1 149	1 574	1 702
Newfoundland	239	263	290	322
Irish Free State	—	2 972	2 968	2 955

Sources: B R Mitchell, *International Historical Statistics: Africa and Asia* (1982), p 41; *International Historical Statistics: The Americas and Australasia* (1982), pp 47, 49, 53; *European Historical Statistics 1750–1970* (1975), p 21

Colonial Empire: components

(Modern names are given in brackets)

British West Indies Bahamas, Barbados, Grenada, Jamaica and Dependencies, Leeward Islands, St Lucia, St Vincent, Trinidad and

Tobago, Bermuda, British Guiana (Guyana), and British Honduras (Belize).

British West Africa Gambia, Gold Coast (Ghana), Nigeria, and Sierra Leone.

British East Africa Kenya, Northern Rhodesia (Zambia), Southern Rhodesia (Zimbabwe), Nyasaland (Malawi), British Somaliland (part of Somalia), Uganda, and Tanganyika (after First World War) and Zanzibar (both Tanzania).

Eastern colonies British North Borneo, Sarawak, British Malaya (all Malaysia); Brunei, Ceylon (Sri Lanka), Hong Kong, Mauritius, Seychelles, Fiji, Gilbert and Ellice Islands, Solomon Islands, Tonga, and New Hebrides.

Mediterranean colonies Cyprus, Gibraltar, Malta, and Palestine.

Other colonies Aden (South Yemen), Falkland Islands, and St Helena.

Colonial Empire: trade with UK as percentage of total trade

	Imports	Exports
British West Indies	35	48
British West Africa	55	46
British East Africa	38	34
Eastern colonies	16	18
Mediterranean colonies	30	46
Other colonies	19	36
Colonial Empire	25	27

Source: F V Meyer, *Britain's Colonies in World Trade* (1948), p 3

Biographies

Biographies

Addison Dr Christopher (1869–1951): Liberal (later Coalition Liberal) MP, 1910–22; Labour MP 1929–31, 1934–5; 1st Baron (later Viscount) Addison, 1937; junior minister under Asquith; under Lloyd George Minister of Munitions (1916–17), Reconstruction (1917–19), Health (1919–21); dismissal from latter post generally seen as marking end of Lloyd George Coalition's radical pretensions; joined Labour party. Minister of Agriculture (1930–1); opposed benefit cuts and resigned, August 1931. Labour leader in House of Lords 1945–51.

Amery Leopold Stennett (1873–1955): Journalist and writer; Conservative MP 1911–45; First Lord of Admiralty 1922–4, Secretary of State for Dominions and Colonies 1924–9, Secretary of State for India 1940–5; protectionist and campaigner for imperial unity.

Anderson Sir John (1882–1958): Leading civil servant (Permanent Under-Secretary at the Home Office 1922–32; Governor of Bengal 1932–7); Independent MP 1938–50; Lord Privy Seal 1938–9, Home Secretary 1939–40, Lord President of the Council 1940–3; as Chancellor of the Exchequer 1943–5, cautioned against too extensive social reform and commitment to full employment policies.

Asquith Herbert Henry (1852–1928): Liberal MP 1886–1918, 1920–4; Earl of Oxford and Asquith, 1925. Leader of Liberal party 1908–26; Prime Minister 1908–16; ousted by Lloyd George. A more effective peacetime than wartime premier, he was widely criticized before his fall in 1916, after which he was ineffectual as Liberal leader.

Attlee Clement Richard (1883–1967): Labour MP 1922–55; Earl Attlee, 1955. Parliamentary Private Secretary to MacDonald, 1922–4, Under-Secretary for War 1924, Chancellor of Duchy of Lancaster 1930–1, Postmaster General 1931. Narrowly held seat, 1931; became deputy leader of Labour party; leader, 1935–55. Member of war cabinet, 1940–5, and deputy Prime Minister, 1942–5, playing major role in the smooth running of the wartime Coalition; Prime Minister, 1945–51.

Baldwin Stanley (1867–1947): Conservative MP 1908–37; Financial Secretary to Treasury 1917–21; President of Board of Trade,

1921–2. Spoke against Coalition at Carlton Club meeting, 1922; Chancellor of the Exchequer, 1922–3; party leader 1923–37; Prime Minister 1923–4, 1924–9, 1935–7; as Lord President of Council, was effectively deputy Prime Minister of National government, 1931–5; Earl Baldwin of Bewdley, 1937. His apparent lethargy and failure to take a strong lead have to be balanced by consideration of his accommodation of Labour into the parliamentary system, his ability to unite the bulk of the political right in Britain, and his competent handling of the General Strike and the Abdication Crisis.

Balfour Arthur James (1848–1930): Conservative MP 1874–1922; created Earl Balfour, 1922. Prime Minister 1902–5; resigned party leadership 1911. Attended war cabinet meetings as a member of Committee of Imperial Defence 1914. First Lord of Admiralty, 1915–16; Foreign Secretary, 1916–19; Lord President of Council 1919–22. Supported Coalition, 1922; Lord President of the Council, 1925–9.

Beatty David (1871–1936): Admiral in First World War; commanded first battle cruiser squadron 1912–16; played a prominent role at battle of Jutland 1916; commanded Grand Fleet 1916–19; Earl, 1919; First Sea Lord 1919–27, helping to improve conditions for ordinary seamen and resist attempts to cut naval expenditure.

Beaverbrook 1st Baron (Sir Max Aitken) (1879–1964): Canadian press magnate, owner of newspapers including *Daily Express* and *Evening Standard*. One of the 'press barons' who helped change face of British press. Passionate advocate of imperial unity. Conservative MP 1910–16; Baron Beaverbrook, 1916. Chancellor of Duchy of Lancaster 1918. Led Empire Crusade 1929–31. Member of war cabinet 1940–2; Minister of Aircraft Production 1940–1; Minister of State 1941; Minister of Supply 1941–2; Lord Privy Seal 1943–5.

Bevan Aneurin (1897–1960): miner; Labour MP 1929–60; leading left-winger; expelled from Labour party 1939 for advocating a popular front; readmitted later in year; leading critic of Churchill Coalition; Minister of Health 1945–51, founding National Health Service; Minister of Labour 1951.

Beveridge William (1879–1963): Economist and writer on social policy, especially unemployment; leading civil servant as director of labour exchanges 1909–16 and at Ministry of Food 1916–19; director of London School of Economics 1919–37; master of University College Oxford from 1937; author of report on *Social Insurance and Allied Services* (1942) (the 'Beveridge Report'); Liberal MP 1944–5.

Bevin Ernest (1881–1951): Rose to prominence in Dockers' Union; united fifty unions into Transport and General Workers' Union, of which he was general secretary (1922–40); played leading role on general council of TUC (1925–40), especially in General Strike, in opposing MacDonald and Snowden during the 1931 crisis, and in determining Labour policy in the 1930s; Labour MP 1940–51; Minister of Labour in war cabinet 1940–5; Foreign Secretary 1945–51, playing a leading role in formation of North Atlantic Treaty Organization (NATO); Lord Privy Seal 1951.

Birkenhead 1st Earl (Frederick Edwin Smith) (1872–1930): Conservative MP 1906–19; Solicitor-General 1915, Attorney-General 1915–19; as Lord Birkenhead, Lord Chancellor 1919–22. A leading Conservative supporter of Lloyd George; opposed withdrawal from Coalition, 1922; refused to serve under Law. India Secretary, 1924–8.

Bondfield Margaret Grace (1873–1953): Labour MP 1923–4, 1926–31; Chief Woman Officer, National Union of General and Municipal Workers, 1921–38; first woman cabinet minister as Minister of Labour 1929–31.

Bourne Cardinal Francis Alphonsus (1861–1935): Catholic Archbishop of Westminster 1903–35, and head of the Catholic Church in Britain; played a leading role in resisting state control of Catholic schools; advised Catholics to support National government in 1931.

Butler Richard Austen (Rab) (1902–82): Conservative MP 1929–65; junior minister at India Office (1932–7), Ministry of Labour (1937–8), Foreign Office (1938–41), earning enmity of Churchill; President of Board of Education 1941–5; passed Education Act 1944. Went on to a series of high offices, 1951–64.

Chamberlain (Arthur) Neville (1869–1940): Son of Joseph Chamberlain, and half-brother of Austen; mayor of Birmingham 1915–17; Director-General of National Service 1917; Conservative MP 1918–40; favoured ending of Coalition 1922; Postmaster-General 1922–3; Paymaster-General 1923; Minister of Health 1923, 1924–9, 1931; Chancellor of Exchequer 1923–4, 1931–7; Prime Minister 1937–40. Chamberlain's rise after 1922 was swift, but justified by his administrative ability. By 1931 he was Baldwin's likely successor, but by the time he became premier in 1937, foreign policy was increasingly important, and he was no match for Hitler, as the failure of his 'appeasement' policy showed. Forced to resign by Commons rebellion of Conservative MPs, May 1940; became Lord President of Council in war cabinet. For many years Chamberlain's reputation suffered because of the 'failure' of appeasement, but in recent times historians have not only revised views of his foreign policy but also directed more attention to his earlier achievements.

Chamberlain (Joseph) Austen (1863–1937): Son of Joseph Chamberlain and half-brother of Neville. Liberal Unionist MP 1892–1906; Conservative MP 1906–37; held a succession of offices, including

Chancellor of Exchequer, 1895–1905; failed in bid for Conservative leadership, 1911; Secretary of State for India 1915–17; member of war cabinet 1918–19; Chancellor of Exchequer 1919–21; party leader and Lord Privy Seal 1921–2; resigned leadership after Carlton Club meeting, 1922, and refused to serve in Law's government; Foreign Secretary 1924–9 (partly responsible for Locarno Pact); First Lord of Admiralty 1931. By mid-1930s his passionate Germanophobia made him a leading critic of the National government's foreign policy.

Churchill Winston Leonard Spencer (1874–1965): Son of Lord Randolph Churchill; Conservative MP 1900–4, then joined Liberals in defence of free trade. Liberal MP 1904–22; Conservative MP 1924–64. Held a variety of offices in Asquith's peacetime government, including President of Board of Trade (1908–10), Home Secretary (1910–11), and First Lord of Admiralty (1911–15). Failure of Dardanelles campaign led to his resignation in 1915. Returned under Lloyd George as Minister of Munitions (1917–19), Secretary of State for War and Air (1919–21), and Secretary of State for Colonies (1921–2). Moved back to Conservatives after losing his seat, 1922. Chancellor of Exchequer, 1924–9. Resigned from shadow cabinet, early 1931, over protectionism and India. He opposed the government's liberal line on India, the abdication of Edward VIII, and the appeasement of Germany. On outbreak of war became First Lord of Admiralty, and in May 1940, became Prime Minister. His inspirational style and combative attitude made him an excellent war leader. In May 1945 Labour withdrew from Coalition; Churchill formed a 'Caretaker' government to rule until a general election could be called, in which the Conservatives were heavily defeated. Prime Minister, 1951–5. Churchill's reputation is no longer beyond reproach: while acknowledging his great contribution in wartime, more attention has been given to Churchill's very mixed career before 1939.

Citrine Walter McLennan (1887–1983): Assistant general secretary of TUC 1925; acting general secretary 1925–6; general secretary 1926–46; president of International Federation of Trade Unions 1928–45; chairman of Central Electricity Authority 1947–57. Leading figure, with Bevin, in reorientation of TUC after General Strike, and of Labour movement as a whole after 1931, helping ensure the growth of British trade unionism on moderate and responsible lines.

Clynes John Robert (1869–1949): Labour MP 1906–31, 1935–45; President, National Union of General and Municipal Workers 1912–37; Minister of Food Control 1918–19; chairman of Labour MPs 1921–2, when defeated by MacDonald; deputy leader 1922–31; Lord Privy Seal 1924; Home Secretary 1929–31. Opposed benefit cuts in Labour cabinet 1931, but refused to become party leader, and again refused to stand in 1935. Not a successful minister, but one of Labour's 'Big Five' leaders between 1922 and 1931.

Cole George Douglas Howard (1889–1959): Oxford don and prolific socialist writer on economics, politics and history; leading advocate of guild socialism through books like *The World of Labour* (1913). With collapse of guild socialism in early 1920s, reverted to a more orthodox position; played important role in Labour policy formulation in 1930s.

Cook Arthur James (1885–1931): English-born south Wales miner; syndicalist agitator before First World War; general secretary, Miners' Federation of Great Britain, 1924–31, and so a leading figure in General Strike and miners' lockout of 1926; seen as firebrand but privately tried to end coal dispute; jointly responsible for Cook-Maxton manifesto 1928; signed Mosley manifesto 1930.

Cripps (Richard) Stafford (1889–1952): Son of Conservative MP who later became a Labour minister; nephew of Beatrice Webb; scientist-turned-barrister; Solicitor-General 1930–1; Labour MP 1931–50; held seat at 1931 election; leading Labour left-winger in 1930s, proposing joint action with Communists; expelled for advocacy of popular front 1939; Ambassador to USSR 1940–2; Lord Privy Seal and Leader of House of Commons (in war cabinet), 1942; Minister of Aircraft Production 1942–5; rejoined Labour party 1945; served in Attlee governments, most notably as Chancellor of Exchequer (1947–50).

Cunliffe-Lister (Lloyd-Greame until 1924), Sir Philip (1884–1972): Conservative MP 1918–35; Viscount Swinton, 1935; junior minister in Lloyd George Coalition, 1920–2; President of Board of Trade 1922–4, 1924–9, 1931; Secretary of State for Colonies, 1931–5; Secretary of State for Air 1935–8; Cabinet Minister Resident in West Africa 1942–4; Minister of Civil Aviation 1944–5; served in Churchill's cabinet, 1951–5. Ardent protectionist who profited from exclusion of Coalitionists in 1922.

Curzon George Nathaniel (1859–1925): Conservative MP 1886–98; Baron 1898, Earl 1911, Marquess 1921; Viceroy of India 1898–1905; Lord Privy Seal 1915–16; President of Air Board 1916; Lord President of Council 1916–19, 1924–5; Foreign Secretary 1919–24; leader of House of Lords 1916–24. One of few leading Coalitionists to serve under Law, 1922–3, and widely expected to succeed as premier, 1923, but Baldwin thwarted him.

Dalton (Edward) Hugh John Neale (1887–1962): Son of tutor to future King George V. Economist; Labour MP 1924–31, 1935–59; under-secretary at Foreign Office under Arthur Henderson 1929–31;

155

played important role in Labour's recovery in 1930s; Minister of Economic Warfare 1940–2; President of Board of Trade 1942–5; Chancellor of Exchequer 1945–7; further cabinet posts 1948–51.

Davidson John Colin Campbell (1889–1970): Conservative MP 1920–3, 1924–37; Viscount Davidson, 1937; Chancellor of Duchy of Lancaster 1923–4, 1931–7; junior Admiralty minister 1924–6; Conservative party chairman 1926–30. Never a cabinet minister but of great importance in reorganizing and modernizing party machinery, and as a 'fixer' for Baldwin. This did not, though, prevent Baldwin from sacrificing him as party chairman in the face of strong attacks in 1930.

Davidson Randall Thomas (1848–1930): Archbishop of Canterbury 1903–28; Baron Davidson 1928. Leading role in resisting Welsh disestablishment, steadying Church in First World War, and calling for reconciliation during General Strike. Worked for Christian unity, improving relations with Nonconformists and Catholics. However, parliamentary refusal to accept Revised Prayer Book in 1928 meant his career ended in disappointment.

Dutt Rajani Palme (1896–1974): Son of Indian and Swedish parents; imprisoned as conscientious objector in First World War; member of Communist party 1920; launched *Labour Monthly* 1921; took over party leadership (with Pollitt) with start of 'class against class' period, 1928; leading ideologue of party until late 1950s; general secretary 1939–41; vice-chairman 1950–65. The leading English-speaking exponent of Stalinism until his death, giving the party a distinctive voice but crushing out dissent and debate.

Eden (Robert) Anthony (1897–1977): Conservative MP 1923–57; Earl of Avon 1957. Foreign Office minister, 1931–3; Lord Privy Seal 1933–5; Minister for League of Nations Affairs 1935; Foreign Secretary 1935–8, resigning in protest at Chamberlain's conciliatory policy towards Italy; thereafter a half-hearted opponent of government; Secretary of State for Dominions 1939–40; Foreign Secretary 1940–5, 1951–5; Prime Minister 1955–7, resigning after Suez Crisis.

Fisher Sir (Norman Fenwick) Warren (1879–1948): Civil servant from 1903; senior posts at Inland Revenue 1913–19; Permanent Secretary to Treasury and head of Civil Service 1919–39, where he ensured dominance of 'generalist' approach to recruitment, and made the Treasury the dominant government department. Defence commissioner, north-west region 1939–40; special commissioner, London 1940–2.

Grey Sir Edward (1862–1933): Liberal MP 1885–1916; Viscount 1916; Foreign Secretary 1905–16, and widely blamed by Liberal radicals for his part in 'secret diplomacy' which they believed had led to war; followed Asquith into opposition, 1916; the leading Asquithian after 1926, and president of Liberal Council from 1927.

Haig Sir Douglas (1861–1928): Commissioned as Army officer 1885; led 1st Army corps at Mons 1914; commander of First Army 1915; commander-in-chief, Western Front 1915–19; masterminded battles of Somme (1916) and Passchendaele (1917) as well as final victory in 1918; Earl 1919; commander-in-chief, home forces 1919–21. Haig has aroused massive controversy: his commitment to winning war of attrition on Western Front led to allegations of callousness and incompetence, but he had many supporters and Lloyd George was never strong enough to get rid of him.

Haldane Viscount (Richard Burdon Haldane) (1856–1928): Liberal MP 1885–1911; Viscount 1911; Secretary of State for War 1905–12; Lord Chancellor 1912–15, when he was dropped because Asquith's new Conservative Coalition partners saw him as too pro-German; moved towards Labour party; Labour Lord Chancellor 1924.

Halifax Earl of, (Edward Frederick Lindley Wood) (1881–1959): Conservative MP 1910–25; Colonial Under-Secretary 1921–2; President of Board of Education 1922–4, 1932–5; Minister of Agriculture 1924–5; Viceroy of India (as Baron Irwin) 1926–31; responsible for 'Irwin Declaration' (1929) that India would move towards Dominion status; 3rd Viscount Halifax 1934; Secretary of State for War 1935; Lord Privy Seal 1935–7; Lord President of Council 1937–8; as Foreign Secretary, 1938–40, favoured appeasement, but quicker than Chamberlain to realize its failure, and pushed latter into taking a sterner line. Labour's choice as Prime Minister, 1940, but did not press his claim and Churchill succeeded instead. Important role as Ambassador to Washington 1941–6; Earl 1944.

Hankey Sir Maurice Pascal Alers (1877–1963): Secretary of Committee of Imperial Defence 1912–38; Baron Hankey, 1938; secretary of war cabinet 1916–18, and of cabinet 1918–38; Minister without Portfolio 1939–40, Chancellor of Duchy of Lancaster 1940–1, Paymaster-General 1941–2. Helped establish cabinet secretariat on a permanent footing.

Henderson Arthur (1863–1935): Labour MP 1903–18, 1919–22, 1923, 1924–31, 1933–5; general secretary of Labour party 1912–34; chairman of Labour MPs 1908–10, 1914–17; President of Board of Education and labour adviser to government 1915–16; member of war cabinet 1916–17; architect of Labour's new constitution 1918; Home Secretary 1924; Foreign Secretary 1929–31; split with MacDonald over benefit cuts; leader of Labour party, 1931–2; president of world disarmament conference 1932–5; won Nobel Peace Prize 1934. A moderate, believing in need for Labour to counter extreme left threat. Christianity was his leading motivation. His most successful period in office came 1929–31, but most of his achievements there were ephemeral.

Hoare Samuel John Gurney (1880–1959): Conservative MP 1910–44; Viscount Templewood 1944; Secretary of State for Air 1922–4, 1924–9, 1940; Secretary of State for India 1931–5, passing 1935 Government of India Act in face of right-wing opposition; Foreign Secretary 1935, when forced to resign after Hoare-Laval Pact; First Lord of Admiralty 1936–7; Home Secretary 1937–9; Lord Privy Seal in war cabinet 1939–40; Ambassador to Spain, 1940–4. Widely seen as able but unscrupulous.

Horne Sir Robert Stevenson (1871–1940): Conservative MP 1918–37; Viscount 1937; Minister of Labour 1919–20; President of Board of Trade 1920–1; Chancellor of Exchequer 1921–2; opposed ending of Coalition; refused to serve under Law and, in 1924, Baldwin. Seen as possible Conservative leader, 1930–1.

Horner Arthur Lewis (1894–1968): Miner; joined Independent Labour party before 1914; joined Communist party 1920; leading figure in South Wales Miners' Federation; president 1936–45; secretary, National Union of Mineworkers 1946–59. The leading Communist trade unionist in 1930s and 1940s, Horner was never easy for the party to control.

Jellicoe John Rushworth (1859–1935): From naval family, entered Royal Navy 1872; commander, Grand Fleet 1914–16; First Sea Lord 1916–17; Chief of Naval Staff 1917–19; Governor-General of New Zealand 1920–4; President of British Legion 1928–32. Widely criticized over battle of Jutland and later for resisting convoys.

Jones Thomas (1870–1955): University lecturer; first secretary of National Health Insurance Commission (Wales) 1912–16; deputy secretary to cabinet 1916–30, becoming a confidante and personal assistant to Baldwin; secretary of Pilgrim Trust 1930–45; member of Unemployment Assistance Board 1934–40.

Keynes John Maynard (1883–1946): Economist; worked at Treasury 1915–19, resigning in protest at peace settlement; wrote *The Economic Consequences of the Peace* (1919); opposed return to gold standard, 1925; member, Liberal industrial inquiry 1927–8; member, Macmillan committee on finance and industry 1929–31, and of economic advisory council from 1930, emerging as leading critic of deflationary policies; argued, especially in *General Theory of Employment, Interest and Money* (1936), for state intervention to secure higher levels of employment; returned to Treasury 1940; influenced change in budgetary policy (1941) and *White Paper on Employment* (1944); Baron Keynes 1942; important role in Bretton Woods conference, 1944; negotiated US loan to Britain 1945. Whether a 'Keynesian solution' could have cut interwar unemployment is still debated.

Kitchener Horatio Herbert, 1st Viscount (1902) Earl (1914) (1850–1916): Soldier; commander-in-chief in South African War (1899–1902); commander-in-chief, India 1902–9; field marshal 1909; consul-general in Egypt 1911–14; Secretary of State for War 1914–16. Anticipating a long war he organized a massive volunteer army, for which he became famous due to his 'Your Country Needs *You*' posters. A difficult colleague. Drowned on sea voyage to Russia, 1916.

Lang (William) Cosmo (1864–1945): Archbishop of Canterbury 1928–42; Baron Lang 1942; agreed to total abolition of tithes 1936; opposed Edward VIII's plan to marry Mrs Simpson.

Lansbury George (1859–1940): Pacifist Labour MP 1910–12, 1922–40; imprisoned with other Poor Law guardians in Poplar, east London, in 1921 for paying too generous scales of relief; First Commissioner of Works 1929–31; opposed cuts and went into opposition, 1931; only ex-cabinet minister to survive 1931 election; leader of Labour MPs 1931–2; party leader 1932–5, resigning in 1935 in protest at party's support for League of Nations economic sanctions against Italy. A popular figure, but ultimately his pacifism clashed with political realities.

Law Andrew Bonar (1858–1923): Born in Canada; son of an Ulsterman; raised in Scotland; Conservative MP 1900–10, 1911–23; junior minister 1902–5; elected leader of Conservative party 1911; gave strong backing to Ulster Unionists in Home Rule crisis, 1912–14; Colonial Secretary 1915–16; Chancellor of Exchequer and member of war cabinet 1916–19; Lord Privy Seal 1919–21, resigning through ill-health; spoke against Coalition at Carlton Club, October 1922, and re-elected party leader; Prime Minister 1922–3. His willingness to take the party leadership in 1922 was possibly crucial in convincing Conservative MPs that they could abandon the Coalition.

Lloyd George David (1863–1945): Born in Manchester, raised in north Wales; Liberal MP 1890–1931, Independent Liberal 1931–45; President of Board of Trade 1905–8; Chancellor of Exchequer 1908–15; Minister of Munitions 1915–16, masterminding a substantial increase in supplies of war materials; War Secretary 1916; Prime Minister 1916–22, falling from power when Conservatives withdrew support; leader of Liberal party 1926–31, revitalizing its policy and organization; failed to keep the party united after 1929 election; finally resigned over alliance with Conservatives in National government, 1931; launched 'New Deal' aiming at policies to reduce unemployment, 1935; visited Hitler 1936; refused office under Churchill 1940. His greatest achievements came before 1918, especially his dynamic wartime premiership; but the record of his peacetime administration made him many enemies, and his love of intrigue and apparent lack of principle consigned him to the political wilderness.

Macarthur Mary Reid (1880–1921): Elected to executive of Shop Assistants' Union 1903; secretary of Women's Trade Union League 1903–21; founder and secretary of National Federation of Women Workers 1906–21; worked to defend and improve position of women workers in First World War as member of War Emergency Workers' National Committee; defeated as a Labour candidate in 1918 election; member, Labour party national executive committee 1919–20.

MacDonald James Ramsay (1866–1937): Born illegitimate in northern Scotland; secretary to a Liberal MP; joined Independent Labour party 1894; secretary, Labour representation committee (Labour party) 1900–12; Labour MP 1906–18, 1922–31; National Labour MP 1931–5, 1936–7; chairman of Labour MPs 1911–14, resigning because of Parliamentary Labour party's support for war; fiercely attacked in 'patriotic' circles for his stance; leader of Labour party 1922–31; Labour Prime Minister 1924 (when also Foreign Secretary), 1929–31; formed National government 1931 and expelled from Labour party; National Prime Minister 1931–5; Lord President of Council 1935–7. An inspirational figure for Labour, doing as much as anyone to make it a major party, but the 1931 'betrayal' was never forgiven by Labour; he soon became a lonely and despised figure at head of a largely Conservative government.

McKenna Reginald (1863–1943): Liberal MP 1895–1918; President of Board of Trade 1907–8; First Lord of Admiralty 1908–11; Home Secretary 1911–15; Chancellor of Exchequer 1915–16, giving name to tariffs on 'luxury' imports; followed Asquith into opposition 1916; chairman, Midland Bank 1919–43; offered the Exchequer by Law in 1922 and Baldwin in 1923; critic of deflationary policies; member of Macmillan committee on finance and industry 1929–31; more sympathetic than most bankers to unorthodox policies.

Maclean John (1879–1923): Schoolteacher and socialist lecturer in Glasgow; joined Social Democratic Federation 1903; popularized Marxism through lectures; opposed First World War, taking a revolutionary defeatist line; imprisoned repeatedly for sedition 1916–22; appointed first Bolshevik Consul to Scotland by Lenin 1918; efforts to form Scottish workers' republican party in opposition to Communist party of Great Britain came to little; heavily defeated at 1922 election. Not an original thinker, but helped inculcate Marxism into a generation of Scottish Labour activists, and inspired many by his example.

Macmillan (Maurice) Harold (1894–1986): Publisher; Conservative MP 1924–9, 1931–64; junior minister at Supply (1940–2) and Colonies (1942–3); Minister Resident in North West Africa 1942–5; Secretary of State for Air 1945; cabinet posts 1951–63 including Prime Minister, 1957–63. Between the wars called for radical employment policies, emerging in the 1930s as an advocate of planning, as seen in his book *The Middle Way* (1938); opponent of appeasement. Maverick reputation held him back until 1940.

Maxton James (1885–1946): Glasgow schoolteacher; imprisoned for sedition 1916; Labour MP 1922–31, Independent Labour party 1931–46; chairman, ILP 1926–31 (helping radicalize party through such efforts as 1928 Cook-Maxton campaign), 1934–9 (working for closer cooperation with other working-class bodies and especially Communists); opposed war 1939. A fiery orator and man of strong left-wing views.

Milner Viscount (Sir Alfred Milner) (1854–1925): High Commissioner for South Africa 1897–1905; member, war cabinet 1916–18; War Secretary 1918–19; Colonial Secretary 1919–21; retired 1921. His social imperialism inspired many, and led to creation of short-lived National Democratic party as 'patriotic' working-class body.

Mond Sir Alfred Moritz (1868–1930): Liberal MP 1906–26; Conservative MP 1926–8; Baron Melchett 1928; First Commissioner of Works 1916–21; Minister of Health 1921–2. Industrialist and head of Brunner-Mond, which he later merged with other firms to form Imperial Chemical Industries (ICI); desire for cooperation with unions led to Mond-Turner talks in 1928.

Montgomery Bernard Law (1887–1976): Became Army officer 1908; served in India, on Western Front, and in Ireland and Middle East; one of few generals to emerge with credit from Belgian campaign, 1940; British commander in North Africa and Italy 1942–4, leading British forces to victory at El Alamein, 1942; commander-in-chief of ground forces (under US General Eisenhower) for D-Day landings 1944; accepted German surrender 1945; Viscount Montgomery of Alamein 1946; served in various high-ranking posts 1946–58. A difficult colleague, but an inspirational figure in Second World War.

Morrison Herbert Stanley (1888–1965): Son of a policeman; conscientious objector during First World War; Labour MP 1923–4, 1929–31, 1935–59; Lord Morrison 1959; Minister of Transport 1929–31 (in cabinet 1931); leader of London County Council 1934–40; defeated by Attlee for party leadership, 1935; Minister of Supply 1940; Home Secretary 1940–5 (in war cabinet 1942–5); Lord President of Council 1945–51, masterminding passage of Labour's nationalization programme; Foreign Secretary 1951.

Mosley Sir Oswald Ernald (1896–1980): Wealthy scion of gentry family; Conservative MP 1918–22; Independent MP 1922–4; Labour MP 1926–31; New party MP 1931. Chancellor of Duchy of Lancaster and part of ministerial team on unemployment 1929–30; rejection by cabinet of his 'memorandum' advocating more interventionist policies led him to resign; formed New party 1931; moved towards fascism, forming British Union of Fascists 1932; interned 1940–3; formed Union Movement 1948. Remains a highly controversial figure.

Norman Montagu Collet (1871–1950): Banker; joined Bank of England, 1915; deputy-governor of Bank 1918–20; governor 1920–44; Baron Norman 1944; helped Baldwin renegotiate US debt 1923; strong advocate of return to gold standard 1925; helped reorganization of industry in 1930s through Bankers' Industrial Development Corporation. Responsible for reorganizing and modernizing the Bank; clashed with economic radicals like Keynes.

Northcliffe Baron (1903), Viscount (1918) (Alfred Charles William Harmsworth) (1865–1922): Journalist; launched many periodicals in 1880s and 1890s, including *Daily Mail* (1896), the first paper to target a lower-middle class audience; launched *Daily Mirror* 1903; bought *The Times* 1908; opposed Asquith in First World War; strongly critical of Lloyd George after war. Crucial figure in popularizing, commercializing and sensationalizing the British press.

Pollitt Harry (1890–1960): Boilermaker; joined Independent Labour party 1909, and British Socialist party 1911; fierce critic of Labour party; opposed First World War; secretary, Hands off Russia Movement, 1919; joined Communist party 1920; secretary, National Minority Movement 1924–9; imprisoned for twelve months, 1925; supported 'new line' of 'class against class' 1928; secretary, Communist party of Great Britain 1929–39 (forced to resign for supporting war against Germany), 1941–56; chairman 1956–60. The popular Pollitt was an ideal foil for the more remote Palme Dutt; together they dominated British Communism for more than three decades.

Rathbone Eleanor Florence (1872–1946): Independent MP 1929–46; 'new' feminist accepting 'separate spheres' ideology in 1920s; a leading advocate of family allowances through such books as *The Disinherited Family* (1924) and *The Case for Family Allowances* (1940).

Reading Baron 1914, Viscount 1916, Earl 1917, Marquess 1926 (Sir Rufus Daniel Isaacs) (1860–1935): Liberal MP 1904–13; Solicitor-General 1910; Attorney-General 1910–13; Lord Chief Justice 1913–21; Viceroy of India 1921–6; Foreign Secretary 1931. Aloof from Liberal feuds of 1916–26, Reading was keen to reunite the party, but his efforts were to no avail.

Reith John (1889–1971): General manager of British Broadcasting Company 1922; director-general of British Broadcasting Corporation 1925–38; chairman of Imperial Airways 1938–9, and of British Overseas Airways Corporation 1939–40; National MP 1940–5; Minister of Information 1940; Minister of Transport 1940; Minister of Works (as Baron Reith) 1940–2. His firm views, based on severe religious convictions, did more than anything to shape the BBC as it existed in this period.

Robertson William Robert (1860–1933): Joined Army 1877, working way up through ranks; Quartermaster-General, British Expeditionary Force (BEF) 1914–15; Chief of General Staff, BEF 1915; Chief of Imperial General Staff 1915–18; seen with Haig as leading proponent of 'western' strategy; effectively dismissed by Lloyd George 1918; commander-in-chief, Home Forces 1918–19, and of British Army on Rhine 1919–20, when he became Field Marshal; retired 1921.

Rothermere 1st Baron (1914), Viscount (1919) (Harold Sidney Harmsworth) (1868–1940): Younger brother of Lord Northcliffe, and financial brains behind his press empire; took over *Daily Mirror* 1914; Minister for Air 1917–18; took over Associated Newspapers, 1922; took an increasingly prominent public role, joining with Beaverbrook in Empire Crusade 1930–1, and calling for an improved Air Force and reconciliation with Hitler and Mussolini in 1930s; supported Mosley and British Union of Fascists 1933–4. Much distrusted in Conservative circles.

Samuel Herbert Louis (1870–1963): Liberal MP 1902–18, 1929–35; junior minister 1905–14; President of Local Government Board 1914–15; Postmaster General 1915–16; Home Secretary 1916; followed Asquith into opposition; knighted 1920; High Commissioner for Palestine 1920–5; chairman of Royal Commission on Coal 1925–6; tried to act as intermediary during General Strike; chairman of Liberal party organization 1927–30; deputy leader of Liberal party 1929–31; acting leader (in illness of Lloyd George) during 1931 crisis; leader 1931–5; Home Secretary 1931–2, resigning over protection; Viscount 1937; Liberal leader in House of Lords 1944–55. Passionate Zionist.

Simon Sir John Allsebrook (1873–1954): Liberal MP 1906–18, 1922–31; Liberal National MP 1931–40; Viscount 1940; Solicitor-General 1910–13, Attorney-General 1913–15, Home Secretary 1915–16 (resigning over introduction of conscription); followed Asquith into opposition; strong opponent of General Strike 1926; chairman of Indian Statutory Commission 1927–30; resigned Liberal whip 1931, later leading new Liberal National group; Foreign Secretary 1931–5; Home Secretary 1935–7; Chancellor of Exchequer

1937–40; Lord Chancellor 1940–5. Simon's long career left behind few solid achievements and he has been widely criticized, especially for his record as Foreign Secretary.

Sinclair Sir Archibald (1890–1970): Scottish landowner; Liberal MP 1922–45; Viscount Thurso 1952; Liberal chief whip 1930–1; Secretary of State for Scotland 1931–2, resigning over protection; leader of Liberal party 1935–45, trying to modernize the party's image; Secretary of State for Air 1940–5.

Snowden Philip (1864–1937): Joined Independent Labour party, 1890s; Labour MP 1906–18, 1922–31; opposed conduct of First World War; Chancellor of Exchequer 1924, 1929–31; joined National government 1931, and played a major role in attacking Labour at 1931 election; Viscount Snowden 1931; Lord Privy Seal 1931–2, resigning over protection; broadcast for Liberals at 1935 election. Crippled by illness from early adulthood. An inspiring speaker and propagandist in early years, but a rigid and rather old-fashioned Chancellor.

Tawney Richard Henry (1880–1962): Historian, socialist thinker; books like *The Acquisitive Society* (1921) advanced ethical socialist views based firmly on Christian morality; educational reformer as member of Board of Education consultative committee, 1912–31; took a leading part on Sankey Coal Commission, 1919; drafted Labour's 1928 programme *Labour and the Nation*, which he later repudiated. His moral approach appealed to many but was weak on economics; he was better at inspiration than prescription.

Temple William (1881–1944): Son of Frederick Temple (arch-bishop of Canterbury 1896–1902); Bishop of Manchester 1921–9; Archbishop of York 1929–42, and Archbishop of Canterbury 1942–4. President, Workers' Educational Association 1908–24; member, Labour party 1918–25; headed Pilgrim Trust investigation *Men Without Work* (1938). Best-remembered as 'People's Archbishop', reflecting his political radicalism and preaching of a Christian social gospel. An advocate of church unity, founding British Council of Churches in 1942.

Thomas James Henry (1874–1949): Railway worker; assistant general secretary, Amalgamated Society of Railway Servants, 1910, and of National Union of Railwaymen (NUR), 1913; NUR general secretary 1917–29; political general secretary 1929–31; expelled for joining National government; Labour MP 1910–31; National Labour MP 1931–6; criticized by left for collapse of Triple Alliance (1921) and General Strike (1926); Colonial Secretary 1924; Lord Privy Seal and minister for employment 1929–30; Secretary of State for Dominions 1930–5, and for Colonies 1935–6; career ended by budget leak 1936.

Often seen as a drunken buffoon, but no mean political operator, doing much to build up the NUR and to make Labour acceptable in the 1920s.

Trenchard Hugh Montague, 1st Baron (1930), Viscount (1936) (1873–1956): Chief of Air Staff 1918, 1919–29, and seen as 'father of the RAF'; particularly important in its formation and its preservation in 1920s; commissioner, Metropolitan Police 1931–5. Emphasis on offensive potential of air power has been much criticized.

Webb Sidney (1859–1947): Civil servant; joined Fabian Society 1885, becoming dominant figure; member of London County Council 1892–1910; married (1892) (Martha) Beatrice Potter (1858–1943); they worked together on massive books on local government, trade unionism, etc; member of Labour party NEC 1915–25; played a leading role in drafting new Labour programme, 1918; MP 1922–9; Baron Passfield 1929; President of Board of Trade 1924; Secretary of State for Dominions and Colonies 1929–30, and Colonies 1930–1. In the 1930s the Webbs became extremely pro-Soviet, though not Communist.

Wheatley John (1869–1930): Catholic businessman in Glasgow; joined Independent Labour party 1908; Labour MP 1922–30; as Minister of Health, responsible for Housing Act 1924; resigned from Labour front bench 1925, and moved to the left; possibly saw Cook–Maxton campaign as prelude to a new party, but its disastrous launch discouraged him; not considered for office 1929. In Glasgow his careful work opened the way for Irish Catholics to move towards Labour after the First World War.

Wilson Sir Horace John (1882–1972): Clerical civil servant 1898; rose high, joining the new Ministry of Labour 1916; in charge of its industrial relations department from 1919; Permanent Secretary 1921; played leading role in negotiations preceding General Strike 1926; government chief industrial adviser 1930–9; personal adviser to Prime Minister 1935–40; Permanent Secretary to Treasury and head of civil service 1939–42. Able administrator, but controversial for his alleged encouragement of Chamberlain in appeasement.

Wood Sir (Howard) Kingsley (1881–1943): Conservative MP 1918–43; junior health minister 1924–9; Postmaster-General 1931–5; Minister of Health 1935–8; Secretary of State for Air 1938–40, Lord Privy Seal 1940, and member of war cabinet 1939–40; Chancellor of Exchequer 1940–3 (member of war cabinet 1940–2). In latter role, cautioned against the massive social expenditure implications of the Beveridge Report.

Woolton Baron 1939, Viscount 1953, Earl 1956 (Sir Frederick James Marquis) (1883–1964): Head of a retail chain; Director-

General of Equipment and Stores, Ministry of Supply 1939–40; Minister of Food 1940–3; Minister of Reconstruction 1943–5; member of war cabinet 1943–5; Lord President of Council 1945, 1951–2; joined Conservative party after 1945 election; party chairman 1946–55.

SECTION VI

Glossary of terms

Glossary of terms

Abdication crisis   In 1936 King Edward VIII wanted to marry a twice-divorced American woman, Wallis Simpson. The cabinet, supported by the Dominions, advised him that he could not do so and remain King. On 11 December he renounced the throne and became Duke of Windsor, marrying Mrs Simpson in 1937.

air raid precautions   Scheme set in motion in 1935 to prepare civil defence against enemy bombardment in event of war; ARP wardens were important in alerting civilians to dangers of air raids, and in maintaining services after raids during Second World War.

appeasement   Principle whereby Britain aimed to reduce potential tensions through limited concessions and conciliation; more specifically, used to describe Chamberlain's foreign policy, 1937–9. It aimed to satisfy Hitler, while building up Britain's defences in case of war, but its failure to prevent German aggression made 'appeasement' a dirty word in Britain.

Auxis/Black and Tans   Irregular forces used in Ireland by British government from 1920 to try to stamp out IRA. Their often brutal methods aroused considerable criticism in Britain and abroad, and severely impaired Lloyd George's Liberal credentials.

Baedecker raids   Air raids in 1942 by German bombers on British cultural centres like Bath and Exeter in reprisal for British raids on Rostock and Lübeck, named after the famous guidebooks.

balance of payments   Net surplus or deficit of exports over imports.

Black Friday   Friday 15 April 1921, when transport workers and railwaymen decided not to support the miners, their partners in the Triple Alliance, in their dispute over pay cuts and the end of national wage bargaining.

Blackshirts   Members of British Union of Fascists who wore the black shirt uniform, which was banned by Public Order Act 1936.

Blitz, the   Meaning 'storm' in German, the 'big Blitz', a series of major night-time air raids on London and most other major British cities and ports, lasted from 7 September 1940 to 10 May 1941, with many large raids on London, and raids also on cities like Coventry, Sheffield and Plymouth. In all, there were 43 000 civilian deaths due

169

to raids in 1940 and 1941. However, the raids failed to seriously impair morale or war production. The 'little Blitz' (Jan.–Mar. 1943) was both shorter and less damaging.

British Broadcasting Corporation (BBC) Publicly-owned body set up with a monopoly in 1925 to replace the old British Broadcasting Company. Under its director-general, Reith, it gained a dour image, but it did maintain its independence against intermittent political attacks.

British Expeditionary Force (BEF) Small body of professional soldiers created by the Liberal government of 1905, which on the outbreak of war in 1914 went to fight on the French left on the Western Front. It helped stop the German advance but was virtually wiped out by the end of the first battle of Ypres (November 1914). In 1939 the BEF was again sent to France, but in 1940 was forced to withdraw from mainland Europe at Dunkirk.

British Gazette Government newspaper, edited by Churchill, issued during the General Strike. It strongly attacked the strike as unconstitutional. The TUC countered with the less effective *British Worker*.

cabinet secretariat Set up by Lloyd George when he became Prime Minister in 1916 to produce formal agendas and minutes of cabinet meetings for the first time. Despite pressure to cut costs, a reduced secretariat was retained after 1922.

Campbell Case Sequence of events following the publication in July 1924 by the Communist *Workers' Weekly* of an appeal to soldiers not to fire on workers. The original decision to prosecute the acting editor, J R Campbell, was withdrawn by the Attorney-General, leading to opposition charges of Communist influence on the Labour government. Following the success of a Liberal motion for an inquiry, the government resigned and called a general election.

capital levy Proposal that part or all of the war debt should be paid off by a wealth tax, particularly associated with Labour although with some wider support. But the 1924 Labour government made no attempt to introduce it and the idea died a quiet death.

Chanak crisis Clash between Britain and the Turkish nationalists under Kemal Atatürk in Sep.–Oct. 1922. Lloyd George supported Greek claims to territory on the Turkish mainland and wanted to stand firm against Atatürk, but had little foreign or Dominion support, and the local British commander, Harington, made a pact with the Turk forces. The incident marked the final failure of the Treaty of Sèvres and aroused further Conservative hostility towards Lloyd George, who was soon overthrown as premier by the Tories.

collectivism   Term given to policies which aim to use power of the state to further aims of social equality and common good, often at the expense of individual liberty, although New Liberals and others claimed that only through state action could individual freedom be guaranteed. Usually associated with welfare politics and the increase in state power which had proponents in all parties.

colonial development   Policy aiming to increase the economic benefits of Empire to Britain and, in theory, to native peoples through financial assistance for industrialization and agricultural and infrastructure development.

colonies   Those (mostly non-white) territories of the British Empire ruled without any formal structures of self-government or autonomy.

conscientious objectors   People who refused to fight on moral grounds despite the introduction of conscription in 1916. Many were exempted, but others were sent to France or imprisoned. Their disfranchisement for five years by the Representation of the People Act 1918 reflected considerable popular hostility. They were generally better treated during the Second World War.

conscription   Compulsory military service; introduced in January 1916 for unmarried men between 18 and 41, and later extended, it lapsed in 1919. In April 1939 it was reintroduced in readiness for war; it remained in force until 1960.

council houses   Dwellings built and owned by local authorities, for rent to tenants. Councils had been able to build them before 1914, but only with the Housing Act 1919 were they obliged to do so, with the help of government subsidies. The proportion of people living in them rose from less than 1 per cent in 1918 to 10 per cent in 1938, mainly at the expense of the private rented sector.

coupon   Derogatory nickname for the letters of support sent by Lloyd George and Law to Coalition candidates at the 1918 election.

demobilization   Process whereby armed forces were stood down after the World Wars. In 1918–19 the process was chaotic, and attempts to release 'essential' workers first led to mutinies, which in turn led to the adoption of a more equitable 'first in, first out' principle. The process after 1945 was rather better managed.

depressed areas   Term used from the 1920s for regions suffering from high levels of long-term unemployment, mainly due to the near-collapse of the old staple industries. They included south Wales, central Scotland, west Cumberland and the north-East. Policies of industrial transference to move the 'surplus' population to more prosperous areas collapsed in the face of general depression after 1929. In 1934 the Special Areas Act represented a more meaningful

171

attempt to bring new hope to some of these areas, but even then the funds provided were very limited. The Act was mainly political window-dressing, and some hard-hit areas like Lancashire were not included. Rearmament was to provide a far bigger boost.

Depression, the Term often used for the 1930s as a whole, but really referring to the period of acute economic difficulty and generally increasing unemployment between 1929 and early 1933; thereafter the economy recovered quite strongly, although there was renewed recession in 1937–8.

derating System introduced in 1929 whereby agriculture was wholly relieved from paying local authority rates, and industrial and railway properties were relieved of 75 per cent of their burdens. Local authorities were compensated by central government block grants.

dilution Process of unapprenticed labour, often female, replacing skilled workers during the World Wars. It caused great discontent during the First World War, despite its acceptance by union leaders; in the Second World War it was accepted more readily, though not without friction. Its temporary nature was made clear by the passing of Restoration of Prewar Practices Acts during both conflicts.

Dominions Territories of the British Empire which were largely self-governing. They were all areas of considerable white settlement: Australia, Canada, Newfoundland, New Zealand and South Africa. In 1921 the Irish Free State also acquired Dominion status, which it virtually repudiated in 1937. Newfoundland's Dominion status was suspended in 1933: ultimately it became part of Canada.

Dunkirk Evacuation of 338 226 men from France between 31 May and 3 June 1940. Although hailed as a success, most of their equipment had to be left behind and the Allies were driven from mainland Europe for four years. 'The Dunkirk Spirit' became an increasingly tired allusion for politicians for many years thereafter.

Easter Rising Abortive rebellion in Dublin on Easter Monday, 25 April 1916. Promised German help did not materialize. The rebels seized the Post Office and proclaimed an independent republic, but after five days of fighting the rising was suppressed. Most of the leaders were executed. The authorities' ruthless response helped galvanize Irish opinion against Britain and in favour of Sinn Fein.

economic advisory council Set up by the Labour government in January 1930, comprising economists, business people, trade unionists and scientists, to advise ministers on policies to counter the slump. Too diffuse to produce any kind of unanimous response, its effects were minimal.

economy   Slogan of those who wanted to see public expenditure cut back and the power of the state restricted: however, economy drives in the early 1920s and early 1930s had only temporary success.

evacuation   Programme whereby urban children and, in some cases, their mothers were moved to 'safer' areas on the outbreak of war in 1939; many soon drifted back. A second wave followed the Blitz, but only a minority of children were involved.

exchange equalization account   Fund set up in 1932 following the departure from the gold standard, to manage the exchange rate by buying and selling sterling inversely to market trends. It showed that the exchange rate could be kept reasonably stable without having to depend on the straitjacket imposed by gold.

fellow-traveller   Derogatory description for Communist sympathizers who were not actually members of the Communist party: John Strachey was a leading example in the 1930s. In more recent years historians have used the term 'fellow-travellers of the right' to describe people who, while not active Fascists, showed sympathy for fascist regimes abroad.

flying bombs   Or 'V-weapons', were used by the Germans in air raids in 1944–5. The V1s (pilotless planes) were used from June 1944, and killed over 6 000 people; the V2s (rockets) were used from September 1944 and killed more than 2 500. Anti-aircraft defences soon got to grips with the V1s, but the V2s were less easily dealt with.

free trade   The principle whereby imports should enter any country without being subjected to tariffs, supported in this period by the Liberals, Labour and a dwindling number of Conservatives. Free trade sentiment was hard-hit by the slump after 1929; in 1932 Britain adopted protection, although some imports were exempted.

Geddes Axe   Refers to the report (February 1922) of the committee on national expenditure, set up under Sir Eric Geddes in August 1921 in response to the vigorous 'anti-waste' press campaign. It recommended cuts totalling £75 million in spending on the armed forces, education, and other areas. Usually seen as the final end of the reconstructionist aspirations of the Lloyd George Coalition.

General Strike   Following the owners' decision to impose wage cuts in coal mining from 1 May 1926 the TUC General Council ordered a general stoppage of work by members in transport, printing, heavy industry, building and the power industries. The strike lasted from 3 to 12 May, and a second wave of workers was called out towards the end, but although it remained solid the government was firm in its opposition and the General Council had no alternative but to surrender unconditionally after nine days. The miners remained locked out until the end of the year when they were forced to return to work at the new lower wages.

gold standard   International mechanism determining exchange rates according to gold reserves, and seen as basis of London's financial pre-eminence before 1914. Britain in effect abandoned it during the war, and formally left it in 1919, but financial opinion was strongly in favour of an early return. In March 1925 this was done at pre-war exchange rates despite Britain's weakened position, arousing criticism from Keynes and sections of business: they believed it overpriced British exports by around 10 per cent. The financial crises of 1931 forced Britain off gold that September, and from then onwards exchange rates were managed more loosely.

Grant affair   Scandal of September 1924 when the Labour premier, MacDonald, received a Daimler car from wealthy biscuit manufacturer Alexander Grant, who was then given a baronetcy. Though not corrupt, it proved embarrassing to MacDonald, and arguably made him less resilient to the Campbell Case than he would otherwise have been.

guild socialism   Theory devised in the 1900s as a reaction against Fabian collectivism, attempting to marry collectivism with syndicalism. The state would still exist in a socialist society, to protect consumers, but producers' democratic rights would be covered by 'guilds', glorified trade unions each covering a particular industry. Its main popularizer after 1910 was G D H Cole. The wartime rise of state control and the shop stewards' movement seemed to augur well, but the rapid decontrol of industry and collapse of the post-war boom from 1920 onwards led to decline, and many left to join the new Communist party of Great Britain. By 1923 the movement was moribund.

Hansard   The official reports of parliamentary debates.

hire purchase   The purchase of goods by instalments, which increased twenty-fold during the interwar period; its expansion especially during the 1930s did much to stimulate the industries producing household consumer durables.

Hoare–Laval Pact   Agreement reached in Paris between Sir Samuel Hoare and the French premier, Pierre Laval, in December 1935 by which Abyssinia was to be partitioned in favour of the invading Italians. Hoare's line, though approved in general by the cabinet, aroused an outcry when it was leaked to the press, and Hoare was forced to resign, allegedly prompting George V's dry comment: 'No more coals to Newcastle, no more Hoares to Paris'.

Home Guard Organization (originally known as the Local Defence Volunteers) set up in May 1940 to deal with a possible invasion threat. More commonly known as 'Dad's Army', it is now best remembered for the successful BBC TV series of that name.

honours scandal Outcry at Lloyd George's alleged abuse of the honours system in the early 1920s. Honours had been given by Conservative and Liberal governments to people contributing to party funds since the 1890s, but the more blatant 'touting' of the Lloyd George period, allied to Lloyd George's use of the money for his own political fund (rather than that of a party) and the disreputable nature of some of the recipients aroused an outcry which helped turn Conservative MPs against him. In 1925 trafficking in honours was outlawed, but it was still taking place in at least the early 1930s.

hunger marches Name given to marches on London organized by the Communist-led National Unemployed Workers' Movement in 1922, 1929, 1930, 1932, 1934 and 1936 to protest about unemployment and the level of benefits. However, they were often met with police force and none achieved the publicity accorded to the 1936 Jarrow March.

imperial conferences Gatherings of British and dominion leaders held on a regular basis to discuss matters of common interest.

International Brigades Volunteers fighting for the Republican side in the Spanish Civil War (1936–9), of whom around 2 000 were British. Many, but by no means all, were Communists; many died.

Invergordon Mutiny Strike of Royal Navy seamen at the Scottish port of Invergordon, 15 September 1931, in protest at the wage cuts many were facing due to the National government's economies. It was soon settled, but fears of renewed unrest led the government to announce that no cuts in salaries or wages would exceed 10 per cent.

Irish Republican Army (IRA) Formed as the army of Sinn Fein in 1919, the IRA played a leading role in the Anglo-Irish war of 1919–21, but split on the formation of the Free State. Some sections became the basis of the new Free State Army, but others ('Irregulars') continued to fight against the treaty. The IRA was later banned in the Free State, but continued to exist and launched a major bombing offensive on the British mainland in 1939.

Irwin Declaration Official statement by the Viceroy, Lord Irwin, in October 1929 that 'the natural issue of India's constitutional progress . . . is the attainment of Dominion status'. It formed the basis of British policy for the remainder of the inter-war period.

Jarrow March   March to London in 1936 organized by the local council of the north-eastern shipbuilding town to draw attention to heavy unemployment. The dignity and good behaviour of the marchers aroused widespread sympathy, but little practical action. It was to become a symbol of the 1930s in the popular memory.

Jubilee, Silver   Celebrations in May 1935 to mark the twenty-fifth anniversary of George V's accession to the throne.

Keynesianism   Name given to economic ideas associated with John Maynard Keynes, whose *General Theory* was published in 1936, advocating state intervention to ensure a fuller use of resources than market forces alone could achieve. Such ideas were largely rejected by governments before 1939. More generally, the term was used for the economic/financial policies of governments from 1941 onwards, though historians now debate when and to what extent the Treasury adopted 'Keynesian' methods at all.

laissez-faire   The doctrine of minimal state interference in economic affairs, which was coming under increasing attack in this period.

League of Nations   Organization formed in 1920 to ensure inter-national co-operation and preserve peace. The USA refused to join, however, and the League lacked the force to put its decisions into action and was rarely effective. By the 1930s it was largely discredited in the eyes of the British government.

Lend-Lease   US legislation of March 1941 which allowed the President to authorize the supply of war materiel to Britain without immediate payment. The Americans paid for the goods, which Britain then received on a loan or lease basis until the end of the war, when it would have to pay for them. The abrupt ending of Lend-Lease in August 1945 caused major problems for Britain.

Living Wage   Policy adopted by the Independent Labour party in its 1926 programme, *Socialism in Our Time*. Based on the 'under-consumptionist' arguments of J A Hobson, the radical economist, it advocated nationalization of basic industries and working-class incomes of about twice their present average, to be achieved by means of a 'living wage' and family allowances. The underlying aim was to set wages at levels that industry could not afford, so forcing them to accept state ownership. The policy made little headway in the wider Labour party: even family allowances were not adopted, because of union hostility.

Lloyd George political fund   Money collected from the sale of honours and from rich benefactors in his period as Prime Minister, and used by Lloyd George to pursue political ends of which he approved. Although he made generous use of the fund for Liberal party purposes between 1926 and 1929, his high-handed methods of managing the fund at other times (like the 1924 election) aroused considerable Liberal hostility.

mandates   Name given to former enemy colonies taken over by the Allies under the League of Nations in the 1919 peace settlement. Class A mandates, to be prepared for early independence, included Palestine (Britain) and Syria (France); Class B mandates, deemed unfit for self-government and to be ruled indefinitely as colonies, included most of Germany's former African colonies; Class C mandates were generally 'backward' territories which could be annexed.

Maurice debate   House of Commons debate (9 May 1918) on an Asquithian Liberal motion for an inquiry into the allegations by General Sir Frederick Maurice that Lloyd George had misled parliament as to the strength of the British army in France at the start of 1918. Despite a convincing rebuttal, Asquith forced a vote, in which 98 Liberals and 1 Conservative voted against the government. This was the only time in the war that the official opposition divided the House against the government.

May Report   Report of the committee on national expenditure, published July 1931, and predicting a budget deficit of £120 million. It recommended increased taxation of £24 million and cuts in public expenditure of £96 million, to include cuts of up to 20 per cent in public servants' salaries and a 20 per cent cut in unemployment benefit. The report intensified the financial crisis and the Labour government's failure to agree on economies remotely close to the level demanded led to its downfall in August 1931.

means test   System introduced in 1931 for recipients of transitional benefit. All household income was taken into account in determining the level of benefit a person should receive. It applied the stigma of the Poor Law in all but name to many unemployed people, and was often administered in a petty way. The test, abolished during the Second World War, came to be seen as the embodiment of a perceivedly penny-pinching and unsympathetic National government.

national debt   Money owed by the government as a result of its having taken out loans. It rose massively during the First World War, which was financed mainly from borrowing rather than taxation. The problem was compounded by falling prices for most of the interwar period, which meant the real value of the debt rose. By the early 1930s around one-third of central government expenditure was spent on servicing the debt, and this burden increased the hostility of ministers and civil servants towards proposals for large-scale loan-financed public works schemes.

Nonconformists   Those Christians who, while protestant, rejected the established Churches. Their approach laid less emphasis on the miraculous side of Christianity. The main groups were the Baptists, the Congregationalists and the various Methodist sects (united in 1932 as the Methodist Church). They declined faster than other Christian Churches in this period.

peace ballot   Five-question survey of 11 million people by the League of Nations Union, 1934–5. The results (June 1935) showed massive support for the League of Nations, disarmament, and the prohibition of private arms sales; and strong support for the abolition of military and naval aircraft and 'economic and non-military measures' against aggressor nations. Although 6.8 million voted for the use of force against aggressors, 2.4 million voted against. It helped define the rhetoric but not the reality of British diplomacy in 1935–6.

political levy   The Trade Union Act 1913 banned unions from making contributions to the Labour party from their general funds, but allowed them, subject to a membership ballot, to set up a separate political fund to be raised by a political levy payable in addition to the ordinary subscription. (Members who objected were allowed to 'contract out' of the levy.) This gave Labour a fairly assured source of income, but the Trade Disputes Act 1927 introduced 'contracting in' whereby the onus was placed on the member to state that s/he wanted to pay the levy. The result was a serious fall in union funding. In 1946 the Labour government restored 'contracting out'.

Poor Law   Historic system of relief for destitute people, involving the election of local Boards of Guardians to oversee payments, etc. The guardians were abolished in 1929; their functions passed to locally appointed public assistance committees under firmer central control.

popular front   Term used for coalitions of Communists, socialists and centrists, adopted as a strategy by Communists in 1935, leading to popular front governments in Spain and France. Pressure for such a front in Britain was sometimes strong in the later 1930s, but Labour's leaders rejected the idea, and Cripps and others were expelled from the party in 1939 for continuing to advocate it.

protection   System whereby imports are subjected to duties ('tariffs') on entry. The Conservatives called for protection in the 1923 election and were defeated, and as a result renounced protectionism, but in 1930 reverted to a pro-tariff policy as free trade sentiment evaporated in a year when unemployment virtually doubled. In 1932 the Import Duties Act imposed tariffs on most non-food imports.

Public Assistance Committees   Set up in place of the Poor Law Boards of Guardians in 1929; unlike the latter bodies, they were not directly elected but run by local authorities, and in 1931 took over responsibility for the payment of transitional benefits as well.

public works   Work ordered by central and local government, usually with the aim of reducing unemployment. During the interwar period public works were in operation, but on too small a scale to reduce significantly the unemployment figures. Extensive works on housing and road-building were periodically advocated, most notably by the Liberals in the late 1920s and by Keynes, but were not implemented.

rationing   System whereby the sale of goods in short supply was restricted during the World Wars.

reconstruction   Term for the plans devised during the World Wars for the post-war world. A Ministry of Reconstruction was set up in 1917 under Addison, who devised a series of plans which came to fruition in, for example, the Housing Act 1919. However, the ministry was abolished in June 1919, and the economic downturn led to the scrapping of most of these plans in 1920–1. In 1943 a similar body was set up, under Lord Woolton.

Red Friday   Name given by Labour movement to Friday 31 July 1925, when, after the TUC threatened an embargo on the movement of coal in the event of the threatened mining lockout taking place, the government agreed to pay a nine-month subsidy to the mining industry to avert wage cuts. In the event the relief was temporary; the ending of the subsidy saw the calling of the General Strike.

safeguarding   Policy of limited protection, whereby industries suffering from demonstrably unfair foreign competition (dumping) could apply for duties of 33.3 per cent to be imposed on such imports. It was introduced in 1921, repealed by Labour in 1924 and reintroduced in 1925. The industries which benefited were mostly small, such as lace and cutlery: applications from the iron and steel industry were repeatedly rejected. In 1929 the Labour government announced its intention to allow the duties to lapse when they came up for renewal, and some industries suffered as a result.

sanctions   Economic measures designed to make an aggressor country obey international law, imposed by the League of Nations on Italy in 1935 over its invasion of Abyssinia. The sanctions, which did not include oil, were ineffective and probably did more to turn Italy towards Germany than to affect its policies in Africa.

Sankey Report   Report of the Royal Commission on the Coal Industry under Justice Sankey, 1919. The commission, economists,

179

business people, and representatives of miners and owners, reported a narrow majority in favour of nationalization, but the government ignored this and also the less radical proposals to carry through a general scheme of reorganization under private enterprise. Sankey profited by becoming a hero of the miners and Lord Chancellor in the second Labour government. Coal was not nationalized until 1946.

Shells Scandal   Press campaign in May 1915 alleging that Britain's war effort was being impaired by shortages of ammunition. With the failure of the Dardanelles campaign it helped lead to the formation of the Asquith Coalition, and led to the appointment of Lloyd George at the head of a new Ministry of Munitions to speed up production.

shop stewards' movement   Grew up in reaction to the compromises of official union leaders with government during the First World War, especially in engineering centres like Clydeside and Sheffield. Mainly concerned with the interests of skilled workers, its impact was more limited than has seemed the case to some historians, and it was smashed in the early 1920s by economic slump and the engineering lockout of 1922. The Communist party of Great Britain's fervent support for the Second World War effort after June 1941 meant no comparable movement was thrown up in that conflict.

staple industries   Trades producing mainly for export that had been the backbone of British prosperity since the Industrial Revolution: coal, textiles, shipbuilding, and iron and steel. The commitment to the staples even by 1939 remained considerable, and their difficulties to a large extent accounted for the high levels of unemployment during the period, especially in the 'depressed areas'.

sterling area   Comprised those states which used sterling as the medium of exchange in trade, and London as their central banker. It included most of the Empire plus certain other countries as well.

syndicalism   Revolutionary doctrine arguing that unions should be reorganized on the basis of one union per industry, and stating that capitalism should be overthrown by means of a general strike; after the revolution the state would be abolished and society run on industrial union lines. It had some popularity on the far left before the First World War, but the milder guild socialism won more adherents.

Ten Year Rule   Ruling adopted by British governments in 1919, 1926, 1927, and on a rolling basis from 1928, that the forces should operate on the assumption that there would be no major war for the next ten years. It was abandoned in 1932.

transitional benefit   Payment made to unemployed people who had exhausted their right to insurance benefit, in order to relieve them of having to apply for Poor Law relief. Known also as uncovenanted benefit at various times.

Treasury view   Line followed by interwar governments, and supported by the mass of financial and business opinion, that, as Churchill put it in 1929, 'very little additional employment and no permanent additional employment can . . . be created by State borrowing and State expenditure'. This line was repeatedly used against critics who argued for radical interventionism and public works.

Triple Alliance   Agreement of 1915 between the Miners' Federation of Great Britain, National Union of Railwaymen and National Transport Workers' Federation to provide mutual support in the event of one of them being in an industrial dispute. Though much feared by some in government circles, it collapsed in 1921 on 'Black Friday'.

unemployment insurance   System introduced in 1911 as Part II of the National Insurance Act for 2.25 million workers in specified trades (building, shipbuilding, mechanical engineering) who, in return for small weekly payments by themselves, their employers and the state became eligible for benefits of 7s per week for up to 15 weeks. In the face of massively increased unemployment, the scheme was extended in 1920 to cover almost all industrial workers, and 'uncovenanted' (later 'transitional') benefit was introduced to save the unemployed from recourse to the Poor Law. The high levels of unemployment throughout the interwar period meant that the insurance fund was increasingly insolvent, leading to cuts in benefits (1931) and a major restructuring of the system (1934–5).

Unionist   The 'Union' referred to was that between Britain and Ireland; the name was generally applied to Conservatives and Liberal Unionists. With the end of the Union in 1921 the term 'Conservative' returned to general use, but many continued to call themselves 'Unionist' or 'Conservative and Unionist'.

United Nations   Organization set up in place of the League of Nations during the latter part of the Second World War.

war cabinet   Term associated with the small executive bodies formed by Lloyd George in 1916 and by Churchill in 1940. In the latter, most ministers continued to represent departments, but Lloyd George's was more radical in that most members had few formal departmental responsibilities as such. The full-size cabinet of about twenty members was restored with the coming of peace in each case.

Welfare State   The idea that the state should act to protect vulnerable groups, to provide social services on a universal basis, and to maintain minimum income levels. The welfare state is generally believed to have been created by the post-war Labour government, building on the Beveridge Report, but the extent to which this had been prefigured by interwar developments is much debated: it seems fairest to say that while social provision was generally extended between the wars, it was the Second World War itself which made the extensive changes of the later 1940s possible.

Welsh Church disestablishment   Process whereby Anglican Church and state were separated in Wales. Its popularity reflected widespread Welsh and nonconformist hostility towards Anglicanism; it was passed by parliament in 1914, although because of the First World War it did not come into effect until 1920.

Western Front   Arena of battle in France and Belgium on which British efforts were concentrated throughout the First World War and in 1939–40 and 1944–5.

Zinoviev Letter   Letter allegedly written by the president of the Communist International, Zinoviev, to British Communists. It was published in British newspapers shortly before polling in the 1924 general election, advising them to prepare for revolution. Since the Labour government had been trying to improve relations with the USSR, it was seen as damaging to Labour's electoral prospects. This was not really the case; Labour would have lost anyway. The letter has usually been seen as a forgery, but there are grounds for believing that it was genuine.

SECTION VII

Topic bibliography

Topic bibliography

Abbreviations

AEHR	*Australian Economic History Review*	*JEEH*	*Journal of European Economic History*
BIHR	*Bulletin of the Institute of Historical Research*	*JICH*	*Journal of Imperial and Commonwealth History*
CC	*Continuity and Change*	*JMH*	*Journal of Modern History*
CH	*Church History*		
EcHR	*Economic History Review*	*MH*	*Midland History*
		PBA	*Proceedings of the British Academy*
EH	*Economy and History*		
EHR	*English Historical Review*	*PH*	*Parliamentary History*
		PP	*Past and Present*
H	*History*	*PubA*	*Public Administration*
HE	*History of Education*	*RH*	*Rural History*
HJ	*Historical Journal*	*SCH*	*Studies in Church History*
HW	*History Workshop*		
IHS	*Irish Historical Studies*	*ScHR*	*Scottish Historical Review*
IRSH	*International Review of Social History*	*SH*	*Social History*
JBS	*Journal of British Studies*	*TCBH*	*Twentieth Century British History*
JCH	*Journal of Contemporary History*	*TRHS*	*Transactions of the Royal Historical Society*
JEcclH	*Journal of Ecclesiastical History*	*WHR*	*Welsh History Review*

Introductory note

This bibliography aims to provide a theme-by-theme introduction to the main areas of interest, but is of course by no means exhaustive. The essay titles are intended as a very general guide to further thought and reading, but no more than that. The bibliographies are fuller than would be expected in an average essay, but at the same time can only scratch the surface of the masses of material that are available; suggestions in the footnotes and bibliographies of the works cited will take the interested reader further into each subject. With each topic, original sources are also suggested.

1. General texts

There are many general histories, but most are heavily political in outlook. Among older works, C L Mowat, *Britain between the Wars 1918–1940* (1955) remains pre-eminent. A J P Taylor, *English History 1914–1945* (1965) is well-written and witty, although not always reliable. M Beloff, *Wars and Welfare: Britain 1914–1945* (1984) and R Blake, *The Decline of Power 1915–1964* (1985) are mainly about politics. T O Lloyd, *Empire to Welfare State: English History 1906–1985* (rev edn, 1986) is solid, if a little dull. K Robbins, *The Eclipse of a Great Power: Modern Britain, 1870–1975* (1983) covers this period in a very different way.

Among books which make no claim to be anything but political history, see especially R R James, *The British Revolution vol 2: British Politics 1914–1939* (1977) and M Pugh's stimulating *The Making of Modern British Politics, 1867–1939* (1986). M Kinnear, *The British Voter: An Atlas and Survey since 1885* (2nd edn, 1981) is a mine of information on electoral matters; see also F W S Craig, *British Electoral Facts 1832–1980* (1981) and *British Parliamentary Election Results 1918–49* (3rd edn, 1983). D E Butler and G Butler, *British Political Facts* (5th edn, 1985) is indispensable.

On social history, see especially J Stevenson, *British Society 1914–1945* (1984). A Crowther, *British Social Policy 1914–1939* (1988) is a useful short study. F Bedarida, *A Social History of England 1851–1990* (1990) and E Royle, *Modern Britain: A Social History 1750–1985* (1987) both include material on this period. H Perkin, *The Rise of Professional Society: England since 1880* (1989) combines 'standard' social history with a compelling thesis.

On the economy, see S Pollard, *The Development of the British Economy 1914–1980* (1983); D H Aldcroft, *The British Economy vol 1: The Years of Turmoil 1920–1951* (1986) and *The British Economy between the Wars* (1983); and J Tomlinson, *Problems of Britain's Economic Policy 1870–1945* (1981). G C Peden, *British Social and Economic Policy: Lloyd George to Margaret Thatcher* (2nd edn, 1991) combines the two succinctly. For reference, see B R Mitchell, *British Historical Statistics* (1988) and R Pope (ed) *Atlas of British Social and Economic History since c1700* (1989).

2. Conservative party

The Conservatives dominated political life, being out of office for just four of the thirty-one years in this period, but this dominance has not really been reflected in the historical writing. Even so, there is no shortage of literature. The party's leaders have always aroused interest. In recent years attention has been turned towards policy and organization, although broader issues, such as the reasons for the party's dominance, have also attracted attention.

Essay topics
Why did the Conservatives dominate government in this period? What were the main aims of Conservatives, and how far were they fulfilled by the party in office?

Sources and documents
A Beattie (ed) *English Party Politics*, vol 2 (1970) remains useful. The party's workings are seen in J C C Davidson, *Memoirs of a Conservative*, ed R R James (1969). Extracts from Chamberlain's papers can be found in K Feiling, *The Life of Neville Chamberlain* (1946). H Macmillan, *The Middle Way* (1938) presents the more radical view of a younger Conservative. Diary sources of value include Lord Bridgeman, *The Modernisation of Conservative Politics: The Diaries and Letters of William Bridgeman 1904–1935*, ed P Williamson (1988).

Secondary works
J Ramsden, *The Age of Balfour and Baldwin, 1902–1940* (1978) looks at all aspects of the party. Alternatives include R Blake, *The Conservative Party from Peel to Churchill* (1970) and T F Lindsay and M Harrington, *The Conservative Party 1918–1979* (1979). J Ramsden, *The Making of Conservative Party Policy* (1980), is a history of the Conservative Research Department. P Goodhart, *The 1922: The Story of the Conservative Backbenchers' Parliamentary Committee* (1973) has some interest. M Pugh, *The Tories and the People, 1880–1935* (1985) is a history of the Primrose League. On party finance for this and the following two sections on the Labour and Liberal parties, see M Pinto-Duschinsky, *British Political Finance 1830–1980* (1981) and G R Searle, *Corruption in British Politics 1895–1930* (1987).

On specific sub-periods: for 1914–22 see J Turner, *British Politics and the Great War* (1992); K O Morgan, *Consensus and Disunity: The Lloyd George Coalition Government 1918–1922* (1979); M Cowling, *The Impact of Labour, 1920–1924* (1971); and M Kinnear, *The Fall of Lloyd George: The Political Crisis of 1922* (1973). For the late 1920s and early 1930s, see P Williamson, *National Crisis and National Government: British Politics, the Economy and Empire, 1926–1932* (1992); S Ball, *Baldwin and the Conservative Party: The Crisis of 1929–1931* (1988); and A Thorpe, *The British General Election of 1931* (1991). For the 1930s, see M Cowling, *The Impact of Hitler: British Politics and British Policies 1933–1940* (1975); T Stannage, *Baldwin Thwarts the Opposition: The British General Election of 1935* (1980); and N Thompson, *The Anti-Appeasers: Conservative Opposition to Appeasement in the 1930s* (1971).

The war years can be followed in P Addison, *The Road to 1945*

(1977), and K Jefferys, *The Churchill Coalition and Wartime Politics, 1940–45* (1991).

Useful biographies include R Blake, *The Unknown Prime Minister: The Life and Times of Andrew Bonar Law* (1955); D Dutton, *Austen Chamberlain: Gentleman in Politics* (1985); K Middlemas and J Barnes, *Baldwin: A Biography* (1969); D Dilks, *Neville Chamberlain, vol I: 1869–1929* (1984); M Gilbert, *Winston S Churchill* (8 vols, 1966–88). Also worth mentioning are J A Cross, *Sir Samuel Hoare* (1977); J Campbell, *F E Smith: First Earl of Birkenhead* (1983); and R R James, *Anthony Eden* (1986).

Articles
M Pugh, 'Popular Conservatism in Britain: continuity and change 1880–1987', *JBS* (1988) is a good overview. Particularly useful are J Stubbs, 'The impact of the Great War on the Conservative party' and G Peele, 'Revolt over India', in G Peele and C Cook (eds), *The Politics of Reappraisal 1918–39* (1975); D H Close, 'The collapse of resistance to democracy: Conservatives, adult suffrage and second chamber reform 1911–28', *HJ* (1977); T J Hollins, 'The Conservative party and film propaganda between the wars', *EHR* (1981); S Moore, 'The agrarian Conservative party in parliament 1920–9', *PH* (1991); S Ball, 'The 1922 committee: the formative years 1922–45', *PH* (1990); B I Coleman, 'The Conservative party and the frustration of the extreme right', in A Thorpe (ed) *The Failure of Political Extremism in Inter-War Britain* (1989); K Jefferys, 'May 1940: the downfall of Neville Chamberlain', *PH* (1991); and J Ramsden, '"A party for owners or a party for earners"? How far did the Conservative party really change after 1945?', *TRHS* (1987).

3. Labour party
This period was one of great advance but also much disappointment for Labour. The party's rise at the expense of the Liberals has received considerable attention, with many historians turning to local case studies to investigate the phenomenon. The question of why Labour was so rarely in office has been discussed widely. However, analysis of the formulation of policy has been rather patchy.

Essay topics
Why did Labour replace the Liberals as the main non-Conservative party?
What had the Labour party achieved by 1945?

Sources and documents
See K Laybourn (ed) *The Labour Party, 1881–1951* (1988) and F Bealey (ed), *The Social and Political Thought of the British Labour Party*

(1970). A Wright (ed), *British Socialism* (1983) has readings on socialist thought. B Webb, *Beatrice Webb's Diaries*, ed M I Cole (2 vols, 1952–6) and H Dalton, *The Political Diary of Hugh Dalton*, ed B Pimlott (1986) give valuable insights.

Secondary works

The most detailed account (though very dated) remains G D H Cole, *A History of the Labour Party from 1914* (1948). Other general histories include H Pelling, *A Short History of the Labour Party* (9th edn, 1990); K Laybourn, *The Rise of Labour: The British Labour Party 1890–1979* (1988); C Cook and I Taylor (eds) *The Labour Party: An Introduction to its History, Structure and Politics* (1980); and the more critical R Miliband, *Parliamentary Socialism* (2nd edn, 1972). J Hinton, *Labour and Socialism: A History of the British Labour Movement 1867–1974* (1983) and J E Cronin, *Labour and Society in Britain 1918–79* (1984) are broader than most. On ideology, see J Callaghan, *Socialism in Britain since 1884* (1990) and G Foote, *The Labour Party's Political Thought: A History* (1986). K O Morgan, *Labour People: Leaders and Lieutenants from Hardie to Kinnock* (1987) is a collection of short biographies.

R I McKibbin, *The Evolution of the Labour Party 1910–1924* (1974) must now be read with D Tanner, *Political Change and the Labour Party 1900–1918* (1990). The party is less well served for the 1920s, but see R W Lyman, *The First Labour Government, 1924* (1957); R Skidelsky, *Politicians and the Slump: The Labour Government of 1929–1931* (1967); P Williamson, *National Crisis and National Government* (1992); and A Thorpe, *The British General Election of 1931* (1991). B Pimlott, *Labour and the Left in the 1930s* (1977) and T Buchanan, *The Spanish Civil War and the British Labour Movement* (1991) are the best works on the 1930s. For the Second World War, see T Burridge, *British Labour and Hitler's War* (1976); P Addison, *The Road to 1945* (1975); and K Jefferys, *The Churchill Coalition and Wartime Politics, 1940–1945* (1991). On regional growth see especially M Savage, *The Dynamics of Working-Class Politics: Preston 1880–1940* (1988); R J Waller, *The Dukeries Transformed: the Social and Political Development of a Twentieth-Century Coalfield* (1983); and R C Whiting, *The View from Cowley: The Impact of Industrialization upon Oxford 1918–39* (1983).

Among the better biographies are D Marquand, *Ramsay MacDonald* (1977); C J Wrigley, *Arthur Henderson* (1990); J Schneer, *George Lansbury* (1989); K Harris, *Attlee* (1982); B Pimlott, *Hugh Dalton* (1985) and B Donoughue and G W Jones, *Herbert Morrison* (1973).

Articles

K D Wald, '"Advance by retreat": the formation of British Labour's election strategy', *JBS* (1988) and A Thorpe, 'The only effective bulwark against revolution and reaction: Labour and the frustration of the extreme left', in A Thorpe (ed) *The Failure of Political Extremism in Inter-War Britain* (1989) are useful overviews. For the First World War, see C Howard, 'MacDonald, Henderson and the outbreak of war in 1914', *HJ* (1977) and R Harrison, 'The War Emergency Workers' National Committee 1914–20', in A Briggs and J Saville (eds) *Essays in Labour History 1886–1923* (1971). Important articles on the interwar period include S Macintyre, 'British Labour, Marxism, and working-class apathy in the 1920s', *HJ* (1977); C Howard, 'Expectations born to death: local Labour party expansion in the 1920s', in J M Winter (ed) *The Working Class in Modern British Politics* (1983); R I McKibbin, 'The economic policy of the second Labour government 1929–31', *PP* (1975); and R Eatwell and A Wright, 'Labour and the lessons of 1931', *H* (1978). On the Second World War see H Pelling, 'The impact of the war on the Labour party', in H L Smith (ed) *War and Social Change: British Society in the Second World War* (1986) and S Brooke, 'Revisionists and fundamentalists: the Labour party and economic policy during the Second World War', *HJ* (1989).

4. Liberal party

In 1914 the Liberals were the party of government; by 1945 they were a tiny sect. The bulk of writing on this period has concentrated on the Asquith-Lloyd George split and its consequences. While recent years have seen some work on the interwar years, the period after 1929 remains something of a historiographical 'black hole'.

Essay topics
Account for the collapse of the Liberal Party in this period.
   'Strong on ideas, weak on everything else.' Discuss this view of the Liberals between 1914 and 1945.

Sources and documents
C P Scott, *The Political Diaries of C P Scott 1911–1928*, ed T Wilson (1970) is invaluable. The later sections of A Bullock and M Shock (eds) *The Liberal Tradition from Fox to Keynes* (1956) remain useful. Lord Samuel, *Memoirs* (1945) covers the whole period. Earl of Oxford and Asquith, *Memories and Reflections*, vol 2 (1928) provides some insights. For Lloyd George, see especially K O Morgan (ed) *Lloyd George Family Letters, 1895–1936* (1973) and A J Sylvester, *Life with Lloyd George*, ed C Cross (1975).

Secondary works
R Douglas, *The History of the Liberal Party, 1895–1970* (1971) remains the standard work. C Cook, *A Short History of the Liberal Party, 1900–92* (4th edn, 1993) is a useful alternative.
   The issue of the decline of the Liberal party has excited a great

deal of speculation. Among works viewing decline as inevitable, see G Dangerfield, *The Strange Death of Liberal England* (1935); H Pelling, *Popular Politics and Society in Late-Victorian Britain* (1968); and G L Bernstein, *Liberalism and Liberal Politics in Edwardian England* (1986). But at present the prevailing view is that the pre-1914 Liberal party was capable of seeing off the Labour challenge: see P F Clarke, *Lancashire and the New Liberalism* (1971); T Wilson, *The Downfall of the Liberal Party 1914–1935* (1966); and D Tanner, *Political Change and the Labour Party, 1900–1918* (1990). J Turner, *British Politics and the Great War: Coalition and Conflict 1915–18* (1992) is an important work. Much of the debate is summarized in M Bentley, *The Climax of Liberal Politics: British Liberalism in Theory and Practice 1868–1918* (1987).

The period after 1918 is much less studied. For the Lloyd George Coalition, see K O Morgan, *Consensus and Disunity: The Lloyd George Coalition 1918–1922* (1979) and M Cowling, *The Impact of Labour, 1920–1924* (1971). C Cook, *The Age of Alignment: Electoral Politics in Britain 1922–9* (1975) remains useful. M Bentley, *The Liberal Mind, 1918–1929* (1977) is complex but rewarding. M Freeden, *Liberalism Divided: A Study in British Political Thought 1914–39* (1986) looks at ideology. There is at present no published book-length work on the Liberals between 1931 and 1945, though see P Williamson, *National Crisis and National Government: British Politics, the Economy and Empire 1926–1932* (1992); A Thorpe, *The British General Election of 1931* (1991); and T Stannage, *Baldwin Thwarts the Opposition: the British General Election of 1935* (1980).

For party leaders, see S Koss, *Asquith* (1976); P Rowland, *Lloyd George* (1974); M Pugh, *Lloyd George* (1988); J Campbell, *Lloyd George: The Goat in the Wilderness 1922–31* (1977); B Wasserstein, *Herbert Samuel: A Political Life* (1992).

Articles

On the 'decline of the Liberals debate', see H C G Matthew, R I McKibbin and J Kay, 'The franchise factor in the rise of the Labour party', *EHR* 1976; M W Hart, 'The Liberals, the war and the franchise', *EHR* (1982); D Tanner, 'The parliamentary electoral system, the "fourth" reform act and the rise of Labour in England and Wales', *BIHR* (1983). On Asquith, see R Quinault, 'Asquith's Liberalism', *H* (1992); on his fall, see M Fry, 'Political change in Britain, August 1914–December 1916: Lloyd George replaces Asquith: the issues underlying the drama', *HJ* (1988). The post-war party is studied in S Koss, 'Asquith versus Lloyd George: the last phase and beyond', in A Sked and C Cook (eds) *Crisis and Controversy: Essays in Honour of A J P Taylor* (1976); M Dawson, 'The Liberal land policy 1924–9: electoral strategy and internal division', *TCBH* (1991); and S Koss, 'Lloyd George and nonconformity: the last rally', *EHR* (1974).

5. Communism and the far left

In contrast to many countries in mainland Europe, Britain did not have a strong or powerful Communist party. Despite this, British Communism has excited a lot of historical research, although much of it is marred by excessive partisanship one way or another. In recent years attention has moved increasingly to the broader campaigns with which the party was involved in order to assess more accurately its actual impact.

Essay topics
How significant a force was the far left in Britain?

Account for the vicissitudes in the fortunes of the Communist party, 1920–1945.

Sources and documents
J Degras, *The Communist International 1919–1943: Documents* (3 vols, 1956–65) contains material relating to the British party. The memoirs of leading Communists vary in what they reveal, but at least give some idea of what impelled them towards the far left: H Pollitt, *Serving my Time* (1940); H McShane and J Smith, *Harry McShane, No Mean Fighter* (1978); W Gallacher, *Revolt on the Clyde* (1936); and W Hannington, *Never on our Knees* (1967).

Secondary works
H Pelling, *The British Communist Party* (1958) remains the only single-volume work to cover the whole period. The official history's three volumes all relate to this period: J Klugmann, *The History of the Communist Party, vol 1, 1919–24* (1968) and *vol 2, 1925–26* (1969), are dull; better is N Branson, *History of the Communist Party of Great Britain, 1927–1941* (1985). H Dewar, *Communist Politics in Britain: The CPGB from its Origins to the Second World War* (1976) is a Trotskyite perspective. W Kendall, *The Revolutionary Movement in Britain, 1900–1921* (1969) and R Challinor, *The Origins of British Bolshevism* (1977) argue that the CPGB was a huge mistake, foisted on the British by Moscow. L J Macfarlane, *The British Communist Party: Its Origin and Development until 1929* (1966) remains useful. S Macintyre, *A Proletarian Science: Marxism in Britain 1917–33* (1980) looks at ideology. J Jupp, *The Radical Left in Britain 1931–41* (1982) covers more than just the CPGB. K Morgan, *Against Fascism and War: Ruptures and Continuities in British Communist Politics 1935–41* (1989) argues that the party was of some importance during the 1930s. On the NUWM see R Croucher, *We Refuse to Starve in Silence: A History of the National Unemployed Workers' Movement 1920–46* (1987) and P Kingsford, *The Hunger Marchers in Britain 1920–39* (1982). On the rise of Trotskyism, see S Borstein and A Richardson, *Against the Stream: A History of the Trotskyist Movement in Britain 1924–38* (1986).

Articles

See especially R I McKibbin, 'Why was there no Marxism in Great Britain', *EHR* (1984); M Durham, 'British revolutionaries and the suppression of the left in Lenin's Russia 1918–24', *JCH* (1985); H Harmer, 'The failure of the Communists: the National Unemployed Workers' Movement 1921–39, a disappointing success', in A Thorpe (ed) *The Failure of Political Extremism in Inter-War Britain* (1989); A Howkins, 'Class against class: the political culture of the Communist party of Great Britain 1930–5', in F Gloversmith (ed) *Class, Culture and Social Change: A New View of the 1930s* (1980); M Ceadel, 'The first Communist peace society: the British anti-war movement 1932–5', *TCBH* (1990); D Childs, 'The British Communist party and the war 1939–41: old slogans revisited', *JCH* (1977); and J Hinton, 'Coventry Communism: a study of factory politics in the Second World War', *HW* (1980).

6. Fascism and the far right

A far right can be identified in Britain from the 1880s onwards. But the spread of fascism across interwar Europe was not reflected in Britain. Even in the 1930s, when Sir Oswald Mosley launched the British Union of Fascists, it was never able to make much of an impact. Most writing has concentrated on the BUF and Mosley, although there is increasing interest in other aspects.

Sources and documents

O Mosley, *The Greater Britain* (1932) and his autobiography, *My Life* (1968) are full of valuable material. H Nicolson, *Diaries and Letters 1930–1939*, ed N Nicolson (1966) describes Mosley's move to fascism in 1930–2. A Leese, *Out of Step* (1947) is the autobiography of a non-Mosley fascist.

Secondary works

The standard work is R Thurlow, *Fascism in Britain: A History, 1918–1985* (1987). D S Lewis, *Illusions of Grandeur: Mosley, fascism and British society, 1931–81* (1987) is a narrower alternative. G Anderson, *Fascists, Communists and the National Government* (1983) looks mainly at political violence. Among older works, see R Benewick, *The Fascist Movement in Britain* (1972) and C Cross, *The Fascists in Britain* (1961). On Mosley himself, see R Skidelsky, *Oswald Mosley* (1975); and N Mosley, *Rules of the Game: Sir Oswald and Lady Cynthia Mosley, 1896–1933* (1982) and *Beyond the Pale: Sir Oswald Mosley, 1933–80* (1983). J Brewer, *Mosley's Men* (1984) looks at the BUF in the west Midlands. G Webber, *The Ideology of the British Right, 1918–1939* (1986) assesses the overlap between Fascism and Conservatism. For admirers of fascism, see R Griffiths, *Fellow Travellers of the Right:*

British Enthusiasts for Nazi Germany (1980). K Lunn and R Thurlow (eds) *British Fascism* (1980) and T Kushner and K Lunn (eds) *Traditions of Intolerance* (1989) are good collections of essays.

Articles
R Thurlow, 'The failure of British Fascism, 1932–40', in A Thorpe (ed) *The Failure of Political Extremism in Inter-War Britain* (1989) is a good overview. Other important articles include S Cullen, 'The development of the ideas and policy of the British Union of Fascists, 1932–40', *JCH* (1987) and 'Leaders and martyrs: Codreanu, Mosley and Jose Antonio', *H* (1986); G C Webber, 'Patterns of membership and support for the British Union of Fascists', *JCH* (1984); and M Newman, 'Democracy versus dictatorship: Labour's role in the struggle against British fascism 1933–6', *HW* (1978).

7. The British state
The growth of the state is one of the most important features of this period. It can be argued, in fact, that this period saw a transformation in the unwritten British constitution, as government moved towards intervention in an increasing proportion of the nation's life. Interest has focused on the machinery of government, the constitutional implications, and the idea that government was executed increasingly through outside organizations in these years.

Essay topics
How far can this period be seen in terms of a shift from *laissez-faire* to collectivism?
   Was the growth of government inexorable?
   How valid is Middlemas's concept of the evolution of 'corporate bias' in this period?

Sources and documents
G Le May, *British Government 1914–1963* (1965) reproduces key documents. H Laski, *The Foundations of Sovereignty and Other Essays* (1921) and G D H Cole, *Self-Government in Industry* (1917) show left-wing fears about the growth of the state; attacks from the right can be seen in H Belloc, *The Servile State* (1913) and F A Hayek, *The Road to Serfdom* (1944). For the Civil Service, see T Jones, *Whitehall Diary*, ed K Middlemas (3 vols, 1969) and the memoirs of a leading civil servant, P J Grigg, *Prejudice and Judgement* (1948).

Secondary works
Study of this subject must begin with W H Greenleaf, *The British Political Tradition, vol 1: The Rise of Collectivism* (1983) and *vol 2: The Ideological Heritage* (1984), but see also J E Cronin, *The Politics of State*

Expansion: War, State and Society in Twentieth-Century Britain (1991).
G K Fry, *The Growth of Government* (1978) looks at administrative
expansion. K Middlemas, *Politics in Industrial Society* (1979) suggests
that the state evolved a system of 'corporate bias' during this period,
mediating between government, employers and unions. R Miliband,
Capitalist Democracy in Britain (1982) offers a Marxist perspective. For
specific areas of the growth of state power, see J Morgan, *Conflict
and Order: The Policing of Labour Disputes 1900–39* (1987); G Rubin,
*War, Law and Labour: The Munitions Acts, State Regulation and the
Unions 1915–21* (1987); and K Burk (ed) *War and the State: The
Transformation of British Government 1914–19* (1982). For the Civil
Service, see R Lowe, *Adjusting to Democracy: The Role of the Ministry
of Labour in British Politics 1916–39* (1986); E O'Halpin, *Sir Warren
Fisher*; and S W Roskill, *Hankey: Man of Secrets* (3 vols, 1970–4).

Articles
General views include S Hall and B Schwarz, 'State and society
1880–1930', in M Langan and B Schwarz (eds) *Crises in the British State
1880–1930* (1985). For the Civil Service, see J R Greenaway, 'Warren
Fisher and the transformation of the British Treasury 1919–39', *JBS*
(1983); and G C Peden, 'The Treasury as the central department of
government, 1919–39', *PubA* (1983). For the winding down of state
control after 1918 the classic article is P Abrams, 'The failure of
social reform: 1918–20', *PP* (1963) but see also R Lowe, 'The erosion
of state intervention in Britain 1917–24', *EcHR* (1978). Discussion
of 'corporatism' can be found in L P Carpenter, 'Corporatism in
Britain 1930–45', *JCH* (1976) and D Ritschel, 'A corporatist economy
in Britain? Capitalist planning for industrial self-government in the
1930s', *EHR (1991)*.

8. Population
During this period population rose steadily but much more slowly
than in the nineteenth century. A whole host of causes, including
two World Wars, the realization that larger families suffered greater
poverty, and the spread of artificial contraception all had profound
demographic results. By the 1930s people were beginning to fear
that the population would actually fall unless drastic measures were
taken. This is a somewhat neglected, though fascinating and vitally
important, issue.

Essay topics
What grounds had people for fearing that the population would
decline?
   Account for the main demographic trends in this period.

Sources and documents

The raw material can be found in the *Censuses* of 1911, 1921, 1931 and 1951. For fears of depopulation, see *The Declining Birthrate: Its Causes and Effects* (1916); Mass-Observation, *Britain and her Birthrate* (1945); and E M Hubback, *The Population of Britain* (1947).

Secondary works

A number of general histories cover this period: see especially R Mitchison, *British Population Change since 1860* (1977) and N Tranter, *Population and Society 1750–1940* (1985). T Barker and M Drake (eds) *Population and Society in Britain 1850–1980* (1982) has some good essays. For family size and birth control see R Soloway, *Birth Control and the Population Question in England 1870–1930* (1982); D Gittins, *Fair Sex: Family Size and Structure 1900–39* (1982); B Brookes, *Abortion in England 1900–67* (1988); and A Leathard, *The Fight for Family Planning* (1980). J Saville, *Rural Depopulation in England and Wales 1851–1951* (1957) looks at migration; for immigration, see K Lunn (ed) *Race and Labour in Twentieth-Century Britain* (1985) and C Holmes, *John Bull's Island: immigration and British society 1871–1971* (1988). J M Winter, *The Great War and the British People* (1986) looks at that aspect.

Articles

See especially P Thane, 'The debate on the declining birth–rate and the menace of an ageing population', *CC* (1990); G Jones, 'Eugenics and social policy between the wars', *HJ* (1982); and W Seccombe, 'Starting to stop: working-class fertility decline in Britain', *PP* (1990). For the period after 1939 see J M Winter, 'The demographic consequences of the war', in H L Smith (ed), *War and Social Change: British Society in the Second World War* (1986).

9. Education

This is a rather neglected area, yet one of considerable importance and occasionally quite impassioned debate. Views that the education system was chronically underfunded and underdeveloped have to be placed against the occasional spurts of intense legislative activity and the wider concerns of governments battling against war and depression.

Essay topics

Did education fail the nation in this period?

What were the purposes of education policy and how far were they fulfilled?

Sources and documents

The best collection is J S Maclure, *Educational Documents: England and Wales 1816–1963* (1965; 5th edn 1986); see also P H J H Gosden (ed), *How They Were Taught: An Anthology of Contemporary Accounts of Learning and Teaching in England 1880–1950* (1969).

Secondary works

General accounts start with three studies by B Simon, *Education and the Labour Movement 1870–1920* (1965); *The Politics of Educational Reform 1920–40* (1974); and *Education and the Social Order 1940–90* (1991). C Barnett, *The Audit of War: The Illusion and Reality of Britain as a Great Power* (1986) offers a powerful critique. The effects of the First World War are covered in G Sherington, *English Education, Social Change and War 1911–20* (1981). On various aspects, see F Hunt, *Gender and Policy in English Education 1902–44* (1990); M Cruikshank, *Church and State in English Education* (1963); M Parkinson, *The Labour Party and the Organization of Secondary Education 1918–65* (1970); R Barker, *Education and Politics 1900–51: A Study of the Labour Party* (1972); C Griggs, *The Trades Union Congress and the Struggle for Education 1868–1925* (1983); G Sutherland, *Ability, Merit and Measurement: Mental Testing and English Education 1880–1940* (1984) and I F Goodman (ed) *Social Histories of the Secondary Curriculum: Subjects for Study* (1985). On the universities, see R D Anderson, *Universities and Elites in Britain since 1800* (1992); M Sanderson, *The Universities and British Industry 1850–1970* (1972); T Kelly, *For Advancement of Learning: The University of Liverpool, 1881–1981* (1981); and C H Shinn, *Paying the Piper: The Development of the University Grants Committee 1919–46* (1986). Adult education is considered in J F C Harrison, *Learning and Living 1790–1960* (1961).

Articles

Useful articles include W D Rubinstein, 'Education and the social origins of British elites 1880–1970', *PP* (1986); G L Savage, 'Social class and social policy: the civil service and secondary education in England during the inter-war period', *JCH* (1983); H M Paterson, 'Incubus and ideology: the development of secondary schooling in Scotland 1900–39', in W M Humes and H M Paterson, *Scottish Culture and Scottish Education 1800–1980* (1983); B Simon, 'The 1944 Education Act: a Conservative measure?', *HE* (1986); K Jefferys, 'R A Butler, the Board of Education and the 1944 Education Act', *H* (1984); and D Thom, 'The 1944 Education Act: the art of the possible?', in H L Smith (ed), *War and Social Change: British Society in the Second World War* (1986).

10. Health, poverty and social policy

All aspects of this question have aroused vigorous debate among contemporaries and historians. The effects of total war, depression and partial recovery have been fiercely debated. So too has the response of government. Policy rarely seemed dynamic, and has been criticized strongly for that reason. Yet others have argued that the foundations of the 'welfare state' were laid here, and that Britain was healthier and more prosperous than ever before.

Essay topics

How far and why did the nation's health improve in this period?

Was health and welfare policy marked more by continuity or change?

Sources and documents

J R Hay (ed) *The Development of the British Welfare State, 1880–1975* (1978) is a sound collection. E R Pike (ed) *Human Documents of the Lloyd George Era* (1972) has material on the First World War. Of the 1930s social investigations, see especially H L Beales and R S Lambert, *Memoirs of the Unemployed* (1934) and Pilgrim Trust, *Men Without Work* (1938). The classic text of welfare politics is the Beveridge Report on *Social Insurance and Allied Services* (1942).

Secondary works

Good general accounts include D Fraser, *The Evolution of the British Welfare State* (2nd edn, 1984); P Thane, *The Foundations of the Welfare State* (1982); A Crowther, *British Social Policy 1914–39* (1988); S Constantine, *Social Conditions in Britain 1918–39* (1983); and B B Gilbert, *British Social Policy 1914–39* (1970).

Various aspects of health services and medicine are covered in B Abel-Smith, *The Hospitals 1800–1948* (1964); D M Fox, *Health Policies, Health Politics: The British and American Experience 1911–65* (1986); N R Eder, *National Health Insurance and the Medical Profession in Britain 1911–39* (1982); J Lewis, *The Politics of Motherhood: Child and Maternal Welfare in England 1900–39* (1980); F F Cartwright, *A Social History of Medicine* (1977); C Webster, *Biology, Medicine and Society 1840–1940* (1981); and F B Smith, *The Retreat of Tuberculosis 1850–1950* (1988).

On the wider field, see J Harris, *William Beveridge* (1977); J Macnicol, *The Movement for Family Allowances 1918–45* (1980); R M Titmuss, *Problems of Social Policy* (1950); A Leathard, *The Fight for Family Planning* (1980); and J Burnett, *Plenty and Want: A Social History of Food in England from 1815 to the Present Day* (1989).

Articles

Among many good articles are A Digby and N Bosanquet, 'Doctors and patients in an era of national health insurance and private practice 1913–38', *EcHR* (1988); D M Fox, 'The National Health Service and the Second World War: the elaboration of consensus', in H L Smith (ed), *War and Social Change: British Society in the Second World War* (1986); and J Lewis, 'The prevention of diphtheria in Canada and Britain 1914–45', *JSH* (1986).

For an 'optimistic' view of health see the work of J M Winter: 'The impact of the First World War on civilian health in Britain', *EcHR* (1977); 'Military fitness and civilian health in Britain during the First World War', *JCH* (1980); 'Unemployment, nutrition and infant mortality in Britain 1920–50', in J M Winter (ed) *The Working Class in Modern British History: Essays in Honour of Henry Pelling* (1983); 'Infant mortality, maternal mortality, and public health in Britain in the 1930s', *JEEH* (1979); and 'The demographic consequences of the war', in H L Smith (ed), *War and Social Change: British Society in the Second World War* (1986). For the 'pessimistic' view, see L Bryden, 'The First World War: healthy or hungry?', *HW* (1987); C Webster, 'Healthy or hungry thirties?', *HW* (1982) and 'Health, welfare and unemployment during the Depression', *PP* (1985); M Mitchell, 'The effects of unemployment on the social condition of women and children in the 1930s', *HW* (1985); and M Mayhew, 'The 1930s nutrition controversy', *JCH* (1988).

11. Housing

Changes in housing were one of the most significant developments of this period. The scale of new building is still attested to today, especially on the outskirts of our larger towns and cities. A number of issues were involved, like the rise of council housing and owner-occupation, increasing government involvement, and the wider social consequences of housing change.

Essay topics

How and why did housing change?

Why did housing grow in importance as a political issue?

Sources and documents

E D Simon, *How to Abolish the Slums* (1929) is a classic text. Improvements in York can be seen in B S Rowntree, *Poverty and Progress* (1941). More anecdotal sources include R Roberts, *The Classic Slum* (1971); G Orwell, *The Road to Wigan Pier* (1937); and J B Priestley, *English Journey* (1934).

Secondary works

J Burnett, *A Social History of Housing, 1815–1970* (1978) is a good introduction; see also J Melling (ed) *Housing, Social Policy and the State* (1980). On council houses, see M Daunton, *Councillors and Tenants: Local Authority Housing in English Cities 1919–39* (1984); S Merrett, *State Housing in Britain* (1979); and M Swenarton, *Homes Fit for Heroes: The Politics and Architecture of Early State Housing in Britain* (1981). S Merrett, *Owner-Occupation in Britain* (1982) is useful. J Melling, *Rent Strikes: People's Struggles for Housing in West Scotland* (1983) and K Morgan, *Against Fascism and War: Ruptures and Continuities in the British Communist Party 1935–41* (1989) place tenants' struggles in a wider context.

Articles

Important articles include M Swenarton, 'An "insurance against revolution": ideological objectives of the provision and design of public housing after the First World War', *BIHR* (1981); A Ravetz, 'From working-class tenement to modern flat: local authorities and multi-storey housing between the wars', in A Sutcliffe (ed), *Multi-Storey Living: The British Working-Class Experience* (1974); M Swenarton and S Taylor, 'The scale and nature of owner-occupation in Britain between the wars', *EcHR* (1985); M McKenna, 'The suburbanization of the working-class population of Liverpool between the wars', *SH* (1991); and J Yelling, 'The metropolitan slum: London 1918–51', in S M Gaskell (ed) *Slums* (1990).

12. Gender and sexuality

The 1970s and 1980s have seen a massive upsurge in women's history, which is now being broadened into more general work on gender and sexuality. Debates have tended to centre around the role of war in improving the position of women, but few would now see it as unproblematic, especially when the post-war periods are examined in detail. Historians are now stressing, in particular, the extent to which women were forced back into traditional women's roles in the interwar period.

Essay topics

What were the effects of total war on the position of women?

Why did 'separate spheres' ideology revive strongly between the wars?

Sources and documents

I O Andrews, *Economic Effects of the World War upon Women and Children in Great Britain* (1923) is a mine of information. For working women, see two books by B Drake, *Women in the Engineering Trades*

(1917) and *Women in Trade Unions* (1920). M Llewellyn Davies (ed) *Life As We Have Known It* (1931) gives a selection of working-class views.

Secondary works

M Pugh, *Women and the Women's Movement in Britain 1914–59* (1992) is comprehensive. Other worthwhile general accounts are J Lewis, *Women in England 1870–1950* (1984); H L Smith (ed), *British Feminism in the Twentieth Century* (1990); and E Roberts, *A Woman's Place: An Oral History of Working-class Women 1890–1940* (1984). On politics, see J Alberti, *Beyond Suffrage: Feminists in War and Peace 1914–28* (1989); S S Holton, *Feminism and Democracy: Women's Suffrage and Reform Politics in Britain 1900–18* (1987); J Liddington, *The Life and Times of a Respectable Rebel: Selina Cooper 1864–1946* (1984); and B Harrison, *Prudent Revolutionaries: Portraits of British Feminists between the Wars* (1987). Work is covered by E Roberts, *Women's Work 1840–1940* (1988); G Braybon, *Women Workers in the First World War* (1981); M Glucksmann, *Workers Assemble: Women Workers and the New Industries in Interwar Britain* (1990); and P Summerfield, *Women Workers in the Second World War* (1984). For trade unionism, see S Lewenhak, *Women and Trade Unions* (1977) and N C Soldon, *Women in British Trade Unions 1874–1976* (1978). On home and family, see C Dyhouse, *Feminism and the Family in England 1880–1930* (1989); J Lewis, *The Politics of Motherhood: Child and Maternal Welfare in England 1900–39* (1980); and J Lewis (ed) *Labour and Love: Women's Experience of Home and Family 1850–1940* (1986).

Aspects of sexuality are covered by J Weeks, *Sex, Politics and Society: The Regulation of Sexuality since 1800* (2nd edn, 1989); L A Hall, *Hidden Anxieties: Male Sexuality 1900–50* (1991); M Roper and J Tosh (eds) *Manful Assertions: Masculinities in Britain since 1800* (1991); and J Weeks, *Coming Out: Homosexual Politics in Britain from the Nineteenth Century to the Present* (1977). On marriage, see J Gillis, *For Better, For Worse: British Marriages since 1600* (1986) and L Stone, *The Road to Divorce: England 1530–1987* (1990).

Articles

S K Kent, 'The politics of sexual difference: World War I and the demise of British feminism', *JBS* (1988) is important, placing the position of women in a broader context of gender relations. On work, see M Zimmech, 'Strategies and stratagems for the employment of women in the British civil service 1919–39', *HJ* (1984) and M Savage: 'Trade unionism, sex segregation and the state: women's employment in the new industries in inter-war Britain', *SH* (1988). On politics, see J V Newberry, 'Anti-war suffragists', *H* (1977); and three articles by B Harrison, 'Women in a men's house: the women MPs 1919–45', *HJ* (1986), 'Class and gender in modern British

Labour history', *PP* (1989) and 'Women's suffrage at Westminster 1866–1928', in M Bentley and J Stevenson (eds) *High and Low Politics in Modern Britain* (1983). On the Second World War see three articles by H L Smith, 'The womanpower problem in Britain during the Second World War', *HJ* (1984); 'The effect of the war on the status of women', in H L Smith (ed) *War and Social Change: British society in the Second World War* (1986); and 'The problem of "equal pay for equal work" in Great Britain during World War II', *JMH* (1981); as well as D Riley, '"The free mothers": pronatalism and working women in industry at the end of the last war in Britain', *HW* (1981).

13. News media

These were years of considerable change in the media. Not only did newspaper-reading spread to the working classes, but also there was the development of new types of media, such as radio and film newsreels. For all that, it is difficult to assess their impact. Even so, there is some agreement that the need to appeal to wider and wider audiences tended to commercialize and vulgarize the press.

Essay topics
Why and how did the press change in this period?
  What was the political impact of the news media?

Sources and documents
Political and Economic Planning, *Report on the British Press* (1938) is full of detail. T Clarke, *My Northcliffe Diary* (1931) is useful. P Kimble, *Newspaper Reading in the Third Year of the War* (1942) is valuable. For the early years of the BBC, see J Reith, *The Reith Diaries*, ed C Stuart (1975).

Secondary works
J Curran and J Seaton, *Power Without Responsibility: The Press and Broadcasting in Britain* (2nd edn, 1985) is a good introduction. On the press, see vol 2 of S Koss, *The Rise and Fall of the Political Press in Britain* (1984); F R Gannon, *The British Press and Germany 1936–9* (1971); R Cockett, *The Twilight of Truth* (1989); R Pound and G Harmsworth, *Northcliffe*; and A J P Taylor, *Beaverbrook* (1972). For radio, see A Briggs, *A History of Broadcasting in the UK* (4 vols, 1961–79) and M Pegg, *Broadcasting and Society 1918–39* (1983). On newsreels, see A Aldgate, *Cinema and History* (1979). For 'public opinion', see an analysis of opinion polling, R Wybrow, *Britain Speaks Out 1937–1987* (1989); P M H Bell, *John Bull and the Bear: British Public Opinion, Foreign Policy and the Soviet Union 1941–45* (1990); and I McLaine, *Ministry of Morale: Home Front Morale and the Ministry of Information in World War II* (1979).

Articles
See especially A Adamthwaite, 'The British government and the media 1937–8', *JCH* (1983); J M McEwen, 'The national press during the First World War: ownership and control', *JCH* (1982); C Seymour-Ure, 'The press and the party system between the wars', in G Peele and C Cook (eds) *The Politics of Reappraisal 1918–39* (1975); and N Pronay, 'British newsreels in the 1930s: 1. Audience and producers', *H* (1971); 'British newsreels in the 1930s: 2. Their policies and impact'; *H* (1972); and 'British documentaries of the 1930s', *H* (1977).

14. Religion

This period saw a general decline of organized religion, with the exception of the Roman Catholics, who expanded in numbers. Britain seemed to be becoming a more secular society. Yet religion still informed the outlook of many people, and was a force which could not be wholly ignored: in particular, it had a continuing political and electoral importance that could not be dismissed by politicians.

Essay topics
Account for the decline in organized religion.
   Did religion have any real influence in this period?

Sources and documents
R Currie, A Gilbert and L Horsley, *Churches and Churchgoers: Patterns of Church Growth in the British Isles since 1700* (1977) is a mine of useful statistics. For Church-State relations, see Church Assembly, *Church and State: Report of the Archbishops' Commission on the Relations between Church and State* (1936). A radical churchman's views are seen in W Temple, *Christianity and Social Order* (1942).

Secondary works
A D Gilbert, *The Making of Post-Christian Britain: A History of the Secularization of Modern Society* (1980) offers a powerful interpretation. More orthodox histories include A Hastings, *A History of English Christianity 1920–85* (1986); D W Bebbington, *Evangelicalism in Modern Britain* (1989); G I T Machin, *Politics and the Churches in Britain 1869–1921* (1987). On the established Church, see R Lloyd, *The Church of England 1900–65* (1966); E R Norman, *Church and Society in England 1770–1970: A Historical Study* (1976); D L Edwards, *Leaders of the Church of England 1828–1944* (1971); O Chadwick, *Hensley Henson* (1983); and F Iremonger, *William Temple, Archbishop of Canterbury* (1948). For Nonconformity, see R Currie, *Methodism Divided* (1968) and K D Brown, *A Social History of the Nonconformist Ministry in England and Wales 1800–1930* (1988). For

the Catholics, see G A Beck (ed) *The English Catholics 1850–1950* (1950). D Jeremy, *Capitalists and Christians: Business Leaders and the Churches in Britain 1900–60* (1990) follows that aspect. Among local studies of significance are P J Waller, *Democracy and Sectarianism: A Political and Social History of Liverpool 1868–1939* (1981); T Gallacher, *Glasgow: The Uneasy Peace* (1987); M Winter, 'Cornwall', and N I Orme, 'Devon', in N I Orme (ed) *Unity and Variety: A History of the Church in Devon and Cornwall* (1991); and E R Wickham, *Church and People in an Industrial City* (1957), a study of Sheffield. Specifically on politics, see S Koss, *Nonconformity in Modern British Politics* (1975). For the Jews, see two books by G Alderman, *London Jewry and London Politics 1889–1986* (1988) and *The Jewish Community in British Politics* (1983).

Articles
Specifically on Anglicans, see D M Thompson, 'The politics of the Enabling Act (1919)', *SCH* (1975) and C A Cline, 'Ecumenism and appeasement: the bishops of the Church of England and the Treaty of Versailles', *JMH* (1989). For Catholics, see P Doyle, 'The Catholic Federation 1906–29', *SCH* (1986); S Mews, 'The sword of the spirit: a Catholic cultural crusade of 1940', *SCH* (1983); T R Greene, 'The English Catholic press and the Second Spanish Republic 1931–6', *CH* (1976); and J Flint, '"Must God go fascist?": English Catholic opinion and the Spanish Civil War', *CH* (1987). On religion and politics, see S Mews, 'Urban problems and rural solutions: drink and disestablishment in the First World War', *SCH* (1979); M Ceadel, 'Christian pacifism in the era of two World Wars', *SCH* (1983); and G I T Machin, 'Marriage and the churches in the 1930s: royal abdication and divorce reform 1936–7', *JEcclH* (1991). On Scotland, see W W Knox, 'Religion and the Scottish Labour movement c1900–39', *JCH* (1988) and T Gallacher, 'Protestant extremism in urban Scotland 1930–9, its growth and contraction', *ScHR* (1985).

15. Leisure
The growth of leisure was one of the most notable aspects of interwar Britain. Real wages rose for those in work, while working hours fell and more people were able to take holidays. Not only did the demand for and supply of leisure provision grow, but also patterns of leisure changed, with the growth of literacy, technological developments like cinema and radio, and the decline of older communal activities like the pub and churchgoing.

Essay topics
How far and why did this period see a 'growth in leisure'?

To what extent and why did leisure pursuits become more home-based in this period?

Sources and Documents
Useful contemporary views include H Durant, *The Problem of Leisure*
(1938); J B Priestley, *English Journey* (1934); and Mass-Observation,
The Pub and the People (1943).

Secondary works
Two good general accounts are S G Jones, *Workers at Play: A Social
and Economic History of Leisure 1918–39* (1986) and J Walvin, *Leisure
and Society 1830–1950* (1978). For radio, see M Pegg, *Broadcasting
and Society 1918–9* (1983) and A Briggs, *The History of Broadcasting
in the United Kingdom, vol II: The Golden Age of Wireless* (1965).
Holidaymaking is covered by J A R Pimlott, *The Englishman's Holiday*
(1947). The cinema has excited much attention: see especially J
Richards, *The Age of the Dream Palace: Cinema and Society in Britain
1930–9* (1984); J Richards and A Aldgate, *Best of British: Cinema and
Society 1930–70* (1983); P M Taylor, *Britain and the Cinema in the Second
World War* (1988); and A Aldgate and J Richards, *Britain Can Take
It: The British Cinema in the Second World War* (1986). For sport and
gambling, see R Holt, *Sport and the British* (1989); N Fishwick, *English
Football and Society 1910–50* (1989) and W Vamplew, *The Turf: A Social
and Economic History of Horse Racing* (1976).

Articles
See S G Jones, 'State intervention in sport and leisure in Britain
between the wars', *JCH* (1987); and 'Trade union policy between
the wars: the case of holidays with pay in Britain', *IRSH* (1986);
J Richards, 'The cinema and cinema-going in Birmingham in the
1930s', in J K Walton and J Walvin (eds) *Leisure in Britain 1780–1939*
(1983); S Farrant, 'London by the sea: resort development on the
south coast of England 1880–1939', *JCH* (1987); R McKibbin,
'Working-class gambling in Britain 1880–1939', *PP* (1979) and
'Work and hobbies in Britain 1880–1950', in J M Winter (ed) *The
Working Class in Modern British Politics* (1983); and A Davies, 'The
police and the people: gambling in Salford 1900–39', *HJ* (1991).

16. Social class

The extent to which British society was divided on rigid class lines
has aroused considerable interest. Work centres on the nature of the
class system and on the individual classes themselves. The view that
this period saw greater class homogeneity has to be set against the
continuing political and religious divisions within the working classes
and the conflicts of earnings and status within all classes.

Essay topics

'Divisions within classes were more important than divisions between them.' Discuss.

How important was class in determining political allegiance?

Sources and documents

A M Carr-Saunders and D Caradog Jones, *A Survey of the Social Structure of England and Wales* (1927) is a classic. For working-class life see G Orwell, *The Road to Wigan Pier* (1937) and R Roberts, *The Classic Slum* (1971). A M Carr-Saunders and P A Wilson, *The Professions* (1933) is full of detail. For a taste of the lifestyle of the wealthy, see H Channon, *Chips: The Diary of Sir Henry Channon*, ed. R Rhodes James (1967).

Secondary works

On class generally, see H Perkin, *The Rise of Professional Society: England since 1880* (1989); W D Rubinstein, *Wealth and Inequality in Britain* (1986); A Marwick, *Class: Image and Reality in Britain, France and the USA since 1930* (1980); and G Routh, *Occupation and Pay in Great Britain 1906–79* (2nd edn, 1980).

On the working classes, E Hopkins, *The Rise and Decline of the English Working Classes 1918–90* (1991) is a good introduction. Other valuable works include R McKibbin, *The Ideologies of Class: Social Relations in Britain 1880–1950* (1990); P Johnson, *Saving and Spending: The Working-Class Economy in Britain 1870–1939* (1985); J Benson, *The Working Class in Britain 1850–1939* (1989); and M Savage, *The Dynamics of Working-Class Politics: The Labour Movement in Preston 1880–1940* (1987).

The middle classes are less well served, but see I Bradley, *The English Middle Classes are Alive and Kicking* (1982); R Lewis and A Maude, *Professional People* (1952); and A H Halsey and M Trow, *The British Academics* (1971).

On the upper classes, see W D Rubinstein, *Men of Property* (1981); D Cannadine, *The Decline and Fall of the British Aristocracy* (1990) and *Lords and Landlords: The Aristocracy and the Towns 1774–1967* (1980); F M L Thompson, *English Landed Society in the Nineteenth Century* (1963), which in fact goes up to 1939; M Beard, *English Landed Society in the Twentieth Century* (1989); and W L Guttsman, *The British Political Elite* (1963).

Articles

General articles include R Price and G S Bain, 'The labour force', in A H Halsey (ed) *British Social Trends since 1900* (2nd edn, 1988); B A Waites, 'The effect of the First World War on class and status in England 1910–20', *JCH* (1976); and P Summerfield, 'The levelling of class', in H L Smith (ed) *War and Social Change: British society in the Second World War* (1986). On the working classes, see R C Whiting, 'Taxation and the working class 1915–24', *HJ* (1990) and E Hopkins, 'Working-class life in Birmingham between the wars 1918–39', *MH* (1990). For their 'social betters' see two articles by F M L Thompson: 'English landed society in the twentieth century: I, property: collapse and survival', *TRHS* (1990) and 'II, new poor and new rich', *TRHS* (1991). See also W D Rubinstein, 'Wealth, elites and the class structure of modern Britain', *PP* (1977); and 'Modern Britain', in W D Rubinstein (ed) *Wealth and the Wealthy in the Modern World* (1980).

17. The interwar economy and economic policy

This subject has aroused great controversy. Debate has centred particularly around the nature, extent and effects of state intervention; the return to the gold standard in 1925; the effects of tariffs; and the extent to which the economy was being restructured in the 1930s. There is now much doubt as to whether a 'Keynesian' policy could have cut unemployment, but government even between the wars took a much higher economic profile than before 1914.

Essay topics
How far was Britain's industrial base restructured, 1914–45?

What did governments see as their main economic objectives, and how successful were they in attaining them?

Sources and documents
B R Mitchell, *British Historical Statistics* (1988), and B W Clapp, H E S Fisher and A R J Jurica (eds) *Documents in English Economic History*, vol 2 (1976) are indispensable. For policy advice, see the documents in S Howson and D Winch, *The Economic Advisory Council, 1930–1939* (1977). For an industrialist's view see R Streat, *Lancashire and Whitehall: The Diaries of Sir Raymond Streate*, (ed) M Dupree (2 vols, 1987).

Secondary works
See especially S Pollard, *The Development of the British Economy 1914–80* (3rd edn, 1983); D H Aldcroft, *The British Economy vol I: The Years of Turmoil 1920–1951* (1986) and *The British Economy between the Wars* (1983). R Floud and D McCloskey (eds) *The Economic History of Britain since 1700, vol 2* (1981) and J Turner (ed) *Businessmen and Politics* (1984) are good collections.

For policy, see J Tomlinson, *Public Policy and the Economy since 1900* (1990); G C Peden, *British Economic and Social Policy: Lloyd George to Margaret Thatcher* (2nd edn, 1991); A Booth and M Pack, *Employment, Capital and Economic Policy: Great Britain 1918–39* (1985); W R Garside, *British Unemployment 1919–1939* (1990); F Capie, *Depression and Protectionism: Britain between the Wars* (1983); P F Clarke, *The Keynesian Revolution in the Making 1924–36* (1988); A Booth, *British Economic Policy 1931–49* (1989); R Middleton, *Towards the Managed Economy* (1985). On Keynes see D E Moggridge, *Keynes* (1976) and *Maynard Keynes* (1992).

On finance, see H Clay, *Lord Norman* (1957); R S Sayers, *The Bank of England 1891–1944* (3 vols, 1976); M Collins, *Banks and Industrial Finance in Britain 1800–1939* (1991); and D B Kunz, *The Battle for Britain's Gold Standard, 1931* (1987). Of numerous works on industry, see especially N K Buxton and D H Aldcroft (eds) *British Industry between the Wars* (1979); B Supple, *The History of the British Coal Industry, vol IV: 1913–46* (1987); S Tolliday, *Business, Banking and Politics: The Case of British Steel 1918–39* (1988); and H W Richardson and D H Aldcroft, *Building in the British Economy between the Wars* (1968). For agriculture, see E H Whetham, *The Agrarian History of England and Wales, vol VIII: 1914–1939* (1978) and D Grigg, *English Agriculture: An Historical Perspective* (1989).

Articles

P K O'Brien, 'Britain's economy between the wars', *PP* (1987) is a good overview. On unemployment and policy, see especially N F R Crafts, 'Long-term unemployment in Britain in the 1930s', *EcHR* (1987); S Glynn and P G A Howells, 'Unemployment in the 1930s: the "Keynesian solution" reconsidered', *AEHR* (1980); W R Garside, 'The failure of the radical alternative: public works, deficit finance and British interwar unemployment', *JEEH* (1985); F M Miller, 'The unemployment policy of the National government 1931–6', *HJ* (1976); and N Whiteside and J A Gillespie, 'Deconstructing unemployment: developments in Britain in the inter-war years', *EcHR* (1991). On gold, see K G P Matthews, 'Was sterling overvalued in 1925?', *EcHR* (1986) and J Redmond, 'Was sterling overvalued in 1925? A comment', *EcHR* (1989). On the 1930s, see A Booth, 'Britain in the 1930s: a managed economy?', *EcHR* (1987); F Capie and M Collins, 'The extent of British economic recovery in the 1930s', *EH* (1980); M Thomas, 'Rearmament and economic recovery in the late 1930s', *EcHR* (1983); F Capie, 'The British tariff and industrial production in the 1930s', *EcHR* (1978); and M Kitson, S Solomou and M Weale, 'Effective protection and economic recovery in the United Kingdom during the 1930s', *EcHR* (1991).

18. Trade unions

This period saw great fluctuations in the fortunes of trade unions. While much of the literature is rather bland, being official history produced at the behest of the union involved, there are also more critical and, sometimes, profound works available. After the events of the 1970s and 1980s it is no longer possible to see the rise of unions as unproblematic or wholly beneficial, but it is still open to historians to point to the appeal which unions had (and retain) among potential recruits.

Essay topics

Account for the fluctuations in trade union membership, 1914–1945.

   To what extent and why were unions incorporated into government during this period?

Sources and documents

W Milne-Bailey, *Trade Union Documents* (1929) remains valuable. J T Ward and W H Fraser (eds) *Workers and Employers: Documents on Trade Unions and Industrial Relations in Britain since the Eighteenth Century* (1980) is a good wide-ranging selection. Lord Citrine, *Men and Work* (1964) is indispensable. For a radical view, see G D H Cole, *Self-Government in Industry* (1917).

Secondary works

H Pelling, *A History of British Trade Unionism* (5th edn, 1992) is a good brief introduction. More substantial are H A Clegg, *A History of British Trade Unions since 1889, vol II: 1911–1933* (1985) and R M Martin, *TUC: The Growth of a Pressure Group 1868–1976* (1980). More profound are R Price, *Labour in British Society* (1986) and K Middlemas, *Politics in Industrial Society* (1979). See also two books by C J Wrigley, *David Lloyd George and the British Labour Movement* (1976) and *Lloyd George and the Challenge of Labour: The Post-War Coalition 1918–1922* (1990); as well as V L Allen, *Trade Unions and the Government* (1960); D F MacDonald, *The State and the Trade Unions* (1976); and S Tolliday and J Zeitlin (eds) *Shopfloor Bargaining and the State* (1985). The impact of the left can be gauged from R Martin, *Communism and the British Trade Unions 1924–1933: A Study of the National Minority Movement* (1969).

   Among the better books on individual unions, see R P Arnot, *The Miners – Years of Struggle: A History of the Miners' Federation of Great Britain (from 1910 onwards)* (1953); J E Williams, *The Derbyshire Miners: A Study in Industrial and Social History* (1962); H Francis and D Smith, *The Fed: A History of the South Wales Miners in the Twentieth Century* (1980); P S Bagwell, *The Railwaymen: The History of the National Union of Railwaymen* (1963); R Hyman, *The Workers' Union* (1971); and

R Croucher, *Engineers at War 1939–45* (1982). For union leaders, see A Bullock, *The Life and Times of Ernest Bevin* (3 vols, 1960–83), and P Davies, *A J Cook* (1987). On rank-and-file movements, see J Hinton, *The First Shop Stewards Movement* (1973); I McLean, *The Legend of Red Clydeside* (1981); and K Fuller, *Radical Aristocrats: London Busworkers from the 1880s to the 1980s* (1985).

For strikes, see J Morgan, *Conflict and Order: The Police and Labour Disputes 1900–39* (1987). For the General Strike see G A Phillips, *The General Strike* (1976); P Renshaw, *The General Strike* (1975); and M Morris, *The General Strike* (1976).

Articles

J E Cronin, 'The peculiar pattern of British strikes since 1888', *JBS* (1979) is useful, as are P Renshaw, 'The depression years 1918–1931' and R Shackleton, 'Trade unions and the slump' in B Pimlott and C Cook (eds), *Trade Unions in British Politics* (2nd edn, 1991). Other important articles include J Melling, 'Whatever happened to Red Clydeside? Industrial conflict and the politics of skill in the First World War', *IRSH* (1990); G R Rubin, 'Law as a bargaining weapon: British labour and the Restoration of Pre-War Practices Act 1919', *HJ* (1989); P S Bagwell, 'The triple industrial alliance 1913–22', in A Briggs and J Saville (eds) *Essays in Labour History 1886–1923* (1971); M Savage, 'Trade unionism, sex segregation and the state: women's employment in new industries in inter-war Britain', *SH* (1988); A J Taylor, 'The miners and nationalization 1931–6', *IRSH* (1983); and A Fowler, 'Lancashire cotton trade unionism in the inter-war years', in J A Jowitt and A J McIvor (eds) *Employers and Labour in the English Textile Industries 1850–1939* (1988).

19. First World War

The First World War has aroused considerable historical controversy, and it would be rash to claim that there is consensus even now in many areas. The debates range across political, economic, social and military history, but include the extent to which a war of attrition on the Western Front was inevitable; whether British society became more cohesive or fragmented; how far it was responsible for the very different political landscape of the interwar period; and whether the conflict accelerated or retarded economic modernization.

Essay topics

'There was no feasible alternative to the 'western' strategy.' Discuss.
Assess the impact of the First World War on British society.

Sources and documents
See D Lloyd George, *War Memoirs* (6 vols, 1933–6) for a taste of
politics. For civilians at war, see E S Pankhurst, *The Home Front* (1932)
and A Clark, *Echoes of the Great War: the diary of the Reverend Andrew
Clark 1914–1919*, ed J Munson (1985). The views of Britain's leading
soldier can be followed in D Haig, *The Private Papers of Douglas Haig*,
ed R Blake (1952).

Secondary works
The best general account is J M Bourne, *Britain and the Great War
1914–1918* (1989), but see also T Wilson, *The Myriad Faces of War:
Britain and the Great War 1914–1918* (1986). On the military side,
see especially E L Woodward, *Great Britain and the War of 1914–1918*
(1967); T Travers, *The Killing Ground: The British Army, the Western
Front and the Emergence of Warfare 1900–18* (1987); D French, *British
Strategy and War Aims 1914–16* (1986); R Hough, *The Great War at
Sea 1914–18* (1983); J Terraine, *Douglas Haig: The Educated Soldier*
(1963); and G J De Groot, *Douglas Haig 1869–1928* (1988). Relations
between politicians and generals are studied in D R Woodward, *Lloyd
George and the Generals* (1983). On recruitment, see W J Reader, *At
Duty's Call* (1988) and R J Q Adams and P P Poirier, *The Conscription
Controversy in Great Britain 1900–1918* (1987).

Many of the books which look at the social, economic and political
aspects of the war are included in other sections of this bibliography.
However, worth noting here are A Marwick, *The Deluge: British Society
and the First World War* (1965); B Waites, *A Class Society at War: England
1914–1918* (1987); J M Winter, *The Great War and the British People*
(1985); J M Winter, *The Experience of World War I* (1988); A S Milward,
The Economic Effects of the Two World Wars on Britain (1972); A Offer,
The First World War: An Agrarian Interpretation (1989); P E Dewey,
British Agriculture in the First World War (1989); K Burk (ed) *War and
the State: The Transformation of British Government 1914–19* (1982); K
Burk, *Britain, America and the Sinews of War, 1914–18* (1985); R J Q
Adams, *Arms and the Wizard: Lloyd George and the Ministry of Munitions*
(1978); and G Rubin, *War, Law and Labour: the Munitions Acts, State
Regulation and the Unions 1915–21* (1987). See also M Sanders and P
M Taylor, *British Propaganda during the First World War* (1983).

Articles
Among the more important articles are M Brock, 'Britain enters the
war', in R J W Evans and H P von Strandmann (eds) *The Coming of
the First World War* (1988); J Gooch, 'Soldiers, strategy and war aims
in Britain 1914–1918', in B Hunt and A Preston (eds) *War Aims
and Strategic Policy in the Great War 1914–1918* (1977); D French,
'The origins of the Dardanelles campaign reconsidered', *H* (1983);
D French, 'The meaning of attrition 1914–16', *EHR* (1988); and P

E Dewey, 'Military recruiting and the British labour force during the First World War', *HJ* (1984). T Balderston, 'War finance and inflation in Britain and Germany 1914–18', *EcHR* (1989) looks at that aspect. See also J Turner, 'The House of Commons and the executive during the First World War', *PH* (1991) and N Hiley, 'Counter-espionage and security in Great Britain during the First World War', *EHR* (1986).

20. The Second World War

The experience of the Second World War has raised major questions among historians of Britain. How significant, for example, was Britain's contribution to the defeat of Germany and Japan? The social and economic impact have also aroused much debate. The effects on Britain's world power status, and especially the Empire, have aroused controversy. And how far was the war responsible for the election of the first majority Labour government in 1945?

Essay topics
Assess the contribution made by Britain to victory over Germany in the Second World War.

Did the Second World War revolutionize British society?

Sources and documents
An obvious starting-point is Churchill's massive *The Second World War* (6 vols, 1948–54). See also J Colville, *The Fringes of Power* (1985) and H Dalton, *The Second World War Diary of Hugh Dalton*, ed B Pimlott (1986). Viscount Montgomery, *Memoirs* (1958) is useful. See also T Harrisson, *Living Through the Blitz* (1976) and A Calder and D Sheridan (eds) *Speak for Yourself: A Mass-Observation Anthology 1937–49* (1984).

Secondary works
General accounts include A Calder, *The People's War: Britain 1939–45* (1969); H Pelling, *Britain and the Second World War* (1970); and H L Smith (ed) *War and Social Change* (1986). On the military side, see R A C Parker, *Struggle for Survival: The History of the Second World War* (1989); HMSO, 'History of the Second World War: United Kingdom Military Series', *Grand Strategy* (6 vols, 1956–76); N Harman, *Dunkirk: The Necessary Myth* (1980); M Hastings, *Overlord: D-Day and the Battle for Normandy* (1984); M Dean, *The RAF and Two World Wars* (1979). Biographies of leading service figures include N Hamilton, *Monty* (3 vols, 1981–6) and D Fraser, *Alanbrooke* (1982). Intelligence is covered by R Lewin, *Ultra Goes to War: The Secret Story* (1978) and R V Jones, *Most Secret War* (1978).

For civilian life, see I McLaine, *Ministry of Morale: Home Front Morale and the Ministry of Information in World War II* (1979) and T H O'Neill, *Civil Defence* (1955).

For politics, see P Addison, *The Road to 1945* (1975) and K Jefferys, *The Churchill Coalition and Wartime Politics 1940–5* (1991). For the economy, contrast the official history, W K Hancock and M Gowing, *British War Economy* (1949), with the critical C Barnett, *The Audit of War: The Illusion and Reality of Britain as a Great Power* (1986); see also A S Milward, *The Economic Effects of the Two World Wars on Britain* (1972). Social aspects are covered in R M Titmuss, *Problems of Social Policy* (1950) and A Marwick, *The Home Front* (1976). D Thoms, *War, Industry and Society: The Midlands 1939–45* (1989) is a good regional study.

Articles
On the fighting, see E F Gueritz, 'Nelson's blood: attitudes and actions of the Royal Navy 1939–45', *JCH* (1981) and T Ben-Moshe, 'Winston Churchill and the Second Front: a reappraisal', *JMH* (1990). On politics, see K Jefferys, 'May 1940: the downfall of Neville Chamberlain', *PH* (1991). Economic matters are the subject of A Booth, 'Economic advice at the centre of British government 1939–41', *HJ* (1986). For social policy, see K Jefferys, 'British politics and social policy during the Second World War', *HJ* (1987) and R Lowe, 'The Second World War, consensus and the foundation of the welfare state', *TCBH* (1990). Propaganda and morale are the subject of N Pronay, 'The land of promise: the projection of peace aims in Britain', in K R M Short (ed) *Film and Radio Propaganda in World War II* (1983) and A Thorpe, 'Britain', in J D Noakes (ed) *The Civilian in War* (1992).

21. Ireland
Ireland was in turmoil for the first part of this period, with the Easter Rising of 1916, the success of Sinn Fein at the 1918 election, the Anglo-Irish war, and then civil war following the Anglo-Irish Treaty of 1921. Ultimately Ireland was partitioned, but trouble flared again in the 1930s with a trade war, and under de Valera the Free State drifted away from the Commonwealth, remaining neutral during the Second World War. This remains a topic of considerable historical interest.

Essay topics
Why was the Irish Free State set up in 1921?

Was the Irish Free State's neutrality in the Second World War the logical outcome of Anglo-Irish relations between 1921 and 1939?

Sources and documents

A O'Day and J Stevenson (eds) *Irish Historical Documents* (1992) and A Mitchell and P O Snodaigh, *Irish Political Documents 1919–49* (1983) are valuable collections. The treaty negotiations can be followed in T Jones, *Whitehall Diary, vol III: Ireland*, ed K Middlemas (1971). M Moynihan (ed) *Speeches and Statements by Eamon de Valera 1917–73* (1980) is important.

Secondary works

Among general works, see especially R F Foster, *Modern Ireland 1600–1972* (1988); K T Hoppen, *Ireland since 1800: Conflict and Conformity* (1989); and the superb J J Lee, *Ireland 1912–1985* (1989). D G Boyce (ed) *The Revolution in Ireland 1879–1923* (1988) is a solid collection. On nationalism, see R Kee, *The Green Flag* (1972); on terrorism, see T P Coogan, *The IRA* (1970) and J Bowyer Bell, *The Secret Army: The IRA 1916–79* (1979). The later parts of C Townshend, *Political Violence in Ireland: Government and Resistance since 1848* (1983) are also useful. K A Kennedy, T Giblin and D McHugh, *The Economic Development of Ireland in the Twentieth Century* (1988) is full of essential information; see also T Brown, *Ireland: A Social and Cultural History 1922–79* (1981).

For the period up to the treaty see S Lawlor, *Britain and Ireland 1914–23* (1983); D Fitzpatrick, *Politics and Irish Life 1913–21* (1977); R Dudley Edwards, *Patrick Pearse: The Triumph of Failure* (1977); D G Boyce, *Englishmen and Irish Troubles: British Public Opinion and the Making of Irish Policy 1918–22* (1972); C Townshend, *The British Campaign in Ireland 1919–21: The Development of Political and Military Policies* (1975); J McColgan, *British Policy and the Irish Administration 1920–2* (1983); and M Hopkinson, *Green Against Green: The Irish Civil War* (1988). For relations after 1921, see P Canning, *British Policy towards Ireland 1921–41* (1983); D W Harkness, *The Restless Dominion: The Irish Free State and the British Commonwealth of Nations 1921–31* (1969); D McMahon, *Republicans and Imperialists: Anglo-Irish Relations in the 1930s* (1984); R Fisk, *In Time of War: Ireland, Ulster and the Price of Neutrality 1939–45* (1983); and J T Carroll, *Ireland in the War Years 1939–45* (1975). For Ulster, see D Harkness, *Northern Ireland since 1920* (1983). Among the better biographies are B Inglis, *Roger Casement* (1973); A Morgan, *James Connolly* (1989); O Dudley Edwards, *Eamon de Valera* (1987); J Bowman, *De Valera and the Ulster Question 1917–73* (1982); A T Q Stewart, *Edward Carson* (1981); B Farrell, *Sean Lemass* (1983); and P Buckland, *James Craig, Lord Craigavon* (1980).

Articles

Among numerous significant articles, see P Jalland and J Stubbs, 'The Irish question after the outbreak of war in 1914', *EHR* (1981); J O Stubbs, 'The Unionists and Ireland 1914–1918', *HJ* (1990);

D Fitzpatrick, 'The geography of Irish nationalism 1910–21', *PP* (1978); R Murphy, 'Walter Long and the making of the Government of Ireland Act 1919–20', *IHS* (1986); S M Lawlor, 'Ireland from truce to treaty: war or peace? July to October 1921', *IHS* (1980–1); D Harkness, 'England's Irish question', in G Peele and C Cook (eds) *The Politics of Reappraisal 1918–39* (1975); D McMahon, 'A transient apparition: British policy towards the de Valera government 1932–5', *IHS* (1980–1); M A Hopkinson, 'The Craig-Collins pacts of 1922: two attempted reforms of the Northern Ireland government', *IHS* (1990); D S Johnson, 'Northern Ireland as a problem in the economic war 1932–8', *IHS* (1980–1); and A C Hepburn, 'The Belfast riots of 1935', *SH* (1990).

22. Scotland

In this period Scotland suffered under the pressure of economic circumstances; living standards generally remained lower than in England. It provided force for the left, with the shop stewards' movement, the Independent Labour party, and the Communists all owing it much for leadership and inspiration. The growth of Nationalist parties began in the 1920s, but their impact in this period was limited. One area of increasing interest is the relationship between the Labour movement and organized religion, particularly the Catholic Church.

Essay topics
Was Scotland's experience in this period significantly different from that of the rest of Britain?

Account for the major fluctuations in the fortunes of the political parties in Scotland, 1914–45.

Sources and documents
I MacDougall, *Voices from the Hunger Marches* (2 vols, 1990) is a good collection, and see the memoirs of Labour leaders: D Kirkwood, *My Life of Revolt* (1933); J McGovern, *Neither Fear nor Favour* (1960); W Gallacher, *Revolt on the Clyde* (1936); H McShane and J Smith, *No Mean Fighter* (1977); and J Maclean, *Into the Rapids of Revolution: Essays, Articles and Letters 1902–23*, ed N Milton (1978).

Secondary works
General histories include T C Smout, *A Century of the Scottish People 1830–1950* (1986) and C Harvie, *No Gods and Precious Few Heroes: Scotland 1914–80* (1981). For politics, see I C G Hutchison, *A Political History of Scotland 1832–1924* (1986); I Donnachie, C Harvie and S Woods (eds) *Forward! Labour Politics in Scotland 1888–1988* (1988); J Hinton, *The First Shop Stewards' Movement* (1973); I McLean, *The*

Legend of Red Clydeside (1983); T Gallacher, *Glasgow, the Uneasy Peace: Religious Tension in Modern Scotland* (1987); B J Ripley and J McHugh, *John Maclean* (1973); D Howell, *A Lost Left: Three Studies in Socialism and Nationalism* (1987); I Wood, *John Wheatley* (1989); and G Walker, *Thomas Johnston* (1988). W Knox (ed) *Scottish Labour Leaders 1918–39* (1984) is indispensable. J Holford, *Reshaping Labour: Organization, Work and Politics – Edinburgh in the Great War and After* (1988) is a useful study; see also T Gallacher, *Edinburgh Divided: John Cormack and Popery in the 1930s* (1988). See also H J Hanham, *Scottish Nationalism* (1969) and B Lenman, *An Economic History of Modern Scotland 1660–1976* (1977).

Articles

P Jalland, 'United Kingdom devolution 1910–14: political panacea or tactical diversion?', *EHR* (1979) assesses how seriously Scottish nationalism was taken before the First World War. On nationalism see J D Young, 'Marxism and the Scottish Nationalist question', *JCH* (1983) and T Dickson, 'Marxism, nationalism and Scottish history', *JCH* (1983). Other useful articles include W W Knox, 'Religion and the Scottish Labour movement c1900–39', *JCH* (1988); T Gallacher, 'Protestant extremism in urban Scotland 1930–39, its growth and contraction', *ScHR* (1985); N K Buxton, 'Economic growth in Scotland between the wars: the role of production structure and rationalization', *EcHR* (1980); R H Campbell, 'The Scottish Office and the Special Areas in the 1930s', *HJ* (1979); and C Harvie, 'Labour in Scotland during the Second World War', *HJ* (1983).

23. Wales

This period saw the transformation of south Wales from an area of prosperity to one of depression as markets for its coal exports dried up: for many, it is the symbol of the 'pessimistic' view of the interwar period. This was reflected in Labour's growing dominance in that part of Wales. Pressure for a Welsh Office on the lines of the Scottish Office was resisted by all governments, but the revival of Welsh nationalism led to the formation of Plaid Cymru. Politically, these were years of advance for Labour, but Liberalism remained strongly entrenched in some parts, most notably the north.

Essay topics

Account for the changing politics of Wales during this period.

Was Welsh nationalism anything more than a literary movement among a minority during this period?

Sources and documents
T Herbert and G E Jones, *Wales between the Wars* (1988) is a useful collection shedding light on a number of different areas of life, with helpful essays.

Secondary works
See especially K O Morgan, *Rebirth of a Nation: Wales 1880–1980* (1981) and *Wales in British Politics 1868–1922* (1980). Other important works include P Jenkins, *A History of Modern Wales 1536–1990* (1992); D Smith (ed) *A People and a Proletariat: Essays in the History of Wales 1780–1980* (1980); D H Davies, *The Welsh Nationalist Party 1925–45: A Call to Nationhood* (1983); B Griffiths, *Saunders Lewis* (1979); H Francis, *Miners against Fascism: Wales and the Spanish Civil War* (1984); M Jones, *The North Wales Quarrymen 1874–1922* (1981); H Francis and D Smith, *The Fed: A History of the South Wales Miners in the Twentieth Century* (1980); A Y Jones and D Beddoe, *The Welsh Maid: A Study of Welsh Women in Domestic Service 1919–39* (1988); and G E Jones, *Controls and Conflict in Welsh Secondary Education 1889–1944* (1982).

Articles
See especially J G Jones, 'E T John and Welsh Home Rule 1910–14', *WHR* (1986–7), and 'E T John, devolution and democracy 1917–24', *WHR* (1988–9); J Aitchison and H Carter, 'Rural Wales and the Welsh language', *RH* (1991); C Cook, 'Wales and the general election of 1923', *WHR* (1969); J G Jones, 'Wales and the new socialism 1926–29', *WHR* (1982–3); M Asteris, 'The rise and decline of South Wales coal exports 1870–1930', *WHR* (1986–7); and G Williams, 'Grand Slam to great slump: economy, society and rugby football in Wales during the Depression', *WHR* (1982–3).

24. Foreign policy

In this period Britain faced many threats abroad, and had to come to terms with a greatly changing world. Most interest has centred on the question of appeasement in the 1930s; here the focus has changed from an unrelenting criticism of the National governments to a more sophisticated view which seeks to lay greater emphasis on the problems they faced. Recent events have also forced scholars to look more closely at Britain's relations with Europe and the United States over the period as a whole.

Essay topics
Were there any consistent principles in British foreign policy?
    What were the aims of British foreign policymakers and how far were they successfully realized?

Sources and documents
See M Gilbert (ed), *Britain and Germany between the Wars* (1964) and
W Kimball (ed) *Churchill and Roosevelt: The Complete Correspondence* (3
vols, 1984). There are many useful 'insider' accounts: see especially
Lord Grey, *Twenty-Five Years* (1925); D Lloyd George, *The Truth about
the Peace Treaties* (1938); and A Cadogan, *The Diaries of Sir Alexander
Cadogan, 1938–1945*, ed D Dilks (1971).

Secondary works
General works include P M Kennedy, *The Realities behind Diplomacy*
(1981) and B Porter, *Britain, Europe and the World 1850–1986* (2nd
edn, 1987). There are useful essays in D Dilks (ed), *Retreat from Power*
(2 vols, 1981).

For the period around the First World War, see V Rothwell, *British
War Aims and Peace Diplomacy 1914–1918* (1971); for critics, see M
Swartz, *The Union of Democratic Control in British Politics during the First
World War* (1971). M Ceadel, *Pacifism in Britain, 1914–1945* (1980)
covers the whole period. For the peace settlements and reparations,
see M Dockrill and J Goold, *Peace without Promise: Britain and the
Peace Conferences 1919–23* (1981); A Orde, *British Policy and European
Reconstruction after the First World War* (1990); and R W D Boyce,
British Capitalism at the Crossroads 1919–32 (1987). Other books on
the 1920s include A Orde, *Great Britain and International Security
1920–6* (1978); B J C McKercher, *The Second Baldwin Government
and the United States 1924–9* (1984); and D Carlton, *MacDonald versus
Henderson: The Foreign Policy of the Second Labour Government* (1970).
On defence policy, see B Bond, *British Military Policy between the Two
World Wars* (1980) and J R Ferris, *The Evolution of British Strategic
Policy 1919–26* (1989).

Of the vast literature on the 1930s, see especially K Robbins,
Appeasement (1988); W R Rock, *British Appeasement in the 1930s* (1977);
N Thompson, *The Anti-Appeasers: Conservative Opposition to Appeasement
in the 1930s* (1971); A Peters, *Anthony Eden at the Foreign Office 1931–8*
(1986); and J Charmley, *Chamberlain and the Lost Peace* (1991).

On relations with specific countries, see D C Watt, *Succeeding John
Bull: America in Britain's Place, 1900–1975* (1984); C Thorne, *Allies of
a Kind: The United States, Britain and the War against Japan 1941–45*
(1979); C Keeble, *Britain and the Soviet Union 1917–89* (1990); P M
H Bell, *John Bull and the Bear: British Public Opinion, Foreign Policy
and the Soviet Union 1941–1945* (1990); and J Edwards, *The British
Government and the Spanish Civil War* (1979).

Articles
Among many important articles, see especially S J Valance, 'There
must be some misunderstanding: Sir Edward Grey's diplomacy of
August 1, 1914', *JBS* (1988); P Yearwood, 'On the safe and right

lines: the Lloyd George government and the origins of the League of Nations 1916–18', *HJ* (1989); J G Darwin, 'The Chanak crisis and the British cabinet', *H* (1980); M Pugh, 'Pacifism and politics in Britain 1931–5', *HJ* (1980); G C Peden, 'Sir Warren Fisher and British rearmament against Germany', *EHR* (1979) and 'A matter of timing: the economic background to British foreign policy 1938–9', *H* (1984); D Dilks, 'We must hope for the best and prepare for the worst: the Prime Minister, the cabinet and Hitler's Germany 1937–9', *PBA* (1987); P W Schroeder, 'Munich and the British tradition', *HJ* (1976); and D Dilks, 'The twilight war and the fall of France: Chamberlain and Churchill in 1940', *TRHS* (1978).

25. Empire

In the classic interpretation of British decolonization, it was believed that this period saw the beginning of the end of Empire. But since the early 1970s there has been a rejection of this view, with the argument that, although imperial control was relaxed in the 1920s, it was then tightened firmly under the impact of depression and the threat of war. Recent writing looks more closely at the effects of the Empire on British society.

Essay topics
Assess the importance of the Empire for Britain.

To what extent did this period prefigure the process of decolonization?

Sources and documents
N Mansergh, *Documents and Speeches on British Commonwealth Affairs, 1931–1952*(2 vols, 1953) is indispensable. A recent volume concentrating also on the later period is A N Porter and A J Stockwell, *British Imperial Policy and Decolonization, vol 1: 1938–51* (1987). For the views of imperialists, see W A S Hewins, *The Apologia of an Imperialist* (2 vols, 1929) and L S Amery, *The Leo Amery Diaries*, ed J Barnes and D Nicholson (2 vols, 1980–8).

Secondary works
A good textbook is B Porter, *The Lion's Share: A Short History of British Imperialism 1850–1983* (2nd edn, 1984). J Gallagher, *The Decline, Revival and Fall of the British Empire* (1982) is a seminal work, while D A Low, *Eclipse of Empire* (1991) is a wide-ranging collection of essays by a leading scholar in the field. See also M Beloff, *Imperial Sunset* (2 vols, 1969–89) and R F Holland, *European Decolonization 1918–1981* (1985). Specifically on this period, see A Clayton, *The British Empire as a Superpower 1919–39* (1986); R F Holland, *Britain and the Commonwealth Alliance 1918–39* (1981); S Constantine, *The*

Making of British Colonial Development Policy 1914–40 (1984); and I M Drummond, *British Economic Policy and the Empire, 1919–39* (1972). For Labour, see P S Gupta, *Imperialism and the British Labour Movement, 1914–64* (1975).

Works on specific parts of the Empire include J Darwin, *Britain, Egypt and the Middle East: Imperial Policy in the Aftermath of War 1918–22* (1981); P J Robb, *The Government of India and Reform 1916–21* (1976); B R Tomlinson, *The Political Economy of the Raj, 1914–47: The Economics of Decolonization* (1979), and *The Indian National Congress and the Raj 1929–42: The Penultimate Phase* (1976); R. J. Moore, *Churchill, Cripps and India 1939–45* (1979); and R D Pearce, *The Turning Point in Africa: British Colonial Policy 1938–48* (1982).

The domestic impact of Empire is studied in J M McKenzie, *Imperialism and Popular Culture* (1986) and *Propaganda and Empire: The Manipulation of British Public Opinion 1880–1960* (1984).

Articles

Important overviews include J Darwin, 'Imperialism in decline? Tendencies in British imperial policy between the wars', *HJ* (1980), and 'Fear of falling: British politics and imperial decline since 1900', *TRHS* (1986); and B R Tomlinson, 'The contraction of England: national decline and the loss of empire', *JICH* (1982). See also A J Stockwell, 'The war and the British Empire', in J Turner (ed) *Britain and the First World War* (1988) and R Hyam, 'Empire and sexual opportunity', *JICH* (1986).

On India, see G Martin, 'The influence of racial attitudes on British policy towards India during the First World War', *JICH* (1986); J M Brown, 'Imperial facade: some constraints upon and contradictions in the British position in India 1919–35', *TRHS* (1976); D Sayer, 'British reaction to the Amritsar Massacre 1919–20', *PP* (1991); C Bridge, 'Conservatism and Indian reform (1929–39)', *JICH* (1976); and B R Tomlinson, 'Britain and the Indian currency crisis 1930–2', *EcHR* (1979). On the Dominions, see N G Garson, 'South Africa and World War I', *JICH* (1979); and R F Holland, 'Imperial collaboration and Great Depression: Britain, Canada and the world wheat crisis 1929–35, *JICH* (1988) and 'The end of an imperial economy: Anglo-Canadian disengagement in the 1930s', *JICH* (1983). On the colonies, see R Robinson, 'The moral disarmament of African Empire 1919–47', *JICH* (1979) and R Smyth, 'Britain's African colonies and British propaganda during the Second World War', *JICH* (1985).

Index

Readers should note that an entry may appear more than once on a page; references in bold indicate main entries; in the interests of economy of space, names etc which only appear in lists are excluded.